LOVE INTEREST

LOVE INTEREST

❧ A Novel ❧

Clare Gilmore

ST. MARTIN'S GRIFFIN
NEW YORK

First published in the United States by St. Martin's Griffin, an imprint of St. Martin's Publishing Group

LOVE INTEREST. Copyright © 2023 by Clare Gilmore. All rights reserved. Printed in the United States of America. For information, address St. Martin's Publishing Group, 120 Broadway, New York, NY 10271.

www.stmartins.com

Designed by Jen Edwards

Library of Congress Cataloging-in-Publication Data

Names: Gilmore, Clare, author.
Title: Love interest : a novel / Clare Gilmore.
Description: First edition. | New York : St. Martin's Griffin, 2023.
Identifiers: LCCN 2023023585 | ISBN 9781250880543
   (trade paperback) | ISBN 9781250880550 (ebook)
Subjects: LCGFT: Romance fiction. | Novels.
Classification: LCC PS3607.I452147 L68 2023 | DDC 813/.6—
   dc23/eng/20230602
LC record available at https://lccn.loc.gov/2023023585

Our books may be purchased in bulk for promotional, educational, or business use. Please contact your local bookseller or the Macmillan Corporate and Premium Sales Department at 1-800-221-7945, extension 5442, or by email at MacmillanSpecialMarkets@macmillan.com.

First Edition: 2023

10 9 8 7 6 5 4 3 2 1

Publishing this book is the scariest thing I've ever done.

The scariest thing I've ever done is dedicated to those looking for the courage to drop-kick their comfort zone into another dimension.

I hope Casey and Alex's love story gets you closer.

LOVE INTEREST

CHAPTER ONE

To: Casey Maitland (Financial Analyst)
From: Molly West (Human Resources Representative)
Meeting Subject: Quick Touchbase!
Time: Monday, August 28, 8:30–9:00 A.M.

The meeting invitation appears on my cell phone screen when I'm halfway up the subway staircase. I pause midstep to read through the details, eyes widening in alarm as I process the date (today), the current time (8:07), and my own translation for what HR really means by "Quick Touchbase!"

In twenty-three minutes, one of two things is going to happen:

1. Molly will tell me I got the new job.
2. Molly will break my heart.

The heart in question thunders, blood beating rhythmically against my eardrums. I didn't think I was getting this news today.

Shouldn't Molly have given me twenty-four hours to mentally prepare? And besides, what if I'd been late to work?

We were going to offer you the new job, Casey, but you were late, so we gave it to Mike from Design. He's never late.

I'm *never late*! my internal monologue stubbornly protests.

Which is . . . probably why Molly scheduled me for an eight thirty.

Someone bumps my shoulder, and my phone nearly slips from my palm. The culprit throws me a glare as he passes. It's my Subway Nemesis: another Brooklyn Heights resident with whom I share every minute of my morning commute. His daily breakfast is a homemade granola bar, which always triggers my airborne allergies. I once thought about forgiving him for this—after all, how could my Subway Nemesis know I'm allergic to almost everything?—but then I learned he's the type to read lengthy *New York Times* articles about air traffic control, and that just seems too boring to forgive.

Taking the last few steps up to the sidewalk with the crush of bodies unleashing its wrath on the Financial District, I dart sideways out of the foot traffic.

I need a moment to get my bearings.

So. Today is the day, then.

Today is the day, today is the day, today is the day—

I suppose—now that my stomach is twisted up in knots, and my breath is coming short, and my brain is going DEFCON 1 on mental health—Molly did me a favor by waiting until the last minute to send that meeting invite. I would have been an anxious wreck for all twenty-four of those hours I wanted.

It doesn't help that I've already had three cups of coffee, brewed in the rose-gold French press I've had since college, which now resides in the apartment I share with my childhood best friend. My heart feels feverish and highly caffeinated.

Also, Aaron Carter is still playing through my AirPods.

The early sunlight grabs me, bouncing off every reflective surface in sight. I press the edge of my palm against my forehead, squinting against the golden beams licking across the city in between scattering clouds. Today's train was just as suffocating as ever—the air hot and stagnant, bodies pressed much too close for even the brief distance we had to travel—but now the aroma of coffee grounds and wet tar roots me in place. I put my hands on my hips and breathe deep, calming gulps into my lungs.

My nose wrinkles, catching the faintest scent of the breakfast burrito I ate this morning. I sniff my hair, drop my bag to the ground, shuffle around until I find the Completely Clean deodorant (clinical strength), an empty bottle of hypoallergenic perfume, and some Listerine strips for good measure. Today is *not* the day to show up at work smelling like a breakfast lover's wet dream.

Standing, I swipe the deodorant as surreptitiously as I'm able and pop a Listerine strip into my mouth. I quickly sweep my hair into a bun with a clip, then turn toward my building with a renewed sense of confidence.

A coffee vendor is staring.

She leans an elbow against her cart and gives me a perfunctory once-over. I tuck my chin down, because I might as well examine myself while she's at it?

I'm in a beige linen pantsuit I got for fifteen bucks at a Reformation sample sale, and fine, it's a bit wrinkled, but isn't linen always? Maybe she's eyeing my Pima-Maricopa hand-beaded earth earrings, clearly visible, since my unruly golden brown hair is now temporarily tamed back. Freckles dust my sun-kissed cheeks. My shoes are black, boring, heinous, but hey, I haven't gotten blisters in months.

All in all, I look the same as always, thank you very much.

The coffee vendor says something aimed at me. I take my AirPods out and say, "What?"

"Do you need some perfume?" she all but screams, lifting her purse into view through her service window.

I toss my own empty bottle into the trash can. The last stragglers from the subway pass between us, completely unfazed.

"Thanks, but I'm probably allergic to that." My voice comes out unused, a guitar with strings that need changing. "I might keel over and die, and what would that do for business?" I say it with a half-hearted chuckle at the end to let her know I'm joking (kind of—honestly, the worst that'll happen is hives erupting all over my neck and wrists), but the woman doesn't laugh. Doesn't even crack a smile. She just stares at me like I'm a travel influencer who asked for seventeen photos by the 9/11 Memorial.

Whatever. Today of all days, she can't get in my head. There's no room left that my anxiety hasn't claimed.

I start walking, my gaze aimed at the skyscraper where I've spent the last two years busting my ass. In front of the building, Manhattan's latest crop of white-collar workaholics mill around like grazing cattle. The lower-floor windows glisten with dewy raindrops. The building is so tall that it's half masked by clouds right now, hanging low from this morning's heavy downpour.

Like "Jack and the Beanstalk," I think about boarding that elevator every workday and reaching a kingdom in the sky.

"Casey!"

My feet do a one-eighty on the sidewalk at the sound of my name, and I smile softly once I recognize who's calling me: Brijesh Krishnu, a recipe editor at *Food Baby*.

He's got one hand wrapped around what I'd guess is at least a six-dollar cappuccino, the other buried deep in the pocket of his light-wash jeans. He probably spent more money on the vintage T-shirt he's wearing than I do on twenty bottles of Trader Joe's wine. The men flanking him are both dressed in Jos. A. Bank suits, but Brijesh's whole aura brooks no argument about how comfortably he fits into FiDi. He was born and raised here, and he knows Manhattan like he knows a good menu—with intimate familiarity.

"Ugh," I groan when he gets close, eyeing his comfy-looking sneakers. "I hate your work attire policy."

"You're *jealous* of my work attire policy," he corrects, falling into step with me as we cross the street toward our building. "And I'm jealous of how close your desk is to the execs. You know what they say about real estate."

"Location, location, location?" Brijesh and I part ways around a slow walker and join up again once we've passed him, nearly across the street. "I'll keep that in mind. Maybe I can get some favors in exchange for my old cubicle."

Immediately, I wince, wanting to the claw the words back the second they leave my lips. Did that sound too cocky? I only meant it as a joke, but the reminder of Molly's calendar invite comes rushing back unbidden.

The company has already made its decision. *Yes*, or *no*. I need to just hold my tongue, wait to be told my future.

Brijesh twists to look at me, his deep-set eyes blown wide with realization. "Oh yeah, that's right. I almost forgot you interviewed for that project manager job." He nudges my shoulder, and the tiny gesture from one of my only friends in this whole city calms my nerves . . . a bit. "If you get the new job, we can trade. Your old desk outside the CFO's office in exchange for mine, outside the cooking studio."

I roll my eyes, not buying his offer to trade for one second but still admiring his attempt to distract me. "You'd never give up being the first person who gets offered the extra food from the cooking studio," I say with a snort. "I bet you'd sooner trade your fame."

Food Baby, the magazine where Brijesh works, is owned by Little Cooper Publications—the larger business conglomerate that employs us both. Brijesh and I are technically coworkers, although we've never coworked a day in our lives. Our departments are, like, third cousins twice removed on your mom's side. His job is hands-on, fun, and flashy. Mine is all about crunching numbers and pleasing corporate executives.

Which isn't the worst, to be honest. I like finance. I'm *good* at finance. Math makes sense to me, and it doesn't play games with you if you don't play games with math (Hello, Wall Street). But truthfully, I've spent my whole life believing I'm supposed to want something *more*. A job that's more creative. A life that's more inspirational. A career track that doesn't make my Brooklyn flower guy release a disappointed "Oh" when he learns what I do all day.

That unshakable feeling is why I applied for this project job with Little Cooper—to stretch my creativity, to see if I can help build something new from scratch—and it's why I'll remain in a panic spiral until I find out if they decided I'm right for it.

Yes, or *no*.

"My fame?" Brijesh repeats, drawing me back to the moment. The word sounds greedy on his lips.

"Following," I correct, stepping around a puddle.

Brijesh has been featured in some of *Food Baby*'s YouTube videos lately, which means he has no small number of social media fans out there. I suspect more than half just like the *look* of him. He's all muscled and bisexual, with black stubble and cheekbones sharper than his very expensive Japanese knife collection. Physically, I understand what the *Food Baby* subscribers see in him, but *they* don't know about his inability to retain how compound interest works.

Also, he and my roommate occasionally bang, so my apologies to the subscribers for introducing them.

"Brijesh." We land on the sidewalk in front of our building, and I still him with a hand to his forearm. He pauses and faces me, eyebrows drawn together, sensing my change in tone. I show him the notification on my home screen.

"Oh," he says, working through the meaning the same way I did when I first got the invite. "Today's the day they're getting back to you?"

I nod solemnly.

It's quiet for a moment. Then Brijesh says, "Well, it's bound to be good news."

His tone is full of unbridled reassurance. I wish it could kinetically transfer to me, but the lead brick in my stomach only sinks deeper.

"You're dynamite, Casey. Like, your whole aesthetic is its own résumé."

"What do you mean?" I tilt my head.

"How hard you work, how many people rely on you, how good you are with numbers. Honestly, LC would be idiotic not to promote you."

I blush, feeling warm blood pool behind my cheeks. Flyaway hairs escape my bun. I tuck them snugly behind my ears. "Thanks, Brijy, but it's not a promotion. It's just a new job."

Even as I say it, I know it's not the whole truth. The job would be an upgrade. A step forward. A venture into uncharted waters. Best of all, a positive affirmation that I don't have to subscribe to the full range of weirdly exclusive Girl Boss Culture to be a successfully functioning adult.

Funny enough, my own boss, Don, was the one to suggest I apply for the opening at Little Cooper's new digital media platform, *Bite the Hand*. What started as a pet project for zany ideas not aimed at our print subscribers—like a list of the best hangover meals for every kind of liquor, activism city guides, quizzes to determine your ideal sex toy, or links to the internet's funniest memes of the moment—has morphed into its own beast with an identity wholly separate from its parent print magazine. It's almost like an amalgamation of *BuzzFeed*, *The Cut*, and whatever content is trending on TikTok right now.

Don didn't suggest I apply in an I'm-trying-to-get-rid-of-you way but more of an I-need-someone-loyal-to-me-on-the-inside way. He's stressed about how fast the platform is growing, how no one seems financially minded. Don went so far as to set up a networking meeting between me and *Bite the Hand*'s deputy director weeks before the job opening posted. He's genuinely confident I have a shot, which has my hopes—and my nerves—*way* up about the whole thing.

I take a deep breath. I'll know, one way or another, in less than fifteen minutes. As a girl who does poorly with unknown variables, that's the consolation I'm clinging to. Even if I get bad news, the waiting will be over.

My skin is sticky from the fog, and I feel a drop of condensation roll between my boobs. I'm so glad I reapplied deodorant. It's a typical August day in the city: sweltering, crowded, muggy, and just miserable enough to be a little bit magic.

We start walking again and hit the lobby of our building a minute later. It's all high ceilings, modern art, escalators leading to straitlaced desk attendants. Brijesh and I swipe our badges by the security kiosk. CASEY MAITLAND, my badge reads in fading blue ink, along with the job title FINANCIAL ANALYST and the company identifier LITTLE COOPER PUBLICATIONS.

I desperately attempt to manifest that, soon, I'll have a newly issued badge to swipe.

We wait in line, eventually piling into an elevator with a crush of bodies that sometimes rivals the subway. Brijesh drains his coffee, then starts muttering the ingredients he needs for a recipe test over and over beneath his breath.

"Ground lamb, white wine, ras el hanout—"

"What's that?" I whisper.

"Tell you when you're older."

His stop arrives before mine; Little Cooper owns nine magazines based in the US, but the staff occupy twelve different floors.

"Good luck. Don't forget my cubicle offer," he whispers as he hops off on thirty-seven.

"Don't forget me when you're famous," I whisper back.

On my way up the beanstalk, my legs grow restless. As the elevator starts and stops, lets people off and lets them on, I tap my right foot in rhythm with the song stuck in my head ("Here I Go Again" by Whitesnake, of all things). The higher we climb, the fewer people remain.

Eventually, as we reach the high nineties, it's just me and one other person.

I've worked here long enough to know that I should keep my gaze forward, on the slowly dwindling number of glowing elevator buttons. Back home in Nashville, I people-watched all the time, but New Yorkers don't like it when you stare. So, I *try* not to look at him. I really, really try. But like a moth inevitably drawn to a bright light in the dark, I can't help but peek over.

And—I swear to God. At first, I think I might be sharing the elevator with a straight-up male model.

LC owns a fashion magazine called *Frame,* so it's not like my thought is outlandish. He's styled impeccably in a lavish but traditional black suit that I *know* without a doubt has been tailored, the jacket slung over his left shoulder and held in place by a couple of loose fingers. A white button-down covers his broad chest.

The man is Asian, maybe biracial, with the calm, bored quality of a person who spends plenty of time *waiting*. The way he's leaning against the opposite side of the elevator looks so aesthetic, it's almost like he's unintentionally posing. One loafer sole is pushed flush against the stainless-steel wall, and there's a slight bend in his knee. I'm halfway expecting a camera to start snapping him ad nauseam as soon as the doors pull open on the next floor.

My next discernment is that he's unabashedly watching me right back.

He's around my age, maybe a year or two older, but definitely in the midtwenties bracket, a few years past the cusp of when the word "man" has permanently overwritten "boy" in your head. He has a couple of tiny lines by his eyes, a tiredness to the set of his mouth that's probably correlated to an absence of work-life balance. But regardless, he's so handsome, it sort of hurts my feelings, with jet-black hair; a straight nose; tawny, freshly shaved skin; and expressive lips that are, at present, pressed together like he's holding back a secret he doesn't want to share. I would describe him as tilt-your-head tall, but not crane-your-neck tall.

So, basically, perfect.

The hand in his pocket is tapping out a rhythm. It's strangely in sync with my restless foot.

I catalog all this with a few careful glances, my eyes moving skittishly over the stranger. With a peek at the solely lit elevator button, I realize we're headed for the same stop. I'm certain I've never seen this person before, which is rare this high up the beanstalk. Outsiders don't frequent my floor. It's really not for the faint of heart, considering business executives—much like volcanoes—tend to erupt spontaneously.

He's . . . still watching me. Staring, honestly. It's unnerving. At least *I'm* trying to be subtle about it. He's not even bothering!

And then—

AND. THEN.

He whispers, in a conspiratorial hiss, "I. Killed. Mufasa."

My jaw drops open, the sticky remnants of my Listerine strip no doubt visibly blue on my tongue. I drop all pretense of subtlety and stare at him, utterly dumbfounded.

Did he just quote Scar from *The Lion King*?

His smile—a gentle, attractive pull of his lips at one corner—dissolves into messy laughter at my expression. He doubles over, clutching his stomach, and a deep, musical sound escapes him like it cannot possibly be contained a moment longer.

I still haven't located my vocal cords.

The elevator pulls to a gradual stop on the ninety-eighth floor, and he pushes off the wall and grins with abandon. "I read that on a *Bite the Hand* list of weird things you can say to strangers in the elevator," he explains.

Somehow, a quick reply jumps out of me. "On a scale of one to ten, how weird was *that* line compared to the rest of the list?"

"Five," he says, not missing a beat. His voice is scratchy. I wonder if I'm his first occasion to speak today.

"You spared me levels six through ten?" I ask.

"I wanted you to smile, not call security."

It works, just as the doors open. My mouth gives in, pulling up into a smile at the absurdity of this man.

"There it is," he murmurs. "You looked like you needed it."

He throws me one last grin—like I made his whole damn *year*—as he strolls into the Little Cooper Publications executive suite.

CHAPTER TWO

Eight minutes later, Molly breaks my heart.

We're in a bland, forgettable conference room I've occupied hundreds of times before when all my frenetic nerves, all that anxious energy, leaks out of me like big corporate oil into the gulf. I have now murdered an ocean with my sadness.

"You were a strong candidate, Casey," Molly says, voice gentle. "But ultimately, *Bite the Hand* went with someone who has more entrepreneurial experience."

They went with someone else.

Which really means, *You're not good enough, Casey.*

"As you know, BTH is kind of like a digital media start-up," Molly says. "And . . . well, they found someone with that exact job history."

My face flushes with mortification, sadness giving way to raging embarrassment in the span of a second. I feel hollow, but I force myself not to break eye contact with Molly as she continues to metaphorically stab me.

"Technically, it's not even the same role you interviewed for," she explains, trying so obviously to soften the blow. "The BTH team changed the job description to match the strengths of their new hire, who has a huge vision for the brand and plans to take a broader approach than we originally considered possible for this position."

"What vision?" I ask, doing my best to disguise any resentment. "What approach?"

Her voice turns admiring, her eyes glassy, and that's when I know Molly's met the new hire herself. Already fallen under their *visionary* spell. "*Bite the Hand* is going to become its own subsidiary company. An independent website for social news, targeting a younger customer than our magazine audience. The new hire will be a project manager helping make that happen."

What Molly's telling me is that they loved this person so damn much, they created a *better* job just for them.

I nod, my focus dropping to the table between us in a signal of acquiescence.

This makes sense, my mind supplies for me. In a self-admitted coping mechanism, I start to rationalize all the reasons this is the only logical conclusion.

I'm too young for a new job already. It's been only two years since I graduated from UT.

I'm too analytical for a project role.

Not enough of a visionary.

It's not like I was *seriously* thinking I'd get that job, right? The description was pretty far outside my wheelhouse, I'll admit. Growth strategy, social media networking, freelance client management. Honestly, I'm better suited to reconciling expense line items.

Applying was interview practice. A what-if question that never merited a real answer. Considering it anything else would be ridiculous.

I should've stayed in my lane. Finance is my lane. And the stupid part is, I love finance. Why did I betray finance?!

Actually. I know exactly why.

I was trying to make a dead woman proud of me.

"But I have some good news, too," Molly goes on.

I look up from where my eyes were burning holes in the table.

"Right now, *Bite the Hand* is still *technically* a magazine vertical. It doesn't have an independent domain or revenue stream."

Come on, Molly. I already know all this. I'm the one who prepares the financial statements.

"Right," I say. "Their revenue and expenses hit *Frame*'s bottom line."

"For now," Molly counters. "The BTH team wants to convince the board to vote in favor of launching a subsidiary, but to hit their timeline, they'll need hard-core financial planning."

I visibly brighten up, intrigued. Molly seems relieved at the sight of it.

"Here's the deal," she says. "You know how your boss has been griping for months that accruals belong with Accounting?"

"Accruals *do* belong with Accounting," I echo.

She fights an eye roll, clearly unimpressed with our inter-departmental warfare. "He got it approved through Change Management, which means you'll have some free time to work with *Bite the Hand.*"

"Really?" I ask, in pure disbelief at my sudden change in luck. No more accruals *and* an opportunity to work for BTH?

"It's not a new job or anything," Molly jumps to add, and my bubble pops just a little. What she's really saying is *it's not a raise or anything.* "But Little Cooper is committed to servicing you in the best way that also services the company."

I do my best to ignore the way she refers to LC as a sentient being. It's weird.

Molly pauses. Leans forward. "And, Casey," she murmurs, "don't forget about your long-term goals we discussed in your last performance review."

Molly, girl, I could never.

"If you help get this vertical ready to launch, you'll be on track for that London transfer you've been considering." Molly chuckles and reclines. "It's a competitive office, but with that level of success under your belt, the transfer is all but guaranteed. You'd probably have your pick from a handful of jobs over there."

My fingers unclasp, nail tips pressing into the wooden tabletop as my mind starts spinning. "The London office?" I might as well have said Narnia or Neverland for all the childlike wonder my voice betrays.

After all, it's not like I've ever visited London in person—even though it's where my mother was raised. To me, the whole concept of "abroad" is just a fairy tale. But I told Molly I was interested in a transfer because at twenty-four, I'm the same age now my mom was when she moved to the United States. And so the whole plan just seemed kind of . . . fated, or whatever.

Molly nods. "As early as next summer."

My teeth pinch at my bottom lip while I process this information. Yesterday, I would have jumped at this opportunity. And if I'm honest, I want a London transfer even *more* than I wanted that project manager job. But I'm scared wishing for London will turn out just like this did. What if, when it comes down to it, I'm told again I'm not good enough? That the beginning and end of my worth is only that I'm a girl who's good with numbers?

But . . . the London office probably needs people like me, too. So maybe I can just . . . be who I am.

In London.

The more I think about it, the more I realize this whole situation is kind of perfect. Because this—moving there—would mean something to her, too. My mother. She would've been proud of this, I think.

"Okay," I tell Molly, a fever of excitement already brewing like the first drips of coffee inside me. Little Cooper may have given the project manager position to someone else, but at least they're making room for me, too.

I make myself a promise as Molly goes over the particulars. Visionary Wunderkind and all their entrepreneurial experience be damned. I'm the one who's going to make this vertical shine like the fucking sun.

CHAPTER THREE

On the way to my cubicle, the vibration of my phone, buried deep inside my black Michael Kors tote (another sample sale find; one handle strap was cut clean through, but I superglued it back together), announces a text. As I walk into the Hive—my affectionate nickname for the cubicles sitting outside our chief financial officer's glass office—I'm thankful no one up here besides my own boss knows I interviewed for something else.

Fari, my work counterpart, looks up from her desktop as I stroll past. "Morning, Case."

"Morning," I reply as I settle into my swivel chair.

Fari is two years younger than me, Black, a three-months-ago Stanford grad, and originally from Seattle. We have the same job title, but since I've been with LC for two years longer, our boss likes to call me her mentor.

I'm pretty sure Fari hated me at first, which tracks, because my best friends have told me I don't make great first impressions. In Fari's defense, on her first day of work, I grilled her in what I can now see is a bizarre way about Washington's native horticulture. It's just that I'd never met anyone from Seattle before, and I've got this book from my stepdad where you try to collect a native flower from all fifty states and press them onto a page. Fari semireluctantly brought me a snowberry flower when she came back to New York after her mom's birthday weekend, and I did all her accruals that month.

Two months later, we're sort of friends now. She came around to the fact that I'm just really into plants.

"Guess what?" I say.

"What?"

I throw her a grin. "Molly and Don got accruals pushed to Accounting."

Her mouth drops into a perfect O. "I almost feel bad for them," she mutters.

"Almost," I repeat.

"We paid our dues." She nods to herself. "It's their rightful turn to wrestle with accruals."

My tote bag lands on my desk with a *thunk,* and when I pull out my phone, there's a text from my roommate, Miriam. She threw Brijesh in the chat, too.

How'd it go?

I blow out a dramatic breath. *Of course* Brijesh already texted her that I was hearing back about the job this morning.

I made the B-team, I type back. They gave the job to someone else, but I get to do finance stuff for BTH. Consolation prize.

Miriam's response comes through right away: dang, sorry. Better than the bench tho, right?

I tilt my head from side to side in consideration. Right, I send back.

We could just kill whoever got the job, Brijesh sends.

A laugh slips out of me, but I cover it with a cough. Fari gives me a weird look, but I brush off the question in her eyes and take a sip of my stale Diet Coke from yesterday.

My cubicle is a wreck, but what else is new? I keep my*self* together just fine—clean hair, fresh clothes, charged phone, enough sleep to get me through the day—but the caveat is everything around me remains in a constant state of chaos. Pink sticky notes litter my whiteboard. The trash can, which gets scooped only once a week (on Wednesdays) by the Facilities department, is already overflowing with take-out containers. Highlighters, notebooks, report printouts, and cups of various beverages blanket my desk—including a half-dredged coffee mug that says BITCH I MIGHT!

On the corkboard between our desks, Fari and I have erected a physical meme wall. *Be strong, I whispered to my Wi-Fi signal* is superimposed over the Wi-Fi logo with one bar. On a workplace translation guide: *Per my last email = Can't you fucking read?* There's even a picture of our CFO Tracy Garcia with a thought bubble coming out of her head: *I dream of EBITDA <3.* (Earnings Before Interest, Taxes, Depreciation, and Amortization. Duh.)

My gaze catches on the dusty, framed photo of me and Dad, shoved behind my double-monitor setup. In it, we're lounging in beach chairs on the coast of the Florida Panhandle.

God, I really need to call him back.

I've only just booted up my computer to check through morning emails when Don materializes beside my desk, frazzled as always. He never fails to remind me of a suburban dad who gets roped into coaching his son's peewee soccer league every year. I'm pretty sure he's in his midthirties, but he's nearly bald already. Not sure if the job has anything to do with that.

Don sits on the plastic stool I bought from Target just for him. (Before, he would kneel by my chair, which always made me feel like he was about to propose.) On a winded exhale, he says, "I need you to do that thing where you make the data beautiful."

My lips purse into a smirk. "What data?"

"Just shot you an email. Last-minute meeting with the big boss in twenty minutes." He shakes his head. "She loves the way you make numbers look."

By she, Don means our chief financial officer, Tracy Garcia—an absolute bad bitch and my personal barometer for success.

"After that," Don says, "can you help Fari do a sensitivity test for subscription price increases on that fashion mag?"

"*Frame?*" I raise a single brow.

"Yeah, that one."

For a seven-year employee, you might expect Don to have long memorized the names of all the magazines in our portfolio, but he cares too much about the profit-leverage effect and debt restructuring to let anything else live in his head rent-free.

I click my ballpoint pen against the desk and say, "You got it."

"Thank you, Casey." Then his face changes, and he adds more quietly, "This afternoon, we'll talk about *Bite the Hand,* okay? Just block thirty minutes"—he winces, eyes blinking closed—"actually, block fifteen. But we'll talk. I promise."

The smile I give him is genuine, because Don is an all-rounder. Great first boss, great human being. I hear a lot of first-boss horror stories—especially in the finance world—but even though we're probably all a *little* overworked, I've never regretted accepting this position.

He leaves, and I make his data (a three-year comparison of ad sales for *Garden Girl*) beautiful. Colors, conditionally highlighted cells, pie charts, pick-your-own-poison drop-down lists. After I send off the edited report, I wheel over to Fari's desk and show her how to model a sensitivity test. We make nerdy Excel jokes that would send a right-brained person to therapy and put in emoji qualifiers beside all the variables. Sad face for 20 percent increase. Throw-up face for 30 percent. Sunglasses guy for negative 5, even though there's no *way* that's happening.

By the time I'm back at my own cubicle an hour and a half later, there's a message from Brijesh blinking in the bottom right corner of my screen.

Come down to thirty-seven. Dustin needs a Nashville native to taste test his healthed-up hot chicken. It's criminally good, but you be the judge.

Oh *baby*. Ten A.M. hot chicken? That is . . . exactly what I didn't know I needed right now. He sent the message fifteen minutes ago. I toss up a prayer I'm not too late.

"You're still a vegetarian, right, Fari?"

"Last I checked."

"Cool. I'm going on a walk."

I grab my phone and badge and head for the elevators. On my way, I pass the executive concierge, Benny.

Benny has only two moods: over-the-moon incandescently happy (usually following a successful night's drag performance) or churlish and malcontent (usually following several days in a row he hasn't gotten to perform). Right now, he's on the desk phone, eyes closed, fingers pinching the bridge of his nose. So, the latter. I bet he's on the phone with our COO's ex-wife. She calls several times a week, demanding Benny put her through to her ex-husband. (Benny has been explicitly told never to do so.)

He catches my eye and covers the mouthpiece of the phone. "Later, can you remind me why women deserve rights?" he whispers.

I wink at him and jab my thumb at the button to call the elevator. Once I'm inside, my mind drifts back to the man from this morning.

What was he doing up here on ninety-eight? Who was he here to see? I didn't catch a glimpse of where he was headed after he left me behind, fighting a smile, but he looked more comfortable strolling into the C-suite than I did after I'd worked up here for half a year. It took me a while to adjust, working so closely with the company's head honchos. I still don't even use the bathroom on this floor if I'm sensing gastrointestinal turbulence.

My phone vibrates again.

> **Miriam:** How you doing, lovebug?
>> **Casey:** Fine.
> **Miriam:** Liar.
>> **Casey:** I promise. It just wasn't meant to be.

For a minute I think she's done, and then, this:

> **Miriam:** You know you're allowed to like what you're good at, right? I for one am great at finding the perfect vein for butterfly IVs. I am the best vein finder in the whole peds wing and damn proud of it.

I know she's right. And I do like what I'm good at. The problem is I'm not sure my family likes what I'm good at.

Dad: Songwriter, quasi-famous musician.

Stepdad: Florist who does Bachelor Nation weddings.

Mom: Concert and fashion photographer.

That disconnect is part of the reason I haven't been home in so long. I love my dad and stepdad so much, but in an unexpected twist on the parental disappointment trope, sometimes I feel like I've let them down. Here I am, in the throes of an industry ripe with designers, stylists, photographers, recipe developers, writers. And what do I decide on? The very career my mother was running away from when she fled London twenty-five years ago.

> **Casey:** Can I still hate whoever got the job?
> **Miriam:** Oh yeah girl. Enemy no. 1.

It takes me a while to get all the way down to thirty-seven, and then I have to wait even longer to get buzzed into the cooking studio, since I don't have security clearance. By the time I walk in, I'm worried all the healthed-up hot chicken has been spoken for. I walk past the industrial refrigerator, my nose and taste buds tingling from the pungent scent of garlic and spice.

"Can you blow steam away while I snap this shot by the window?" a recipe developer says to the cooking studio manager. She garnishes a plate of what looks like chickpea curry with a smattering of handpicked cilantro leaves.

My eyes search for Dustin in the recipe dev bay, the same spot I always find Brijesh whenever he invites me downstairs to taste something he's planning to present to the *Food Baby* editors. But neither Dustin nor Brijesh is there, and the bay is covered in remnants of Middle Eastern cooking.

I frown. Did I really miss Dustin's recipe test by that much?

"Case!" a voice calls out from the far side of the studio. I track the sound, my head swiveling.

"Oh. Fuck," I whisper.

Dustin isn't testing this recipe for *Food Baby* consideration. He must have gotten it approved months ago. Because now he's recording at the *film* bay.

I can count on one hand the number of times I've been allowed in here, and it's never been on a film day.

I blink, frozen in place.

Brijesh is standing on one side of the counter, Dustin beside him, aproned up. The videography crew and all their gear are on the other side, sleek and ominous. It's intimidating, how much gear they've got. In my head, I pictured a dinky little camera on a tripod like all my favorite vloggers use.

I was not anticipating my YouTube debut today. Or, like, ever. I can safely say I don't have the right personality to fit in with the rest of *Food Baby*'s "on-camera talent." To say the absolute least.

Brijesh beckons me impatiently. I gulp, walking forward. When I'm close enough to touch, he throws an arm over my shoulder and pulls my side against his.

"This is Casey," he says, addressing the front-and-center camera lens. "She's a financial analyst up on ninety-eight. For all you folks at home, that means she works beside my boss's boss's boss's boss's boss. And she also happens to be a born and bred Nashvillian. So we're going to get her opinion on the healthed-up hot chicken."

"Go easy on me, Casey from ninety-eight," Dustin says, grinning at me widely.

We've never met, but I watch all his YouTube videos—even the ones he does for other brands besides *Food Baby.* Here are just a few of the creepy, parasocial factoids I've learned about Dustin through many hours of cooking-demo consumption. He is: of Jamaican heritage, a barbecue whisperer, scared of turmeric powder stains, and allergic to most nuts (same!).

Also, there is abundant fan fiction about him and Brijesh on the internet.

(I haven't read it.)

(I have.)

"Do *not* go easy on him," Brijesh tells me, countermanding Dustin's request. "It's in the public's best interest for you to be scrupulous."

"Noted," I say, my voice audibly unsteady. I cross my arms over my chest, glancing down at the fancily plated dish on the countertop. I point at it and turn to Dustin, doing my best to ignore the camera. "You know it's normally served on a piece of white bread with a pickle and a toothpick, right?"

Dustin sighs. "This is why I can't have nice things."

Brijesh grabs a fork and knife, cutting a piece of chicken for me as he talks to the camera about *how multifaceted the flavor of the dish is.* I watch (him, not the camera lens), enraptured, unable to do anything but smile at the sight of him in action. This feels ridiculous and panic-inducing to me, but Brijesh and Dustin make it seem like the most natural thing in the world. A couple seconds later, I forget all about the camera. Brijesh and I taste test while Dustin offers up the ingredients and tasting notes he was aiming to hit.

"It's delicious," I say after taking a bite.

"Gas me up, baby girl," Dustin says.

"But it's not Nashville-style. My lips aren't peeling away from my face right now, which isn't a good sign in the way of authenticity."

"It's healthed-up—" Brijesh protests.

"Yeah, I got that," I interrupt. "And I do really like it. But in terms of using this recipe as a comp for Nashville hot chicken, I don't think it works. It's not fried, and the heat profile is totally different. Did you use cayenne?"

"Aleppo."

I sigh. "I was lured here under false pretenses."

"All right, who let her in here?" Dustin complains to no one in particular.

Brijesh mocks kicking me out, whipping a tea towel near my knees, and I back away, hands up in placation.

"That was great, guys," says the video director as he steps away from the equipment. I wince at his implication—that we're acting like this for show—and move toward the sink, firmly out of frame, under the pretense of washing my hands. "Let's take five before the outro," the director adds.

And that is my official cue to GTFO ASAP.

"Hey." Brijesh rushes up to me, handing me a paper towel. "I know something that might make you feel better, or very much worse."

I raise my eyebrows, shutting off the water. "Okay. I can handle it."

"They gave the job you interviewed for to the board chairman's son."

In all fairness, Brijesh has never been one to mince words.

A beat of silence as it sinks in.

They gave . . .

The job I wanted . . .

To the board chairman's *son*?

"You have got to be fucking joking." My voice is deathly soft. Brijesh shakes his head. "Is that even legal?" I hiss.

"No clue. I don't know who all knows. I got suspicious when I learned his last name."

"Harrison?" I ask. Our board chairman is named Robert Harrison.

Brijesh nods. "New guy is Alex Harrison. He's Korean American, biracial."

"How do you know that? Did you already meet him?"

"Not yet, but I spent, like, two hours stalking his LinkedIn and Instagram to confirm his family connection," Brijesh says. "I almost gave up, but then, under his tagged photos, there's one with Robert on the Harvard alumni account from a few years back. His college graduation, I think. I'm sure they're trying to keep the family relation on the down-low, but like, did they think no one was going to find out?"

Wait. A. Damn. Minute.

Korean American, who graduated from college a few years back?

Was Alex Harrison the guy in the elevator?

Blinking, I start to mutter, "I think I—"

"Shut up, shut up, shut up," Brijesh hisses. "He just came in."

I turn on my heels, the squeak of my rubber soles mimicking the sound lodged in the back of my throat.

Sure enough, Deirdre—the cooking studio manager—is walking Elevator Man around. Giving him a goddamn tour like she's a real estate agent on *Selling Sunset* and he's looking to spend a few million. I watch numbly as his gorgeous face lights up from the inside out. He takes in his surroundings, holding out a hand to greet the video crew as Deirdre introduces him.

He says something that makes Dustin laugh. Then he grins, just like he did in the elevator this morning. And it's devastating, just like it was this morning.

My blood is on fire. I am going to sink my nails into something and claw it to shreds, and it'll probably end up being his throat. Are we seriously still giving jobs to people because of their family tree?

Alex Harrison's eyes skate toward Brijesh and me. When he sees me, he does a double take, his expression warming with familiarity. He starts toward us both, but his gaze stays focused on me.

"Simba."

"It's Casey," I barely manage. "Maitland."

Amused, he sticks out a palm. "It's a pleasure to officially meet you. I'm Alex Harrison, the new project manager for *Bite the Hand*." His voice is velvet with tiny scratches, like the morning after a concert or a swallow of whiskey.

I press my palm against his, and my shaking disappears, engulfed by his strong grip. I try to imagine I'm capable of the kinetic transfer of pain. Mine to him. The way I feel right now, just so he'd know. Just to see if he'd care.

As we lock eyes, and he keeps smiling with private amusement, and I try not to start crying or screaming, I realize I don't know what to be more furious about.

That the prince of nepotism got the job I wanted, or that Little Cooper dangled a transfer to London in front of me to keep me quiet about it.

Four weeks later, the video premieres on *Food Baby*'s YouTube channel. And the comments section sets the course for . . .

Well. For everything.

> **Dustin Makes Healthed-Up Hot Chicken,**
> **but Don't Call It Nashville-Style**

The girl who appears at 18:20. A fucking dream.

How do I get Analyst Casey in my subscription queue?

Y'all think she's dating one of them?

Where has the video team been hiding that girl!

OMG! Casey! We went to elementary school together <3

I'd watch a vlog of her just crunching numbers

You can analyze me, babe

When you've got a date with a pro chef at ten and a
    rendezvous with the CFO at eleven

CHAPTER FOUR

Besides Brijesh and Miriam, my only other friend in New York is Sasha Nicholson. Sasha is five eleven—making her a whopping six inches taller than me—with balmy deep-brown skin that belongs in a CoverGirl commercial, Met Gala–ready Afro-teased hair, and a truly comedic number of four-inch stilettos in her closet that should be organized on an episode of *The Home Edit*. The shoe addiction comes from her mom, but her height comes from her dad: NBA Hall of Famer Devon Nicholson.

(I'm embarrassed to admit this, but even after four years of living with Sasha in college, plus a handful of times watching her play for the women's team on campus, I still know less about basketball than a thespian.)

At the University of Tennessee, Sasha and I got randomly assigned as roommates in the honors dorm our first year. We liked each other enough to get an off-campus apartment together after that, but between her basketball obligations, myriad out-of-town boyfriends, and a tight-knit family based out of Chicago, I can count on two hands the number of weekends she was around during college. Even now that we both live in New York, I still wouldn't call us close. I'd call us comfortable.

Comfortable enough that when she calls in a favor, I'm obligated to say yes. Today's favor includes being Sasha's plus-one to her work function: a Yankees season-closing happy hour on a rooftop bar in Chelsea.

(I also know less about *base*ball than a thespian, but maybe I'm underselling the sports knowledge of thespians.)

The venue is gorgeous, with golden-hour evening sunlight and a warm, September wind streaming through the open doors between a balcony facing the river and the U-shaped bar inside. I'm holding a frosty pisco sour and headed back to where I last saw Sasha when I realize she's standing with Dougie Dawson.

My CEO.

The man's hair is thin and graying, his face dimpled in a purplish hue from years of sun damage. Sasha is standing farther away from him than she'd likely stand from anyone else solely because of the size of Dougie's protruding belly. I've never seen him up close like this, only in passing on days he makes it into his office. Which is not all that often.

But I remember in perfect detail the day he took over. The whole Finance department got pulled into the boardroom, and Dougie gave a spiel about *how thankful he was to be working with such a dedicated team* and *how expansive his vision was for LC's future.* To me, he'd looked exactly like our old CEO. Read: thrilled with his own existence.

Half of Sasha's job description is schmoozing rich people, so I take an educated guess and decide Dougie must be a Yankees season ticket holder with a luxury suite.

I approach the two of them, not sure what to do, how to act. Should I introduce myself? Should I pretend there's no connection?

Should I point out the sunspot on his neck in case he'd like to run it by his dermatologist?

"Casey!" Sasha says, her voice chipper and totally fake. "Did you know Dougie is the CEO of Little Cooper? What great exposure for you!"

Sasha is, unfortunately, the type of person who thinks about things like good exposure. I'm starting to think there's more than one reason she invited me here tonight.

I smile anyway. "Hi, Mr. Dawson. I work in Little Cooper's Finance department."

Dougie appraises me and scoffs. "You can't be older than twenty-five." His voice is deep and grandfatherly. It feels like I'm getting scolded for inappropriate conduct at the youth group ice cream social.

"I'm twenty-four."

"When I was your age," he says as his flattened palm taps me lightly against my hip bone, "I had hair down to here—"

My brain short-circuits. Sasha and I lock eyes for a fraction of a second.

"And a mustache down to here." His hand moves to my chest, where he taps my clavicle with the length of his pinkie, just above my breasts. "I was failing business school. A serious career was the last thing on my mind."

Double or nothing, I suppose. If you're going to touch a woman in the Me Too era, you might as well make it worth the headline?

The funny part is that my gut reaction is to come up with something to say next that won't make *him* uncomfortable. What would I do otherwise? Cause a scene? Claim harassment by a man who likely helped pay for the open bar I'm drinking at because he tapped my hip and clavicle? I hate myself a little for the passivity of it, but in professional situations like this, with my *literal livelihood* at stake, I revert to a scared little girl who has internalized that under no circumstances should she ruffle affluent society's feathers.

Don't bite the hand that feeds you.

The irony isn't lost on me. It's not lost on BTH, either. Their slogan? *Bite the hand, feed yourself.* It's just . . . harder than our feisty editorial team makes it look.

Beside me, Sasha swirls the melting ice in her glass and saves me from having to reply. "So, Dougie. You're close with the Yankees marketing VP, right? Do you know if he's considering new advertisers for next season? I have some suggestions—"

"They don't need new advertisers, dear," Dougie interrupts. "The old-school sponsorships are where the Yankees bankroll."

Sasha nods silently and twists her cocktail glass between her fingertips, her lips pressed together, which is how I know she's trying not to say something. Probably that she thinks the sports industry's sponsorship structure is from the dinosaur age.

"Now." Dougie turns back to me. "What exactly do you do for the Finance department?"

"She works with me."

I whip around, hair tickling my bare shoulders as the voice that's been haunting me for *weeks* envelops all three of us like a cloak.

It's him. Alex Harrison.

His eyes lock with mine. As usual, looking into the light brown color of his irises is like diving headfirst into a vat of quicksand that plans to choke me to death. Also as usual, I can't read the expression on his face. He is frustratingly unreadable.

"Alex." Dougie straightens, but his effort to gain height over Alex is fruitless. Dougie is only an inch taller than me, while Alex, by contrast, is about as tall as Sasha.

Alex clears his throat. "Dougie. It's good to see you." But the roll in his jaw, the pinch between his brows says otherwise.

"Since Choate graduation, right?"

"Right," Alex confirms.

What the heck is Choate? Sounds like a fancy private school in, like, the middle of Connecticut.

Something unpleasant settles onto Dougie's features. "Did I hear correctly? You're *working* for Little Cooper?"

"Yes. I'm the project manager for *Bite the Hand*."

Dougie's expression sours even more. There's an awkward, pregnant pause. I glance at Sasha; she's picking up on it, too, her face openly enraptured.

"Your father didn't mention you were back stateside," Dougie says.

Back stateside?

"Just recently." Alex's face softens into an easy smile as he reaches to shake Sasha's hand. "Hey. I'm Alex."

"Sasha Nicholson," she offers, shaking. "You work with Casey?"

"Yep." When he looks at me, a smirk plays on his lips, half there and then gone. "She's . . . a pleasure."

I raise an eyebrow at him, silently challenging the weak attempt at a compliment. A *pleasure*? It's been exactly a month since Alex started with *Bite the Hand,* and in that time, I'm pretty sure I've been nothing short of a headache for him to work with.

It's not that I've ever deliberately sabotaged him. I cordially reply to all his emails, file every expense report he sends my way. But I'm not that helpful, either—not the way I'm helpful to everyone else on the team—and Alex and I both know it. Just this morning, we got into a disagreement over payroll projections. I may have used the word "egregious," and he may have used the phrase "penny-pinching."

But the worst part about the whole thing—the most abhorrent, disgusting aspect of it all—is that Alex Harrison is *good* at his job, and it feels like he's doing that to me *on purpose*. Picking at my insecurities, drawing them to the surface of my skin with all his sparkly ideas and pitches, his easygoing conversations with everyone but me, his casual mentions of knowing a guy who can totally help with that roadblock we just hit.

I've never been the type of person to *know a guy*.

"Can I steal Casey?" Alex asks as the hand not holding his beer dips into the pocket of his slacks. "I've got an idea to run by her that we should get aligned on before a big meeting tomorrow."

"What meeting?" I ask, and Alex lets me read him just long enough that I understand he's telling me *just go with me, for once.*

Dougie still looks like he's trying to swallow a bar of soap. He clearly doesn't like Alex, and that's got to be his only redeeming quality. There's history between them.

If I figure it out, maybe I can use it against them both.

"As long as you're making me money," Dougie concedes.

Alex gives him a tight smile and jerks a nod. He faces me with his body, eyebrows raised in question, and gestures with his beer toward a balcony that overlooks the Hudson River. I walk past the Yankees agents, managers, and bankrollers toward the sunlight whispering along the water. The balcony is broad and gold rimmed, and the warmth of the September evening bathes me as the air-conditioning dissipates.

Resting my elbows on the balcony's ledge, I squint at the horizon. "What do we need to get aligned on?"

"Nothing."

I frown and turn back to look at him.

He's golden and hazy right now, the sun clinging to his frame like he's a magnet for it, with messy black hair after a long day tugging at it and dark circles under his eyes. He's calm now that he's outside of work—no filler conversation, no bright grin.

What I've realized over the past four weeks is that Alex Harrison's personality is like a charge. He makes people happier. Makes them feel more at ease. I've noticed it happen, again and again and again. Alex has an ability to endear people to him on their very first impression.

I have never related to someone less.

But for the first time since our elevator exchange the day he started, his focus on me feels singular, undiluted. Like this man is taking the full measure of me and expending no energy on a single other thought. It's making my head spin, making my body react in a way I don't want to be held responsible for. In fact, the way I'm physically drawn in only makes me more frustrated at the royal flush poker hand the universe dealt him. He's attractive *and* rich *and* charismatic *and* smart. With millions of adoring HR reps.

Where is the fatal flaw?

"If it wasn't about work, what did you really want?" I ask.

"I saw Dougie . . ." Alex drifts off, looking at a spot above my head. He doesn't say it—*touch you*—but I blush anyway, like I'm the one who did something wrong. "Thought you might need an out from that conversation."

I think about saying, *I didn't,* or *I could have walked away on my own,* or even *thank you.* What comes out instead is "Why don't you like him?"

Alex shoots me a flat look. "What gave you that impression?"

I take another sip of my drink, feel the crisp alcohol slide down my throat. "You seemed about as thrilled to see him as my boss is after his expense touchbase with the COO."

Alex smirks. "Well, the COO *is* a nightmare. Did you hear about his ex-wife? Benny was giving me the scoop last week."

"Don't change the subject."

Alex rolls his eyes. It's a gesture I've become distinctly familiar with, since he rolls his eyes at me *a lot.* "I dislike the subject."

"*Why* do you dislike the subject?"

"Aside from the fact that he *touched* you inappropriately?"

"I've fared worse." According to his alarmed expression, this doesn't appease Alex. "Aside from that."

He walks forward and leans against the rail, looking out at the river. I turn my head toward him as a drop of condensation from his beer bottle falls to the street, stories below. "He's got history with my father. If you must know."

This piques my interest. A CEO and a board chairman at odds

with each other? "What kind of history?" I ask, too curious to play it cool.

Alex shakes his head, humming out a gentle laugh. "It's hilarious you think I would just tell you that."

A laugh slips out of me, too, escaping me against my will. It *is* hilarious that I thought he'd tell me that. We play nice at the office, but Alex isn't naive, and I've never been any good at subtlety. He *knows* I'm not his biggest fan. Why would he tell me anything personal?

"That's a first," he murmurs, half smiling. Then adds, "That was a real laugh, too."

I want to shove the sound back down my throat. "How do you know it was real?"

He leans in. Smelling like expensive cologne I'm probably allergic to and freshly laundered sheets. "I know it was real," he says, "because I've never once been around you when your heart wasn't pinned to your sleeve."

Um . . .

What on earth is a girl supposed to say to *that*?

Nothing, apparently. Alex doesn't give me enough time to string together words in rebuttal, but he also can't hide the blush that creeps into his cheeks just seconds before he says, "So. How does it feel to be the internet's latest dream girl?"

When I only continue to look at him dumbly—still reeling from the heart-on-my-sleeve comment—he adds, "What, didn't you hear?"

Oh, I'd heard. After the "Healthed-Up Hot Chicken" video went live two days ago, I got eight hundred new Instagram followers overnight and half a dozen texts from people I used to know. It had felt fun at first, and then fake. Then fun again, and stressful, and back to fake.

"I'm nobody's dream girl." My voice comes out hollower than I mean it to. My mind flashes to my ex-boyfriend, then away before the familiar sting of memory settles onto my skin like a sunburn. "People can't like me if they don't really know me."

Alex frowns. His eyebrows draw together, asking a question I can nearly hear: *Who really knows you?*

I could count the number of people on one hand. That's the difference between us.

"Well." He scratches at his jaw. "Unlike you, *I* have a pathological need to be liked."

I snort. "Why is that?"

"If I had a therapist, I'm sure they'd have ideas." His tone is dark and amused. Then, as if brushing past the admission, he shoots me a pointed look. "It's why you're so frustrating."

"Because I don't like you?"

"Yes," he agrees. "Makes me bitter."

"At least we're in that together."

He drains his beer and deposits it on a waist-high bar table in the middle of the balcony. "Hang on. Has something *I've* done made *you* bitter?"

"Oh, come on." I wait. He waits. "Alex, you can't be serious."

"Rarely." He smirks. "But that *was* a serious question."

I consider him, wondering how to play this. If he wants it all out there, I'm game.

"Tell me what you're doing here," I demand, taking an educated guess at his answer.

He laughs softly, amused at a private joke. But then the expression vanishes, and he admits, "I'm sometimes invited to stuff like this."

"Why?" I ask. It's a dare.

He considers my dare, then turns to me. "I think you probably know why."

"Maybe I want to hear you say it."

My gaze never drops, and eventually Alex sighs in exasperation, glaring at the water. "I got invited to this event because my father has good seats. Not that I've ever been to a game with him. I'm pretty sure he mostly gives the tickets away to business partners, but the team's probably hoping I'll buy some of my own after tonight."

This line of inquiry is going exactly the way I planned.

"Your father sounds rich and important," I say, voice dripping with sarcasm. "What does he do for a living?"

Slowly Alex turns his head, eyes widening. "Oh. That's what it is," he murmurs. Very faintly, and more to himself than to me. He looks like he just decoded the Rosetta stone, and the fact that this cause-and-effect scenario is *only now* dawning on him makes my blood boil. "You hate the nepotism of it," he says at last.

"Duh. Doesn't everyone hate nepotism?"

He tilts his head back and forth. "Except the people who benefit from it."

He's smirking, but not smugly. Why do I feel like I'm missing the punch line of a joke Alex is keeping just out of reach?

He scratches at his neck. "I guess your reaction is fair."

"You *guess* it's fair?"

"I'm *qualified* for this job," he defends, losing patience, but he gives away his unease by fidgeting with his shirt cuffs. "I spent the past two years working in Seoul for a digital media company that's very similar to what *Bite the Hand* is trying to become. We grew that brand from the ground up, and the company is performing well."

"Another family business?" I quip.

Alex pinches the bridge of his nose. "You're intolerable. I don't know why I try."

"Try? Alex, when have you ever had to try at anything?"

He whirls on me, caramel eyes roving hotly over my face. "You don't know anything about me. You don't have a clue."

Maybe he's right, but now that we're finally having it out, I can't find it in me to hold back. "I know that you're well connected, well educated, well traveled—"

"Here I thought we were fighting."

"And I know that for some reason, everybody *loves* you. God forbid I'm the one person who didn't immediately warm to your presence, but please don't delude yourself into thinking it wasn't for lack of trying that hard."

"Just because you're as inviting as a *porcupine* doesn't mean I should be villainized because I'm friendly," he says. "Believe me, you've got the try-hard personality trait covered enough for both of us."

"What's that supposed to mean?"

His eyes gleam. "It means I've never seen anyone so committed to hating a person they hardly fucking know. No wonder you said you're nobody's dream girl."

I flinch, stung, and take a step backward that's more like a stumble.

"Casey." Alex takes a small step forward, and our eyes lock. His face is twisted in regret. "I didn't mean that. I'm sorry."

"It's fine."

"I promise. I didn't mean it," he says again, lower.

Is he reading the heart on my sleeve right now? Am I letting him? It's such a vulnerable feeling that all I can think to do in this moment is find the chink in his own armor and stab him right back.

"Do you really think HR didn't know who your dad was when they offered you your job, Alex? Be serious. At the very least, they were biased in your favor."

I can tell from the fracture in his eyes that he knows I'm right. A twisted satisfaction seeps through me, taking this small thing from him.

"What do you want from me?" He raises his arms, but his voice is soft. "HR said I was their strongest candidate by a mile."

And *that*, I realize with a punch to the gut, is the crux of why his presence hurts me so much.

Not because I lost out on the job to the board chairman's son, but because even if he weren't the board chairman's son, Alex would have edged me out anyway.

He clearly has no idea I applied. As much as I want to dislike him, I can admit he wouldn't have said that to me just now if he'd known.

Alex doesn't deserve to be the source of my insecurity, but still, he landed squarely into it, every edge of him filling the gaps of what I'm not.

Maybe I should say sorry, too. For saying he's never had to try at anything in life, which was unfair. Because Alex is right. I don't know anything about him. Not really. But I can't talk, or look him in the eye again, without risking him discovering that there's something deeper going on here. Like he said, heart's on my sleeve.

We're quiet for a few moments, letting the wave of voices inside and the noise of car horns below fill up the space between us.

"Casey," he says eventually. "Just . . . I just wish—"

But he's interrupted when someone in a navy-blue suit smelling suspiciously of spray tan comes up and claps Alex on the shoulder. "My God. I thought that was you!"

His eyes jerk away from mine, the cord snapping, ricocheting. "Yeah, I'm . . . Hey, Bishop, how've you been?" His voice resets. Now it's the voice Alex uses on others, the one that makes everybody fall in love with him.

My eyes search for Sasha. She's been watching us from the bar inside, too far away to hear much, but when we lock eyes, she jerks her head at the elevator.

I leave the party, and Alex stays, and I never learn what he just wishes for.

CHAPTER FIVE

"Where does he think he gets *off*!"

Sasha hurls her body through my apartment door, stomping inside like the petulant celebrity's daughter she occasionally still emulates. She kicks off her heels while I set the to-go bag of Chinese food on my tiny, scuffed-up kitchen table.

"The entitlement of men never ceases to amaze me," she adds.

"Tiger, stripes," I offer with a shrug.

She exhales, rubbing her hands over the smooth ebony skin of her face. "I'm really sorry about tonight, Case. I know you hate events like that, and normally, I would have brought Miguel—"

"Wait." My head cocks. "I thought you said he had the flu."

"I fibbed!" She winces. "I thought it would be cool for you to network with Dougie outside of work, but I'd never really *talked* to the man before, and, well . . . I didn't realize he'd be such a handsy, father-knows-best asshat."

I wave a hand at her. "I appreciate the thought. I think."

My roommate, Miriam, appears in the doorway of her

bedroom—which is honestly just a partitioned section of our tiny, one-bedroom apartment—still dressed in hospital scrubs. It looks like she's been sleeping; her bleached-blond bobbed hair is a bird's nest, and mascara is rubbed under her eyes.

"Food?" she croaks.

I beckon her with my palm. "Got you, lover."

She smiles sleepily and pads into the kitchen, feet clad in panda slippers. "Whose man is entitled?"

"A mutual acquaintance named Dougie Dawson," I supply while I open the plastic lid of the pork siu mai dumplings.

Miriam sits down beside me. "Sounds like a cartoon character."

"He thinks he's the fucking mayor." Sasha helps herself to a half-drunk bottle of red wine on the bar cart I'm pretty sure is three weeks old. She pours three glasses and hands them out to us. "No offense to your paycheck, Case, but that guy sucks. After you walked away, I tried broaching the subject of female-focused ads on the jumbotrons at sports events, and he all but laughed me out of the room."

"He'll probably die soon," I mutter darkly.

Miriam laughs. "You spend too much time with Brijesh."

"You're the one screwing him."

Miriam flips me the bird.

Sasha divests herself of her Chanel purse and sits down while I start in on the Chinese broccoli in oyster sauce I ordered. Miriam takes careful bites of everything: sticky rice with Chinese sausage, scallion pancakes, pan-fried noodles. Her nursing hours are weird, and I can never keep up with when she'll be here or at work, but her daily eating schedule pretty much relies on whether I've left takeout for her in the fridge. I just Venmo charge her at the end of the month. It's a well-oiled system.

After a few seconds of quiet, Sasha groans. "Okay, I was waiting for you to bring it up, but you're clearly not going to. Can we *please* talk about that hottie, Alex?"

Miriam tilts her head at me. "Alex . . ." She drifts off, grasping for context clues.

I was really hoping Sasha had let that part of the evening slip from her mind.

"Alex Harrison," I grumble.

"Alex *Harrison*?" Miriam repeats. "The jackass who stole your job? You never told me he was a hottie!"

Affecting the tone of a degenerate grouch, I admit, "He is objectively attractive. His hair is nice. And his eyes are . . . nice, and his voice is sort of scratchy. And he's tall enough to loom."

My friends are quiet for a couple of long seconds, staring at me. I shift in my seat, belatedly realizing how much I just admitted.

To them. To myself.

"Oh, Casey." Miriam shakes her head. "You always did swoon for a man who loomed."

"I did not."

She sips her wine and makes an *ahh* sound. "You're in trouble, doll face."

"They looked very romantic together, out there on the balcony," Sasha adds.

Unbidden, the scene from earlier strikes sharp and hard behind my eyes. *No wonder you said you're nobody's dream girl.*

"I'd put money on the fact that romantic is not the way we looked."

I'm prepared to go to the mat on this one with four weeks' worth of grievances to share, but they just laugh together, proud of themselves for riling me up. Miriam and Sasha—who are friends only because I introduced them during Geology 101 our first year of college—love to conspire against me. It'd be annoying if it were not a reminder they cared.

"Did you guys get Jack and Jill's save the date?" Sasha asks. "Mine came yesterday."

Ugh. Hate this subject, too.

Miriam jerks a thumb at the fridge, where the save the date in question is hanging behind a Brooklyn Bridge magnet. "They addressed it to Casey and me together, like we're an old married couple."

"I sometimes wonder," Sasha deadpans. "Weddings are expensive. So what if they didn't want to waste an extra stamp?"

"Especially since Casey's going to bail anyway," Miriam intones.

I glare at her. She smirks back.

I hadn't even . . . How on earth could she *know* that? Mir and I have been best friends since we were eleven, but sometimes I think she's well and truly psychic. I *was* planning to bail on the wedding. I just haven't come up with a creative excuse yet.

Sasha pins me with her mature, woman-about-town look. "Case, you have to go. I know it's gonna be awkward seeing your ex as a groomsman and all—"

"Never said I wasn't going."

"But Jack and Jill were your friends, too."

"Can we *not*? I'm begging." I press my hands to my temples, feigning a headache. After the last couple of hours, thinking about the guy I broke up with on graduation day—and all the reasons why that choice was the right one—is simply too much to bear.

"Fine." Sasha holds up her palms in submission. "Let's talk about New Year's Eve. Are we still planning to go to Nashville?"

Miriam arches her eyebrows, gestures between me and her. "Why are you asking us as if we had any part in that plan?"

"Come *on*, guys," Sasha whines. "I want to go *so* bad, and I need you locals to show me how to ride the mechanical bulls on Broadway."

"The key," I say, propping my foot on the fourth chair, "is to flirt with the guy working the bull so he takes it easy on you for ten whole seconds."

Miriam nods sagely. "Spilling your drink all over your legs a couple of minutes beforehand helps, too. It makes your thighs stick to the leather."

Sasha blinks. "Neither of you have done it, have you."

"Of course not." Miriam sounds genuinely offended.

"Well then." Sasha crosses her arms. "All three of us are riding the mechanical bull in December, and whoever falls off the fastest has to solo-perform 'Rocky Top' at a karaoke bar on wine night."

I laugh deep in my chest. "Hand to God, Sasha, you have never met an experience you couldn't turn into a challenge."

"I probably get that from my dad," she says.

Miriam launches into a retelling of her day at the hospital—"The cutest baby in the PICU, I almost triggered an Amber Alert"—and Sasha and I listen to her describe burping methods in excruciating detail as the city quiets down outside.

I can hear the drip of our leaky faucet, soft and repetitive, into our pint-size enamel kitchen sink, beside a stove that couldn't cook a hard-boiled egg if it tried. This apartment is a disaster—too small, too messy, too run-down, and way, *way* too expensive for all its quirks—but it's perfect to me. Because it represents everything I traded when Lance and I broke up, when Miriam and I decided to move to New York City together.

A life I knew like the back of my hand for a life I never could have predicted.

CHAPTER SIX

Alex Harrison: How much money is left in the
budget for September?
   Casey Maitland: None.
Alex Harrison: None?
   Casey Maitland: You have already eaten into half
   of October's budget.
Alex Harrison: Why can't we just take the L and reset
for Oct?
   Casey Maitland: Please explain how you convinced
   your high school algebra teacher to let you pass.

We never talked about it.

Never sought each other out, never lingered after a meeting to
clear the air. Alex's singular focus isn't on me anymore; he's preoc-
cupied with one thing only.

Well. Two things:

1. Getting the subsidiary primed to launch.
2. Cementing his status as Little Cooper's most flagrant spender.

It's kind of funny, if I stop to think about it. The way his goals are in exact opposition to mine. If I want a recommendation for the London office, I need to spend the next eight months doing my job exceptionally well. Doing my job well means controlling the finances. Problem is, Alex encourages every idea without bothering to consider the cost.

Podcast? Do it. Digital creator conference in LA? Put the airfare on the corporate card! A new Web designer? Hire him.

Whenever we're in the same room, our disharmony comes off both of us in frustrated heat waves. Like right now, for example, as we argue our way through another weekly BTH meeting. It almost feels like the two of us are alone in this conference room. Which is why it startles me when Saanvi interrupts us to say, "You guys should appear together on our YouTube channel."

Alex and I stop bickering long enough to look at Saanvi, one of Little Cooper's on-staff video directors. Her arms are loosely crossed. She's staring at us across the conference table, a flicker of amusement in her eyes.

I think Saanvi views everything in life through the lens of a camera. She's one of those people that have found their capital-P Purpose. Before Saanvi came to Little Cooper, she worked for one of our competitors, where she made a huge name for herself directing all those videos of celebrities walking around their homes showing off the interior design or answering a bunch of rapid-fire questions we shouldn't care about but do.

She has this policy—if you appear on the channel, you get paid. Brijesh explained it to me after the "Healthed-Up Hot Chicken" video, and then I saw it for myself on my next paycheck: there was a line item in the HR portal where they break down your earnings that said *video appearance*. The amount of money I'd earned was minuscule, but I appreciated it all the same.

In response to Saanvi's suggestion, I dumbly mutter, "What?"

"No, seriously." Her face is utterly calm. "I think you two would be great."

Beside me (he *always* sits next to me, and I *never* understand why), Alex laughs. "How on earth did you get there from us debating the social media budget?"

"There's no *debate*," I half growl, growing heated again at what I was *trying* to explain moments ago. "*Bite the Hand*'s budget is too small to handle all these projects at the same time. You need to get your priorities in order."

He leans back in his chair and taps a pen absentmindedly on his notepad. "We'll get the budget expanded. I'm not worried about money right now."

I shake my head, laughing humorlessly. "If I had a dime for every time that sentence has come out of your mouth, I wouldn't be worried about money, either."

"Oh my God, Saanvi," says Amanda, the social media director. "You're totally right. They'd be perfect for that work life segment."

My mouth snaps closed.

Everyone in the room is looking at me and Alex like they just solved a puzzle.

"The *Food Baby* YouTube subscribers already love Casey," Saanvi says, sitting up. "You're relatable to them because your job is—"

"Boring?" I supply.

"Don't be so hard on yourself, Simba," Alex jokes.

"You're both young and—forgive me—attractive, with perfectly typical day jobs, which I think our viewers will find endearing. We've featured chefs, professional athletes, TV personalities,

Lin-Manuel Miranda, even a few politicians. But we've never had business professionals on the 'One Day at Work' segment."

"I'm into it," says Gus, Alex's boss. "They can give our audience a behind-the-scenes look at the industry."

I scowl at him. Gus Moskowitz comes second only to Alex in terms of flagrant spending. *Bite the Hand* was his idea, and he's been heading up its mostly freelance editorial team ever since. When he interviewed me for Alex's job, I'd been temporarily enamored with his big personality and disarming nature—but now, I'm flabbergasted I ever wanted to work for someone so fiscally irresponsible.

"Oh my God," says Social Media Amanda. "They fit a totally untapped niche!"

My eyes widen and my heart rate spikes as I turn to Alex for support. Surely he'll agree this is a *terrible* idea. When our eyes catch, I hold out hopes he'll speak for the both of us. There's a downturn to his lips, and his jaw looks tense.

But then he says, "I'm in if you're in."

Traitor!

I don't even know where to start in rationalizing my forthcoming response of "No fucking way in hell" to the BTH project team.

First of all, what is Alex trying to accomplish here? Does he want to keep his enemy close? How can I justify appearing on a YouTube segment with him when that would be like welcoming him into the fold? It would signal that I'm *okay* with his presence here, which, to reiterate, I am *not*. Lastly, who in their ever-loving right mind could possibly think I'm interesting enough to hold my own through an entire YouTube video? And that's not even to mention my childhood speech impediment, which still rears its head at the most inopportune moments.

"I'm not sure Don's going to like this," I say.

"We'll be transparent with your boss about the time commitment," Saanvi promises. "It wouldn't go beyond normal work hours."

Ha! Normal work hours. That's a good one, Saanvi.

Everyone's staring at me now. Waiting for me to agree. Because honestly, who'd pass up on the chance to be at the center of something new and fun and potentially career altering? After all, isn't this what I wanted? Isn't this why I applied for Alex's job in the first place? To be a part of something that means *something*?

A grainy, sepia image of Mom floods my mind, the edges of her likeness blurred away after sixteen years. The problem with photographers is that they're hardly ever in the picture, and whenever I hold her photos in my hands, I see what *she* saw.

I see everything but her.

Now, though, she's clearer, and so are the words she spoke to me when I was six: *It all comes down to what you leave behind.*

It took me years to figure out what she meant. What she wanted so desperately to communicate to me on her deathbed. When I got older, I learned she was sick for a lot longer than either she or Dad ever let on. Years, in fact. Once I knew that, things started to click.

Mom saw death coming. She had time to think about it. Time to process what good could come from it. And for Mom, in the end, it was all about legacy.

It all comes down to what you leave behind.

I wrestle with that piece of wisdom a lot. Every day, probably. Because Mom has a real legacy, and so does Dad. They've both made works of art that are going to outlive them. But not me. There's nothing I've ever done that might outlive me.

Maybe, though, this choice is the beginning of something that will.

"I guess I'm okay with trying." My voice comes out softer than I mean it to. "Though honestly, I'm not convinced two business professionals bickering in a conference room will translate well on camera."

"Of course it won't, but I have a better idea." Saanvi snaps her fingers, looking at nothing. Her focus comes back to us. "I'll book a small video team. We'll record a working lunch between you two to test this concept out. I'll make some calls, see if we can't reserve a back corner somewhere. Can you guys block off eleven to one o'clock on your calendars tomorrow?"

"Tomorrow?" I squeak. It's like Saanvi knows that if she can't make this happen in twenty-four hours, I'll have time to come up with an excuse to get out of it.

Alex leans over. Low in his throat, he says, "I'll send you a meeting invite."

"I'll send *you* a meeting invite," I whisper back.

He clicks his tongue. "But you might forget to add me again."

"Trust me, I won't."

Five minutes later, we exit the conference room, and I expel a heavy breath when I realize I accomplished the *opposite* of what my boss asked me to do. Instead of putting the brakes on the budget, I got roped into participating in our costliest platform.

I tap my foot, tug at my pink cashmere T-shirt dress as Alex and I wait for the elevator back to ninety-eight. He works here on thirty-seven, but he spends a lot of time traversing my floor, too. Right now, he's leaning a shoulder against the wall, one hand loosely clutching a brown, leather padfolio (Alex never brings his laptop to meetings). He's watching me with a perplexed expression, his eyebrows drawn together in thought.

"Look," he says, rubbing a hand over his face. "I understand you'd rather jump out a ninety-eighth-floor window than be caught on video with me, but I'm committed to doing everything I can to get *Bite the Hand* up and running independently. Can we just . . . put aside our differences for one day to make this work?"

"It's not that. It's not you," I say, belatedly realizing I hadn't meant to say it out loud.

His forehead wrinkles. "Then what is it?"

Now it's Dad swarming my thoughts. Because it's all still tied up in my head like this, memories that are one big slippery slope. Me, eleven years old. The fifth-grade talent show flyer Dad fished out of the recycling bin. I'd been sitting on the kitchen floor, organizing my savings into different coin piles to see if I had enough money for a pair of Sperrys, when he held up that flyer and said, "I've been waiting for this since you were born."

We practiced for weeks. Him on the electric guitar, me on the bedazzled acoustic he'd gotten Taylor Swift to sign for me two years earlier. He'd been so excited for me to perform his latest breakout song (albeit recorded by someone much more famous), blasting that fall on every country music station in Nashville. Dad and Jerry, who was only his boyfriend at the time, had shown up to the school auditorium with a video camera and a bouquet of flowers. But I couldn't even muster up the courage to make it onstage.

They hadn't cared, of course. We left the talent show early and went to Bolton's for hot chicken, then home so I could perform the song for an audience of two. Jerry clipped the flowers and rained the petals down on me. It was a good day, in its way. But thinking about it still breaks my heart a little. Dad leaves his legacy behind with every song he writes, and I couldn't honor it the way we both wanted me to.

"I won't be good at it," I admit to Alex softly, biting my lip. "Even worse, I'll probably choke."

His expression goes soft and open, and maybe even a little bit tortured, like my words have bothered him in a way I didn't intend and certainly don't understand. He opens his mouth and pushes himself off the wall, but right then, the elevator doors open.

We step inside and move to opposite corners, the silence clawing at me. Two older gentlemen stand in front of us, mutely staring at the silver doors. I don't dare look at Alex after what I just admitted to him. But halfway up the beanstalk, the men exit together, and when the doors close, he slides down the rail toward me.

I glance up, expecting that same soft openness, but he's already back to his neutral state. "I've been thinking a lot," he begins, his voice like a scratched-up record in a vintage store. "About you." I gulp, and his eyes drop to my throat. "About the things you said to me during that happy hour. The things I said to you."

"And?"

He sighs. "And we hurt each other's feelings."

"We—" I shake my head. "You didn't . . . hurt my feelings."

"Okay. Fine. I didn't hurt your feelings when I implied nobody would want to be with you. Just like you didn't hurt mine when you boiled my whole job down to my bloodline." He looms over me, casting me in shadow.

"What's your point?" I bite out.

His eyes drop to the narrow strip of space between our bodies just before he steps away. "I guess I don't really have one. But I've been thinking about it. Wondering if it's even possible to prove you wrong about who I am, or if it isn't, because you're right."

The elevator peels open on the ninety-eighth floor, and Benny nods a greeting from behind the concierge desk, halfway finished with the Reese's Peanut Butter Cup he's stress-eating. (I really need to have a conversation with him about allergen-friendly workplace behavior.)

Alex steps toward Benny. But like an afterthought, he throws back to me over his shoulder, "I'm dying to be wrong about you, Casey. You're not making it easy."

CHAPTER SEVEN

There's a note from Miriam stuck to our fridge, scrawled in pink Sharpie on the back of an Ulta receipt:

> BE HOME AT 3 A.M. BRIJ MENTIONED Y'ALL
> ARE GETTING DIN TONIGHT. COULD YOU GUYS
> CONSIDER ITALIAN?? I WANT GNOCCHI!!!

I text him a picture of her request. When we made plans earlier today, he'd had his heart set on tamales, but he also has his heart set on Miriam, and I know for a fact he will recalibrate to Italian so she'll have the leftovers she wants after her shift.

I swipe a tepid Diet Coke from the counter—cluttered with everything that doesn't strictly necessitate refrigeration—and walk into my bedroom.

Once, a three-night stand during my first whirlwind month in New York described this room as what he assumed a thrift store would look like. I've latched on to that ever since like it was the biggest compliment in the world, even though I'm pretty sure the dude meant it as a dig. The furniture is ramshackle, my "closet" is just a freestanding Ikea rack of vintage clothes and sample sale purchases, and I can't see out the window because it's mostly taken up by the AC unit. Also, it smells like Chinese food from the restaurant one building over mellowed out by sage smudges.

I like what he'd said, though, about the room being *thrifted,* because that word never fails to remind me of Mom. She died of lung cancer when I was six—a chain-smoker till the end, as Dad tells it with equal parts annoyance and affection—but in every rare, precious photo of her, she's wearing all these awesome outfits you'd never find in Aritzia. I think part of her fashion sense came from being a Londoner and part came from being a concert photographer. Whatever it was, the woman had *style.* I was too young to remember most things about her, but I remember sitting on her bed while she got dressed every morning, designing her OOTD in the floor-length mirror. That, I remember.

And suddenly, I'm feeling homesick, dialing my father.

"Hi, honey!" Dad shouts on the other end of the FaceTime call. I wince at the piercing shrill of his voice and hold the phone away from my face, but I can't help grinning. Dad has a graying ponytail and weathered skin, and his cheeks get rounder each time I see him.

"Hey, Dad. What's good?"

"Casey!" My stepdad, Jerry, appears, bald with wire-rimmed glasses that frame bright green eyes. He and Dad grin in a way I hardly deserve. "Look at my amaryllis! Here, gimme that."

There's a scuffle, during which I hear, "Jer!" Then the phone drops, and the screen goes black. I bite my bottom lip, fighting a snort.

"Casey!" Dad bellows. "Are you okay?"

"Oh my God, you guys dropping your own cell phone can't hurt—never mind."

The phone is scooped back up, and I get a glorious view of Jerry's nose hairs. "Come with me," he tells me.

"Right behind you."

Thirty seconds later, he flashes me the amaryllis in question after I give him pointers on how to flip the camera to its front view. I sit up in bed, genuinely astounded. The amaryllis is healthy and vibrant, with tall, green stalks and gorgeous pink flowers.

"Wait, is that the same bulb?" I ask in disbelief. "The dried-up one—"

"That I got from the neighbors' compost bin? Yeah!" Jerry sticks a thumb up in front of the camera.

Dad snorts somewhere nearby. "You *stole* it from the neighbor's compost bin."

"I didn't steal it."

"You didn't ask."

"They threw it away."

I tilt my head from side to side. "I mean, they could have been experimenting with how it would fare in an environment of biological degradation."

"Only we would do something that weird. I thought you were on my side with this one." Jerry pouts.

"I am. I can't believe you got it to bloom."

"I did exactly what you suggested," Jerry says proudly. "I mixed three parts Miracle-Gro with one part sandy soil, seven days outdoors and two days in. Water sparingly."

"The student has become the master," I brag.

"Don't push it, sweetheart."

Dad steals the phone back from his husband and flips the camera around. He pushes the glasses up the bridge of his nose and says, as if plants are utterly boring, "Anyway. Listen to this drama about the family across the street. It involves a Serbian cellist and half a dozen illegitimate children, all of whom are named after a pastry. Jer and I got invited to this Yom Kippur break fast. . . ."

I listen obediently to the scandalous tale of my parents' weird new neighbors and the murder-mystery-esque plot that unfolded at

Yom Kippur break fast. I give soft, convincing mm-hmms during the juicy bits, only halfway paying attention, but by the time Dad gets to the part about a hidden message in the cellist's music indicating a *seventh* illegitimate Serbian child named Croissant, I'm laughing my ass off, buried in my mountain of jewel-tone pillows.

"I'm calling bluff," I say at last, bleary tears staining my cheeks.

"Fine," Dad mutters. "Only about half of that is true. You're too sharp these days, kiddo. But they really did name their offspring after pastries."

He talks and talks and talks some more until he's told me every menial detail about whatever floats into his head. Jerry pipes up every now and then, and they have a whole conversation about which Aldi cracker brand they like best for charcuterie boards before they steer themselves back to me.

"How are you doing, Case?" Jerry asks. Before I can answer, he adds, "I heard a story about you from someone you know from college, Andrew something. He works at an event-planning company?"

"Andrew Martinez," I supply.

"Yes! He ordered an apology bouquet for his girlfriend, but that's none of *my* business. I mean, it's technically my *business,* since I'm his florist, but anyway, he saw you on YouTube. Is that part of your finance job?"

I giggle. "No, it's not related to finance." I try to explain, but I think I lose Dad and Jerry somewhere between *vertical* and *profit optimization.* We occasionally fumble in our communications at the junction of where art meets STEM.

"Now I'm craving hot chicken," Jerry says. "Can you show us how to watch the YouTube video?"

"I'll text you guys the link."

"Thanks, hon," Dad says. "Have you thought about coming home for Thanksgiving?"

Ugh. I *knew* that was coming.

I haven't seen my parents in nearly a year. We vacationed in

Key West last Thanksgiving, but I didn't go home for Christmas because the year before, I'd visited Nashville and experienced some sort of . . . geographical depression. It's what I assume people who hate the cold feel like during winter.

If I had to psychoanalyze it, I think it comes back to my college ex. Our knock-down-drag-out-graduation-day breakup. We had *just* exited the auditorium in our black caps and gowns, our stoles and cords draped over our necks, when I got the *call.* From an HR rep at Little Cooper, telling me they were offering me a job as an entry-level financial analyst.

I was shocked. I'd already written off the interview as hopeless, thought my chances of landing the job were especially slim considering the lineup of Ivies the other people in LC's Finance department had graduated from. Miriam was the one who pushed me to apply; she was moving here to work as a nurse, and with Sasha heading to Manhattan, too, I'd thrown a few applications at the wall just to see what might stick.

Little Cooper stuck. And with that brand-new option before me, I realized something.

Moving back to Nashville with Lance would be a given, but moving to New York with Miriam would be a *choice.*

And I wanted it so badly. The city, the job, the lifestyle, the romanticism of coming into your adulthood in a delirious fumble of *Oh my God what the hell am I doing, who cares, this is just as exhilarating as it is petrifying.* I wanted it, knowing it would probably destroy my four-year relationship. Which was, admittedly, the hardest decision I've ever made.

We had it out that night. I was more naive than he always thought, and wasn't I supposed to be smarter than this? Didn't I know everybody in New York bled money faster than they earned it? How did I think I'd ever find someone better than him? Wasn't it selfish to want something different when I could find a job in Nashville that would set us up for the future?

Lance was right about that part. It *was* selfish. But looking back, I'm proud of myself for going after what I wanted.

Because New York makes me feel like I'm on the precipice of something. It's the bridge between Casey before and Casey forever, and now, I just have to figure out what's around the corner, on the other side of this precipice. London, maybe. Or a job that makes people's eyes go starry when they hear about it. Or—call me a romantic, as I suppose that I am one—the love of my life, or whatever.

"Casey? You there?"

I sigh dreamily. "Let me double-check with my boss, and then I'll look at flights."

Jerry whoops, and Dad exhales a huge sigh of relief. It punches me in the gut, the guilt of staying away.

"Honey, it will be amazing. We'll plan your whole trip down to the letter."

Pleeeease don't, I want to say, but I keep my mouth shut as Dad rattles off a list of all the things he wants us to do over Thanksgiving. I love my parents. I really, really do. But sometimes, they are more exhausting and harder to manage than the COO's ex-wife. (And just for some perspective, she once disguised herself as a janitor to get up to ninety-eight so she could berate the COO about his spicy LinkedIn chats. Apparently, he's smitten with the CEO of CycleBar . . . but that's none of *my* business.)

"Can you explain to me why," Brijesh asks as he swirls the wine in his glass, "when it comes to men, I'm only ever interested in toxic himbos?"

We're at a cozy Italian restaurant in Prospect Heights with a plate of garlic ciabatta and an olive oil flight between us. These dinners are scheduled whenever Brijesh needs new material for his *Food Baby* column, Guess That Restaurant.

Sometimes, Miriam comes, too. An outing like this is actually how she and Brijesh first met, exchanging lingering stares and laughing at each other's jokes that weren't that funny, in my opinion. But she can only make it half the time because of work.

I drain my own glass of cabernet. "I literally don't know what a himbo is."

"Don't you have Twitter?"

"Yeah, but I mostly follow Jason Sudeikis fan accounts."

Brijesh looks down and pinches the bridge of his nose. "You're too wholesome for New York. I'm kicking you out. Just not before Friday at eight o'clock, because we have that Oaxacan reservation. Opening night."

"Oh!" I brighten up. "I forgot about that. Didn't we reserve it, like, three months ago?"

"Four. It's an important one, too. *Food Baby* wants the first scoop on the chef, but he's notoriously reclusive." Brijesh's eyes never leave the menu. "Do you like sardines?"

"Allergic," I remind him. "What about the tagliatelle?"

"What about the roasted duck."

"It's a Wednesday," I counter.

He puts his chin on his fist and smiles. "I didn't know you were Catholic."

"I'm not. That's not a thing. You can't just go around having roasted duck on a Wednesday, unless you're, like, as pretentious as the Harrisons."

Brijesh shrugs, as if he's considering whether he'd like to be. With an evil grin he adds, "I'll need a full report of Alex Harrison's food and beverage choices tomorrow during your *lunch meeting.*" He may as well have said *sexual intercourse.* I already regret telling him about Saanvi's weird YouTube idea. "I can tell things about people from the way they order," he explains. "It's my own personal zodiac."

"What does mine say about me?"

"That you're chaotic. Meanwhile, *my* meal choices are intentional. If I had to guess, I'd say Alex runs the creature comfort foods gamut."

I have no idea what he means by that, and I don't want to ask, lest I sound more invested than I've got any right to be. But still, my mind wanders back to what Alex said in the elevator, him questioning if I'd been right about him all along. And in the next breath: *I'm dying to be wrong about you. You're not making it easy.*

My whole body frowns every time I try to decode that exchange.

"You're thinking about him, and you wish you weren't," Brijesh says.

"Good Lord," I groan, mortified. "Am I seriously that easy to read?"

"Yes." He smirks. "You're very expressive."

I find myself much less concerned about Brijesh reading my thoughts than Alex reading them, which is concerning in and of itself. "He just—is so—"

"Intense," Brijesh offers.

I frown. "Intense?"

He leans back, rubs at his chin stubble. "Honestly, Alex kind of reminds me of you in that way. You're like each other's inverses."

My glare is instantaneous. "What did I do to deserve that comparison."

"He's all fueled up with ideas coming out of his ass every thirty seconds, and meanwhile, you're this steady, reliable kind of genius. If people need help with something specific, you're the first person they'd ask, but if they need a soundboard for ideas, they'd go to Alex." He drags another piece of bread through olive oil. "I'd bet my whole cookbook collection you two have an identical podcast lineup."

Our waiter returns with a plate of roasted squash in hand. It's been done up all fancy with pistachios, fennel, and prosciutto. "Compliments of the chef," he says.

Brijesh drops his sliver of bread. "Fuck!"

I flinch. The waiter takes a step back from the table, eyes wide with confusion.

Remembering himself, Brijesh apologizes and thanks the waiter, who sets the food down and scurries away.

"Well," he says. "I can officially cross 'restaurant critic' off my list of future career opportunities. My anonymity is shot."

"Oh. Someone recognized you?"

"Must have."

My eyes track to the hostess and a few waiters in a circle, staring at us and whispering conspiratorially. Brijesh is watching them, too. Specifically, he's watching a waitress with pink hair and doe eyes.

I don't think Miriam minds when Brijesh hooks up with other people, considering their friends-with-benefits arrangement is *her* idea. Then again, I have no clue what's really going on between the two of them. Mostly, I just stay out of it. But right now, there's a carefully concealed smile of intent behind Brijesh's eyes I can't avoid.

He grabs his wineglass. Swirls it. Sips languorously.

I pin him with a knowing look. "You're loving this, you attention whore."

"You can't prove that!"

After dinner, he takes home the hostess, and I take home the gnocchi.

CHAPTER EIGHT

I'm halfway through last month's P&L prep when Alex swings into my cubicle. One of his hands is clinging to the flimsy wall's edge, the other open and lifted. His hair is a wreck and he's wearing a crimson-and-yellow tie striped on the diagonal. With a clip.

"Tie clip," I comment dryly.

"Does it offend you?"

"Depends. Is it engraved with the logo of your personal clothier?"

"Of course," Alex says, just as dryly. "I visit him in the South of France each June after the Cannes Film Festival. Where do you summer?"

"The Florida Panhandle."

He whistles appreciatively.

"What are you doing here?" I ask. "I could have met you in the lobby."

The face Alex aims at me is triumphant, insufferable, and I can already tell he's going to gloat about something. "I wanted to tell you right away that I got the budget expanded."

"What? How?" I spin toward him in my swivel chair and cross my legs beneath my maxi skirt.

"With the right motivation, anything is possible."

My eyes narrow. "Who'd you get fired to cobble together the money?"

"Looking at her."

I blink in rapid succession. "You're hilarious."

He smirks. "Don't worry, Simba. Much as I hate to admit it, I wouldn't get anything done without you. The extra money came out of *Garden Girl*'s budget. I now have enemies on thirty-eight who might try to off me with poisonous flora."

"Worse ways to go."

"Even so, I won't be accepting strange teas for the time being."

"Not even from me?"

"Especially from you." Alex taps on the wall a couple of times, then leans against it, crossing his arms. "I didn't know you wore glasses."

"Oh." I rip them off my face. "They're just blue light."

He hums. "Here I thought we finally had something in common."

"Contacts?" I ask.

He nods. "Since I was a kid."

I get a sudden flash of Alex in the morning, dressed in boxers (with a lacrosse stick motif) and an old HARVARD T-shirt. Glasses on, hair wrecked. The image makes my ears get weirdly hot.

"You ready for lunch?" he asks quietly, as if he really is just asking me if I'm ready for lunch. His expression is warm. After what I admitted to him yesterday, maybe he's trying to be gentle with me.

I put my computer to sleep, grab my bag, and stand. With a weary sigh, I warn him, "This whole YouTube thing might be an absolute shit show."

"Knowing us, it will be." He smiles. But something about it seems kind of sad.

"Alex." My chin tilts down toward my shoes. "I . . ."

When I don't finish, he takes a step forward. "Yeah?" His voice is still soft. Encouraging.

I want to be wrong about you, too.

A more magnanimous person would say it. But if I told him I want to move forward, it would still feel like a betrayal to myself. His employment here is a hump I'm not fully able to get past, and maybe that's okay, but it's not right for me to lord it over Alex's very qualified, hardworking head, either.

"For today, should we just . . . put everything aside? For *Bite the Hand*'s sake?"

He gives me another smile and looks out the window, hands in his pockets. "Sure, Casey. If that's what you want."

I nod. He nods. I start walking, and he follows.

On our way to the elevator, Alex says, "Hey, Benny."

Benny holds up a palm, head hung in defeat from all the schedule wrangling he's had to do this month. "I cannot engage with you today, Alex. I simply cannot."

I stifle a snort.

Behind the closed doors of the elevator, Alex and I settle against opposite walls. "Sometimes I think Benny's attitude is a vibe check for the whole company," he says.

"Bad news for the rest of October," I joke, tucking my hair behind my ears.

He watches me for a moment in that open, plain-as-day way of his, arms crossed over his chest, head resting against the wall behind him. His eyes flicker across my face, then flash briefly down the length of my body and back up. So fast I might have imagined it.

His lips part. But he must decide against whatever was on the tip of his tongue, because he clamps them back together and gives a tiny shake of his head.

"What?" I ask.

He hesitates. "Nothing."

"Liar."

Alex scrubs a hand over his forehead. "It's not professional."

I raise my eyebrows. "Do I really need to remind you what you whispered to me in this very elevator on your first day? Besides, if you don't tell me, my mind's going to autofill with something far worse."

Alex laughs and shakes his head. "I was just going to say you look pretty."

My head perks up like a bird-of-paradise, proud someone noticed my ridiculous preening. "Oh. Thank you."

I tried *not* to put on more makeup this morning than I'd do for my normal workday routine, but I couldn't get the fact that I'd be on camera out of my head every time I looked in the mirror. I picked out an eye-popping outfit, too, praying the bright colors would distract from whatever bland, forgettable nonsense falls out of my mouth. My maxi skirt is pink and pleated, and I'm wearing a lightweight sweater that belonged to my mom. My ears are adorned with big silver stars and my hair's been semi-blown out.

"Don't worry. Tomorrow I'll go back to looking like a gremlin."

Alex shakes his head again, softer this time. Beneath his breath, he says, "You'll look just as pretty tomorrow as you did the day we met."

The elevator doors open to the lobby. I hardly notice. Alex's and my gazes are locked, as if we're both waiting to see if the other person is going to freak out over what he just said.

"Alex?" comes a deep, hoarse voice from outside the elevator.

We both turn forward in sync.

Standing there among a gaggle of old white men, all of whom are dressed in tailored suits and boasting varying states of baldness, is Robert Harrison.

Alex's father.

Their familial designations may as well be written on their foreheads. Robert is tall, like his son. They have the same sharp jawline, the same thin nose, broad forehead, and even broader shoulders. But his father's eyes are blue compared to Alex's light brown, and his hair and skin is pale white against Alex's darker features.

Robert Harrison was the CEO when I first started with Little Cooper two and a half years ago. When he announced he was moving on to the less demanding position of board chairman, Dougie Dawson came onto the scene out of nowhere.

I spot Dougie now in the crowd, too. Must be a board meeting today.

"Dad," Alex says, gulping.

His father looks genuinely taken off guard. "Alex, what are you doing here?"

Alex winces, his face twisted up in what is obviously panic.

I'm so confused.

"Uh." He scratches at the back of his neck and walks out of the elevator, pointing to a spot a short distance away, his head hung low. His dad follows him, abandoning his cohort, and I follow, too, as the other board members press into the elevator we just vacated.

"What's that about?" one of them asks under his breath.

"Robert's bastard works here," another one—Dougie, this time—answers. The sentence is louder than necessary, and Dougie adds on an unkind laugh, which causes Robert to pause and glare back at him. I catch the tail end of what Dougie says as I keep walking. "I thought Robert knew. I thought Robert did it."

Me too.

Out of earshot from the others, Alex says to his father, "I work here now. At Little Cooper, for *Bite the Hand.*"

The older man's face goes beet red, his expression mottled with fury.

Holy crap. His dad had no idea.

Which means . . . Alex didn't get this job because of his father.

"Put in your notice today," Robert threatens quietly, and I'm so jarred by those five words that I stumble back a little.

Both men turn, noticing me for the first time. "I'll wait for you outside," I tell Alex. I shouldn't be present for the fallout of this conversation.

He gives me a terse nod, staring at the floor like he's guilty of something. I walk away as my mind spins in violent pirouettes.

Behind me, Robert starts in on his son. "When did you leave Seoul?"

"I left you three voicemails. I tried to tell you. . . ."

I exit the building, still numb with confusion. Did Robert Harrison just order his own son to put in his *notice*? Without bothering to hear him out?

Brisk fall air replaces the sterile chill on my skin from the lobby. The soles of my shoes scrape along the sidewalk as I attempt to deconstruct an equation I was certain I'd already solved in my head. Nepotism plus Harvard plus Yankees happy hour invites. Seoul start-ups plus goofy elevator jokes plus *You don't know anything about me, you don't have a clue.*

"Casey!" I snap to attention, and Saanvi materializes before me on the sidewalk. Behind her, the glow of the midday sun splayed across the city's financial district jars me back to reality. There's a small video team with her and a portable version of the cooking studio recording setup. "Perfect timing. Where's Alex?"

"He's just . . ." I gesture vaguely behind me. "Talking with someone inside."

A short, curvy woman with curls and milk-white skin clips a microphone to the front of my sweater. "Hi," the stranger says. "I'm Sara. I do sound."

"Casey. I do finance."

Behind Sara, two guys with matching hipster aesthetics are strapped up in camera gear. They eye me suspiciously. I eye them suspiciously right back.

"Oh, there he is!" Saanvi bounces on her heels.

Before I can turn, Alex appears, stoic, speechless, eyes like a finance bro who just realized he fell victim to the sunk cost fallacy. His face is ashen.

I've got an inkling the Alex I know isn't really here at all.

Sara mics him up the same way she did me, and then she runs us through the audio need-to-knows—reminders not to smack the hidden tech with our arms, how to avoid muffling the sound. But I don't think Alex hears a word of it.

I start to panic then. Because I need Alex right now, and he's lost somewhere. Which is a problem, because I can't *be* him. Wouldn't know how to if I tried. His extroverted enthusiasm, his off-the-cuff humor. That's what's going to make this thing work. Not me. Never just me.

"Alex," I say softly when Sara moves away.

His caramel eyes find mine, and he croaks out, "This was a mistake."

He's not talking about the video shoot.

My voice is firm, the words a near hiss under my breath. Once I say this, there will be no taking it back. "It wasn't a mistake. You're good at this job. People want you here. *I* want you here."

And holy shit, but I really do mean it.

His face is turned down toward mine, and his head blocks the sun, his features cast in shadow. But even like this, I can see him plain as day. The demons his father brought forth get banished in the sunlight, and he starts to appear again from beneath them. The longer I look, the more Alex comes back, until that familiar face of casual competence is just as maddening as it's always been—but at least it's fixed right back where it belongs.

He bites the inside of his cheek. "I can't believe you just said those words."

I want you here.

"Don't let it go to your head."

Alex grins softly, pushing a hand through his hair to flatten it down, which is mostly unsuccessful. "It's too late for that."

Saanvi walks Alex and me through the intro she's after, warning us when the mics go live. "Keep it simple," she says. "Name, job title, where you're from. Someone can also mention what you're doing today. Alex, you want it?"

He shrugs. "Sure."

"So, Casey, you'll go first. Don't worry if you don't nail the intro on your first try. It takes a while for anyone to find their sea legs on camera." Saanvi wrinkles her nose with distaste, as if recalling a previous disaster of a video shoot. As long as I don't cause her to make *that* face again, I'll mark this venture as a success.

The team goes through some final checks and last-minute video setup. Then, I'm saying—in a slightly elevated voice, to a tiny black dot on a little machine—"Hey, guys, welcome to another episode of 'One Day at Work.' I'm Casey, a financial analyst here at Little Cooper Publications, and I'm from Tennessee."

Beside me, Alex waves and flashes a brilliant smile that'll probably melt hearts. "And I'm Alex, a project manager. I'm from right here, New York City. And today we're taking you out for a work lunch."

We get it on the first take, and Saanvi's head almost explodes. She spins around in a circle, flapping her arms, potentially trying to take off. The rest of the video team looks substantially impressed, too, and I am slightly less embarrassed than I was a few minutes ago.

"Let's walk," Saanvi directs. "The team will follow behind you two so we don't piss off the pedestrians. I don't like this angle much, but we have to work with nature on this one."

There isn't a scrap of actual nature in sight—nothing but industrial buildings, hot dog carts, and cigarette butts on the ground—but I choose not to point this out to Saanvi.

I start to walk. "Should I just assume everything I say from now on is fair game for the final cut?"

"Yes." Saanvi's expression is dead serious. "That question included. Adorable."

The October sun is warm on my back. Behind me, Saanvi whispers lens-glare-related prayers to the clouds. Since it's only ten past eleven, the lunch crowd hasn't come out in droves yet, and the sidewalks are just this side of bearable.

"What should we talk about?" Alex asks, aiming his question at the team behind us.

"Whatever you want. This angle is shitty, so we won't use much of this footage."

The only thing I want to talk to Alex about right now is the one thing we can't: his dad.

The dad he left three voicemails for that apparently went unplayed. Maybe even deleted.

Somewhere in Seoul, months ago, Alex tried to explain to his father that he was moving to Manhattan, that he got a job at LC. Robert Harrison doesn't strike me as the type to have gotten where he is in life by not following up on loose ends. Which means he was ignoring his own kid on purpose.

His *bastard* kid, according to Dougie Dawson.

I try to recall a single time my dad sent me to voicemail and can't. Once, I called him drunk at three A.M., screaming into the speakerphone, *"Listen, your song! Playing at Radegast, Dad, the guy on the saxophone, listen, he's riffing on your song!"* And he answered, and laughed, and told me to drink water before I went to bed.

He used to take me backstage with him in the days he played in concert bands, strumming guitar and singing backup vocals for the lead. Every few minutes his eyes would drift toward me, and he'd wink, reminding me he was there if I needed him. He taught me how to ride a bike in Percy Warner Park. Never let go of the handlebars until long after I was certain I wouldn't fall. When I was twelve, I did my first mathletes competition, and Dad showed up to watch with three extra calculators in case mine broke.

He was always, *always* there.

I've heard stories about a parent dying, and the child and the surviving parent never repairing what they used to have. Becoming estranged, the space between them swelling with the grief they don't know how to share. But that's not what happened to me and Dad. He made sure of it—with a family therapist and the crying sessions that neither of us shied away from, the Wednesday nights at Mom's favorite restaurants, the songs he wrote about her, about me. He turned something broken into something beautiful, and until I met Miriam when I was eleven, Dad was my best friend.

And Alex's father won't even listen to his voicemails.

How does *his* mom fit into all of this? I'd always assumed Robert's wife must be Alex's Korean mother. But—

"Hey." He bends toward me, his lips level with my ear, and I catch a whiff of that same cologne. There's something else, a nicer, cleaner scent beneath it he's nearly masking. "Across the street, right there." He points with one hand to a Greek street cart with numbered photos of menu items printed on one side. The gesture makes his shirtsleeve pull up, and I catch the barest glimpse of an inked tattoo on his forearm. "Best gyro in FiDi."

"You've tasted them all?"

"Impossible. That one's the best because the owner's name is Alexander."

When I look over, Alex is smirking, but his eyes are tight, the color of his brown pupils somehow muted, despite the daylight. I have the weirdest notion he's trying to distract me because he knows I'm thinking about what happened in the lobby, and he doesn't want me worrying about it.

"Your vanity is humbling," I deadpan.

"By the way, I've been meaning to ask. Do you mind if I copy your email signature? I like your font and company logo."

I stare, wondering if he's serious. "Uh. It's not copyrighted."

"Cool," he says, winking, and I trip a little, on nothing. "We'll match."

Eataly, an Italian market with dry goods and food stalls, is on the third floor of 4 World Trade. It's a popular lunch spot, so I guess if we're going to be filming a "One Day at Work" segment *not* at the office (which is odd, now that I'm thinking about it), this is as good a location as any. The building appears as we round the corner of Church and Liberty, and five minutes later we're inside.

The video team has more space now, swinging around at all angles, making me feel like a fish in an aquarium. Briefly, I plot a daring escape to the bathroom to check my makeup before deciding that I will not be That Girl.

"I had pasta last night," I tell Alex as we board the escalator for the restaurant section of the market. We're kind of facing each other, kind of facing the camera. Stage angle, Saanvi called it.

Alex glares, and the effect it has on me is . . . really something. "Saanvi told us we were coming here at four thirty yesterday. I had a salad for dinner, like, very specifically."

"Can we get pizza instead?" I ask hopefully.

"Sure." He rolls his eyes. "What do you like on it?"

"Anything. What do you like?"

"Anything."

I bite my lip, dancing from one foot to the other as we step off the escalator. "Actually, I have several allergies."

He tilts his head. "Actually, I hate mushrooms."

I freeze. "Why did we lie."

"Nerves." Alex smiles. He doesn't look nervous, but I think he can tell *I* am and is trying to make me more comfortable. Still trying. "Come on. Let's just build our own."

We order for ourselves, Fari and Don (both of whom were so focused on month-end books they would have forgotten to eat if I hadn't offered to pick up lunch), and the video crew. But when we select our tables, the crew under good lighting and us in the corner to protect the sound quality as best we can, everyone else keeps their food in the bag. Our pizza is staged on our table alongside two Topo Chico bottles. Saanvi tells us to "sip and place them, but don't turn the label away from the camera."

"This cannot possibly be sponsored," I say.

"No, but here's hoping."

One of the hipster twins, Andre, gets a bunch of artsy, close-up shots of the food, drinks, and table while Alex and I stand behind our chairs awkwardly. He shakes his head, clearly just as amused as I am unsettled by this entire procedure. Sara's got ear mufflers on, the other hipster, Eric, is working the wide lens, and Saanvi is watching everything like a hawk.

I am this close to slamming Andre's camera to the ground. My stomach is growling, our pizza looks scrumptious, and this is pure torture.

Finally—*finally*—we're allowed to sit down and start eating.

"Talk about work," Saanvi instructs after a few minutes of uninterrupted lunchtime. "But can you make it, like, not boring?"

Alex and I both burst out laughing, and our eyes catch at the same moment. Maybe because it's the first mutual feeling we've ever shared.

My memory flashes to the latest episode of the "One Day at Work" segment I caught on YouTube; it was a female head chef of an upscale Mexican restaurant, and she was making some sort of mole while they filmed her talking about irregular work hours, gender issues in restaurant kitchens, her favorite professional-grade cooking tool, and what she eats off the job. The reminder doesn't give me any ideas about what I could say now that's even remotely interesting.

"Saanvi," Alex says, voicing my concern. "We need more direction than that."

"What's it like to work around here?" she prompts. "The environment, the people, the expectations? Make sure you answer in a complete sentence because my voice will get cut. And say it to Casey, like you're having a conversation."

After thinking for a minute, he leans toward me, both his elbows propped on the table's surface. Eyes on mine, as if it's just the two of us here. "Working in Manhattan is halfway a dream and halfway a living nightmare," he says lowly.

I nod, swallowing. "Couldn't agree more."

"There are so many weird smells." He wrinkles his nose. "I dry-clean my suits so often now that I'm only one punch away from fifty percent off the next time I walk past a garbage truck at high noon."

I laugh, take a sip of my Topo Chico (stalling), and then fiddle with the bottle, making sure the label is facing the camera. My eyes dip up to Alex, then back down again. I can already feel myself starting to choke.

"What's something that surprised you about working downtown?" he asks, pitching me a softball. Still trying to make me feel comfortable.

"Um." My brain produces word vomit: "The mansplaining I get subjected to is more random than you'd think?" Alex arches an eyebrow in silent question, cuing me to go on. "Like, this one time, completely unprompted, a guy at Pret saw me reading a *New York Times* op-ed, and he started lecturing me about the history of newspapers. I've also gotten sailboat anatomy from somebody at Blue Bottle whose coffee order is a decaf drip with two shots of espresso. And another time, on my way to the office, somebody just, like, walked right up to me, and started giving me unsolicited directions to Rockefeller Park."

"Well, you do have a picnic-girl vibe. Very pack-and-play," Alex says.

My eyes narrow. "Excuse me?"

"It's a compliment."

"In what world?"

"In mine. People who upheave themselves at a moment's notice in the name of fun are the best kind of people."

"Guys!" Saanvi says, snapping. "No tangents, please!"

"Sorry." I put the question back on Alex: "What about you? What's something that has surprised *you* about downtown?"

He runs a hand over his jaw, thinking. "I guess it shouldn't have, but the level of security did. If you're forgetful like me, getting around the building with no badge can be a pain."

I nod and add, "Stock market volatility is like FiDi's version of Mercury in retrograde."

Alex grins. "A rat followed me into the revolving door of our building yesterday."

"Young professionals around here thrive on gossip, but they'll disguise it with the word 'networking.'"

"People from the city love to remind you they're from the city," he adds.

"Also, this whole video concept of an hour-long sit-down lunch with a coworker? It's kind of bullshit." I turn toward the camera, half expecting Saanvi to be pissed at me for the honesty, but her lips are pulled up like I'm playing right into her hands, so I keep going. "Low-level grunts like me and Alex don't have time for fancy Italian lunches. I typically eat takeout or vending machine food at my desk."

"I don't even bother most days." Alex absentmindedly twirls his bottle between his thumb and pointer finger, completely reversing the label. Saanvi scowls, and I can't help but smirk. "But I don't mind," Alex goes on, oblivious. "I love my job, and the scope of what we're doing at *Bite the Hand* feels endless. I think that's what's cool about the magazine industry, too."

"What do you mean?"

"If you're willing to evolve, cut your losses when it comes to print, keep things fresh, it's a launchpad for whatever you want it to be."

"Is that why you came here?" I ask. "The launchpad?"

"That's part of it." Alex nods. "But also, I just . . . burned out eventually, I guess. I needed to come home." He drops his eyes to the table and picks up his slice of pizza. "Sorry, Saanvi, that was probably too personal."

"We can cut it if you want," she says. "But to be honest, our subscribers tend to find the personal lives of on-camera talent just as entertaining."

Alex nods while I do a mental checklist of every personal detail I've absorbed about all my favorite entertainers. I hope Amy from @unironicliterarybitch got an A on her senior thesis. And that @gypseaswholesomelife figures out if she's gluten intolerant.

Speaking of personal lives—

"What did you study?" I ask Alex. "That's a good question, right, Saanvi? What majors got us here?"

"Sure," she says.

"I double majored in entrepreneurship and digital media," Alex says.

Which means: All along, even back in college, he wanted this. The whole time, he was figuring out how to be good at it.

Something cracks open inside me, and air rushes in. I *am* starting to know him, and it feels like . . . *relief.* Like an inevitability I wasn't ever going to be able to stop from happening.

"Let me guess." Alex laces his fingers together, pinning me with a knowing look. "Finance?"

"What gave me away."

"The necklace you're wearing is engraved with 'It's Accrual World.'"

My hand flutters to my neck, and I fiddle with the gag gift Miriam gave me for my last birthday. Alex's gaze drops to my neck, too. He frowns and looks away, twirling his Topo Chico bottle.

"Aren't you hungry?" I ask, nodding at his pizza. He's eaten only three-quarters of one slice compared to my two and a half.

He shrugs. "Adderall screws with my appetite." Glancing at the crew, he adds, "Can I say that on camera, Saanvi?"

"That's PG compared to what's ingested on Wall Street," she mutters, more focused on Eric's video frame than the Real Us. "Especially if it's prescribed."

"It's prescribed."

"Guys, don't say anything useful right now, something's wrong with Eric's camera."

"ADHD?" I ask Alex, ignoring Saanvi.

"Yes." He shakes his head, smirking. "Don't say it."

"Don't say what?"

"That finding that out makes perfect sense for me."

I bite my bottom lip. "You were right."

"Yeah?" He grins, crossing his arms over his chest. "Regarding?"

"I didn't know anything about you."

Alex's smile drops. After a beat, he says, "You're starting to." His eyes catch and hold on to mine, and it feels like he's withholding my oxygen. "Here. I'll give you one more thing. I'm an Enneagram seven."

"Okay." I tilt my head, appreciative but confused. "Sorry, I don't know my number."

"Should we do Enneagram tests during our next seminar?" His eyes brighten. "And then, as a follow-up, we could get a comedy contributor to write a spread on how to work with each Enneagram type—but make it snappier and funnier than what's on the internet now."

"You really do shit ideas."

"Casey, say that again for the camera, but less gross," Saanvi says.

"You are an idea factory," I restate, never dropping my eyes from his. "But I don't want to know my Enneagram, because I refuse to believe my personality can be boiled down to a number. Besides, who says my work personality is the same as my regular one, anyway?"

Alex considers. "Wouldn't that get exhausting, though? Showing up as someone else to work every day?"

I get a flash of Dad the way I drew him in crayon when I was a kid. Me, Dad with his guitar, ghost-Mommy, plus my one-eyed corgi, Pirate. I colored a million of those still lifes during aftercare, at church, on road trips to visit Dad's family in Arkansas. Now I see the drawings the way Dad must have seen them then: cookie-cutter portrayals of a family man who worked in a total boys' club environment where everyone assumed he was straight years after he'd self-acknowledged he wasn't.

Try as I might, memory doesn't serve me on the exact day Jerry entered my life. He just . . . bleeds into the past somewhere in the middle of my fourth-grade year. I remember him planting rose bulbs in our weed-ridden, overgrown flower beds. I went outside to loiter, pleased when he gave me his gloves and I stuffed my tiny hands into them, gripping the dirt. We didn't talk a lot in the beginning, and looking back, I think Jerry was treating me like he treated his rose bulbs. Tentative, careful nurturing was what it took to get them to bloom.

Eventually, I started asking him questions about plants. Then about him. A few years later, about who he was to my dad.

"I can only tell you who your dad is to me," Jerry answered. "Someone I want to spend the rest of my life with."

It was that simple for him. That straightforward. But for my dad, it was a bit more complicated. It was the reality of his workplace in the early two thousands, and for years, he showed up as someone else to work every day.

"No," I say to Alex, shaking my head softly. "You're right, actually. That would suck."

The conversation pauses while he watches me, his eyebrows

furrowed, very obviously trying to parse through the thoughts behind my expressive face.

"What floor do you have to visit to get the best cup of coffee in
our building?" Saanvi throws out.

"It's Well, the life coach company on the twelfth floor," I say
quickly. "They've got a drip machine that has this gold setting—"

"Nope." Alex shakes his head. "It's that app start-up three floors
below yours. They have the fancy Breville where you can save your
drink of choice under your name. And a fridge dedicated to milk."

"You're both wrong," Sara pipes in. "The editor in chief of *Frame*
has an assistant who used to be a barista. In *Italy*."

"Settling this debate," Saanvi whispers, "would make for a fan-
tastic video concept."

It goes on like that for another twenty minutes. We talk about
print versus online content, our favorite and most loathsome parts
of our jobs. When the subject drifts, Saanvi always pulls us back
on course. It's silly nothingness, but it's fun. And despite the cameras, and constantly being scared of saying the wrong thing because
these are my literal coworkers, and even though I'm trying to eat,
and chew, and swallow, and talk with a clean mouth while *also*
suppressing some seriously powerful burps from the Topo Chico, I
realize this is *easy*.

Which is, in a word, strange. It usually takes more effort on my
part to make myself come across that way.

Eventually, we pack up and head back to the office. I've got no
clue if the team got what they needed, no clue how I'll come across
on the other side of those cameras. But the universe is out to play,
because if that whole experience could have had a grand, ridiculous
finale, Alex and I give it one on the escalator down.

CHAPTER NINE

All things considered, the spewing thing *is* pretty funny.

I come around to it the next day, watching the footage over Andre's shoulder. More accurately, it's the first thirty seconds of the video draft he's already cobbled together.

"So," Video Alex says on the computer screen. In this shot, we're descending the escalator after lunch. I'm holding Fari and Don's take-out bag in one hand, taking a swig of my drink with my other, and Alex is leaning against the side rail one step above me. "What's your favorite Excel formula?"

That's when I spewed Topo Chico all over his face and chest.

Look. It felt unavoidable in the moment.

The screen switches to gray static, followed by a familiar trade-marked jingle and the BTH logo against a solid black background. Then Andre's editing has the video cut back to our intros. There we are, standing on the skyscraper's front steps, looking as fresh-faced and dorky as two kids about to be subjected to their parents' first-day-of-school photo shoot. Honestly, we seem too young to belong in this part of the city.

"I'm Casey," Video Casey says. I, being Real Casey, cringe a little, blinking hard against the sound of my voice.

Andre hits the space bar on his keyboard and swivels to face me in his desk chair. "That's what I've got so far. All clear?"

I put my hands on my hips and exhale slow. "Clear," I confirm.

I told the crew yesterday I needed to see that part in person before I would even consider letting Andre put it on the internet. Alex, for his part, thought it was hilarious, and said he didn't need to see shit, the clip should go at the beginning.

Andre smiles at me, wide and toothy. "You're not at all like how I thought someone in finance would be. When Saanvi told me about this plan, I thought she was crazy."

"I still think she's crazy," I mutter, staring at the blurry still frame of me and Alex behind Andre's head. "But thanks."

"I guess we'll know in two weeks, won't we?"

"Just two?"

"Yeah. Saanvi wants this expedited."

"Ugh." I pull a baleful face as I back away. "Have you talked to Alex today?"

"No," Andre says. "Should I have?"

"Nah." I swat my hand at the air. "Never mind."

Still, on my way back toward the elevators, navigating the maze of cubicles on his floor, I keep my eyes peeled for Alex. I've never been by his desk before, and I'm not brave enough to purposely seek him out.

He took the afternoon off yesterday. Canceled all his meetings so he could go home and change, claiming he might as well take a half day.

I'd felt guilty. His shirt getting wet was my fault. But even after I offered to procure a new one for him from *Frame*'s fashion closet, Alex just shrugged and said, "It's no big deal. I could use the time off, anyway."

I was confused, until I remembered the fallout with his dad. He buried it so well over the hour and a half we spent filming that I nearly forgot, but that was probably the real reason he didn't want to go back in the building yesterday. I mean, it was just . . . soda water.

Here is a fact about me: I tend to be a private person. Probably, it's a result of growing up around country music stars. My dad isn't one of them—he's only a songwriter and backup vocalist, and frankly, he sings a little off-key in his middle age—but my entire life, he's worked alongside some of the biggest names in the business. I learned the importance of privacy at a young age, and living with Devon Nicholson's daughter in college only exacerbated that tendency.

So of course, on the flip side of that coin, I'm also not interested in prying into *other* people's lives.

Usually.

But, like . . . I *can't* stop thinking about Alex and his dad.

I have concocted a million scenarios in my head and dissected every one of them, just like I do with numbers that don't add up.

He's from New York, he studied at Harvard, and then he moved to Seoul and spent three years working there.

His mother is *not* Robert Harrison's wife. Robert Harrison's wife is a white woman named Linda. Thanks to Google, I know they've been married for thirty years, and thanks to Instagram, I know Alex is only twenty-five.

But his father didn't know he was home . . . because he wouldn't take Alex's calls. Wouldn't even listen to Alex's voicemails. Maybe that would make more sense if Alex hadn't called him Dad. If Alex didn't share his last name. But he *did,* and he *does,* and there's something fishy going on here, and I simply *cannot* focus on month-end books right now because I'm desperate to find out what.

The ninety-eighth-floor break room is never without a baked good, and I head there now for some sugar fuel to get me through the rest of today. But when I arrive, someone has beaten me to the last slice of Benny's no-nut chocolate chip banana bread.

Tracy Garcia: CFO.

Here's the thing. If Tracy told me to commit a murder for her, I would ask in what manner she would prefer it to be done and also if she needs me to frame someone after.

Aggressive but true, and here's why.

I was in a bad place when I interviewed for this job. My boyfriend didn't understand why I was even bothering, since our plan was to move back to Nashville together. Frankly, *I* didn't understand why I was bothering, when every other candidate was a dude from a northeastern Ivy. I passed the technical assessment with flying colors. But during the group interview—which was a mock roundtable discussion in front of a panel including the CFO—I choked. I spoke a grand total of six words the whole time.

Anyway. I wound up in the lady's restroom crying, scolding myself for getting quiet, for ruining my chances, and that's where Tracy found me. She breezed in, spotted me, and then froze, tilting her head.

"The girl who beat the test," she said.

"Um. Sorry?" I mumbled.

"You beat our technical assessment. You know that thing is designed to be failed?"

I had not known that. "Sorry," I said again.

Tracy laughed faintly. When she stepped forward, I straightened, clenching a mascara-stained paper towel in my fist. "Are you okay?" she asked, voice soft.

"Yeah," I assured her, forcing a laugh. "I'm so sorry about this."

"Stop apologizing. That's three in a row."

Another one was on the tip of my tongue. "Yes, ma'am," I said instead.

We fell silent, Tracy studying me, me studying the floor.

"That was harsh. I just wanted you to know you have nothing to apologize for."

I nodded, and Tracy sighed.

"Just because they're saying words doesn't mean they're saying the right words. Okay?"

I nodded again.

"Why do you like finance, Casey?"

When I peeked up, she was leaning against the bathroom counter. Not in a hurry. I had no clue whether this was part of my interview. But I was sick of posturing, so I told her the truth.

"I think it's because . . . math doesn't lie. It always makes sense, always adds up. There's a lot of stuff in life that makes me anxious. But this never has."

"It makes you feel calm," Tracy suggested, smiling softly. "Steady. I know that feeling. I know it well. You should tell what you just told me to Don during your one-on-one interview. He's like us in that way, too."

I have no idea if that conversation is what pushed me over the edge in getting this job or not. But the thing I'll never forget—the thing that makes me willing to commit murder for Tracy Garcia—is because that day, for the first time in my life, I felt wholly, 100 percent known.

It's empowering, to feel that connection to the CFO of a global mass media company. She's stately. Otherworldly. Being near her is like bathing in feminism.

Her career history is mythic. Tracy climbed the ranks of New York City business slowly but surely, year after year, promotion after promotion, and three years ago, she was named the CFO of Little Cooper.

There are stories that float around about Tracy. Legendary stuff she's done at all the companies she's been with. There was the pay exposé at the investment firm she worked at in her thirties, the tech giant antitrust bill she spoke about in her forties (she's heavily credited as the scale tipper in getting the bill passed). When she's not doing her nine-to-five, she talks on panels, gives commencement addresses, and writes articles for *Insider* about how to be a woman of color in the workplace and not let it take a single thing from you.

Obviously, I am obsessed with her.

When she sees me enter the break room from her spot on the other side of the kitchen island, Tracy tilts her head at me. I can almost see the cogs of her mind working on a complicated problem.

"Can you do something for me, Casey?" she says at last.

Naturally, my response is a stuttered but passionate "A-anything."

Tracy keeps watching me, as if calculating just how serious I am about *anything* (very). Her arms cross over her Eileen Fisher cardigan, and she raps dark purple fingernails against her opposite elbow. Between us, the toaster gives a soft *pop* as her slice of banana bread springs up from the heat.

"I'm told you've been working closely with Alex Harrison," Tracy says. "Don assigned you to the *Bite the Hand* launch project. Correct?"

I nod but say nothing, unsure what else to add, so I just stand there quietly and let Tracy size me up. She comes closer, walking around to my side of the island. The click of her heels echoes on the marble floor.

"Something is . . . off," she says at last. "Between the board of directors and the chief executives. We can't agree on anything. I feel like I'm trying to corral unruly children."

Instantly, what Alex told me about Dougie comes back: *He's got history with my father, if you must know.*

I'm convinced Tracy can see the memory cross my mind; that's how carefully she's studying me.

"When Robert decided to step down as CEO," Tracy says, "Dougie Dawson somehow got wind of it all the way from DC. He lobbied our board, proposed himself as Robert's replacement, and got enough members to vote him in despite Robert himself claiming it was a terrible decision."

That's some major tea, I want to say but don't. "Did you get to vote?" I ask.

Tracy shakes her head.

"Well, what did you think about Dougie?"

"I was indifferent at the time, but it's been almost a year, and things haven't smoothed over. Robert and Dougie spend so much time bickering, they're oblivious to their own company struggling to stay afloat."

I wince when she admits this. I'm perfectly aware of our company's financial state, but hearing it from the CFO's own mouth makes my stomach churn. To Tracy's point, we haven't hit an EBITDA target— the financial benchmark our entire bonus structure is based on—since my first quarter with LC, and that was a year and a half ago.

The fact of the matter is the print magazine industry is dying. Some of our brands have pivoted successfully into the digital space, but other editors in chief are dragging their feet.

And our CEO is letting them.

"You think Dougie Dawson is damaging LC?" I ask her.

Tracy's mouth presses into a firm, displeased line. "Yes. We need change, and we needed it yesterday. I don't know why our CEO isn't fixing anything, but I seem to be the only person concerned."

"Well, that's . . ." I hesitate, biting my lip. "That's a violation of his fiduciary duty."

As the words leave my mouth, I brace myself to get smote for blasphemy, but Tracy doesn't backpedal or tell me I crossed a line.

She says, "It would be helpful to me . . . and it would be in the best interest of the company . . . if I could learn the root cause of the hatred between our CEO and chairman."

What Tracy isn't saying comes across loud and clear.

Get Alex to tell you the truth.

I don't fully understand why she's divulging all this to me, why she's asking *me* specifically to do this, and not for the first time, I try to get inside Tracy's head.

I work with Alex Harrison closely.

I'm around his age.

She thinks if I really try, I can get him to spill.

Maybe. Maybe I could. But the word "yes" can't get past my lips because the image of him, shoulders hunched while he got berated by Robert, is telling me to be careful with him. Alex is fragile right now. Maybe digging for and then relaying information about his dubious father is an even more dubious thing to do.

I've never liked underhandedness. It makes my skin itch, my muscles feel tight, and when it comes to Alex, that uncomfortable feeling in the pit of my gut is doubled, tripled. So badly, I wish I could say to Tracy, *Why can't you just ask him yourself?*

"Please help me, Casey," Tracy says. *Heart's on your sleeve,* I warn myself. She's reading my hesitation. "You know me, and I know you. This isn't about petty gossip. It's important."

"Okay," I breathe in the next instant. "I'll try."

Maybe I would have deliberated longer if I trusted Tracy less, or thought more highly of Robert and Dougie, or wasn't *dying* to know the truth myself. But once, Tracy helped me, and now she's calling it in. I owe her.

She nods, satisfied with my answer. She opens her mouth to say something else, but Benny comes into the break room right then, humming the *Hamilton* soundtrack under his breath. Tracy breaks eye contact with me and steps away.

"You can have the last slice of banana bread," she tells me, and then walks out the door.

The sound of Benny opening the fridge interrupts my train of thought. "What was that about?" he asks. "She had her boss lady expression on. You in trouble, Maitland?"

"Erm." I grasp for a fib. I've always been a great secret keeper, but lying is something that makes my neck clammy and my heart race. I open my mouth to make up something mind-numbingly boring, but as if Benny can sense it, he talks first.

"Actually, in the interest of my mental health, I've decided not to care."

My middle finger sticks up as Benny throws me a wicked grin from behind the refrigerator door. All I can see is an annoyingly well-moisturized face and shoulders blanketed in a sky-blue pashmina.

"Your loss," I hedge. "It was juicy."

Benny rolls his eyes, playing into my reverse psychology like a horse led to water. "Casey." He shakes his head as he grabs his Guava Goddess kombucha from the fridge. "If I've learned anything from you about finance, it's that it's never, *ever* juicy."

I roll my eyes back for good measure, grab the banana bread out of the toaster, and stomp out of the break room. Benny follows me all the way back to my desk.

"Casey," Fari whines as I drop into my chair. "I'm sick of reconciliations."

"Why are you doing reconciliations? Pawn that shit off on Accounting."

Her nose wrinkles. "I can't just pawn shit off. I'm a freshman!"

I laugh, uncapping a highlighter, and think to myself, *This is it.* If I had to boil down why I like working in finance, I'd do it by explaining month-end.

It's a little bit of a con we're running here: convincing people of the incredibly high stakes and very intense difference between 7 percent and 8.5 percent ROI. But at the same time, that 1.5 percent really does *matter,* and if you can find it, if you can make it happen, it sometimes feels bigger than anything else you've ever accomplished. Because it could mean a project green light, or maybe a new hire, somebody getting a bonus that helps them finally afford their dream vacation. I've always loved the idea that numbers I analyze might help somebody's dreams come true, and I've always hoped I'm not simply lining the CEO's pocket.

"Right." I nod to Fari. "I forgot we haze with reconciliations. Carry on."

Benny sits on the edge of my desk and smirks. "As a junior in adulthood, I demand you each bring me a fanciful, luxurious coffee on Monday. I'll rank whose choice is better, and the loser has to answer the phone the next time the COO's ex-wife calls."

I eye Benny suspiciously. "Why are you in such a good mood?" He's one of those people who are only allowed to approach *you*, not the other way around. When he comes to see me and Fari, it's either in a state of flurried commotion or because he's in the mood to fuck around.

"It's month-end," Benny answers, examining his multicolored fingernails. "During month-end, everyone else gets so stressed out, they block their calendars all day. No executive babies to corral, since they're holed up in their offices, figuring out how to blame each other for missing last month's targets."

"I'm so glad our misery can be your pleasure," I intone.

"Pipe it down with the attitude, chica." He taps my forehead, scolding me like a toddler. "I heard about your playdate with Alex yesterday. It sounds like Fari's the one doing the legwork around here. You better get to it. Double-time now."

"Go away, Benny. I have a playdate with the income statement."

He laughs, face pointed at the ceiling. "I love it when I'm happy and you're not."

I scowl as he walks away. Fari snorts from her cube.

The next three hours are spent reviewing expense line items until my eyes bleed. After that, I double-check the reconciliations Fari wasn't sure about and then make Don's hedge numbers pretty.

"If we make the numbers pretty," he tells me, "we might get bonuses."

It's incentive enough to take my time making his summary shine.

At some point in the midafternoon, Miriam texts, Today my Co-Star app told me yes to karaoke and no to hibernation. Therefore,

I need you drunk, loose lipped, and ready for a duet when I get off my shift at midnight.

I reply, let's run it back.

Around six thirty, Fari taps out. I high-five her as she leaves. Don is gone fifteen minutes later, muttering something very on-brand about an elementary school music program. I'm not long behind—I want to make it to the Ralph Lauren sample sale in SoHo before the Oaxacan reservation with Brijesh tonight that I just got a calendar reminder for—but right after Don vanishes, I get an unexpected message.

> **Alex Harrison:** It's nearly seven pm on a Friday. Don't you have a life?
>> **Casey Maitland:** I could say the same???
> **Alex Harrison:** I had to work late tonight. Some girl projectiled all over my clothes yesterday and shot my productivity to hell
>> **Casey Maitland:** Yikes, what'd you do to trigger such a bad reaction?
> **Alex Harrison:** I got you to laugh, didn't I? counting that as a win.

The grin on my face right now is frankly just embarrassing.

> **Alex Harrison:** Andre mentioned you were looking for me earlier. Sorry I couldn't get back to you until now, I've been slammed. Anything you need?

I chew on my lip, debating what to say. Truth is, I was only checking to make sure he'd shown up to work today at all. Part of me worried he was hiding out somewhere with his tail between his legs, debating whether to turn in his notice.

I *do* actually need something from Alex now, but I can't type out Tracy's request in our chat box. Getting him to open up to me is going to require more stealth than that.

Another wave of guilt presses in on me. The idea of using Alex for information crawls up my skin like a pest.

I have to remind myself that my intentions are pure. I just want what's best for LC.

> **Casey Maitland:** I didn't need anything. I was just looking

I watch Alex's type bubbles appear, vanish. Appear again.

> **Alex Harrison:** What's your ETA for leaving?
> **Casey Maitland:** Can you really say ETA for leaving when that technically means estimated time of arrival for leaving?
> **Alex Harrison:** fine, what's your ETL?
> **Casey Maitland:** I was about to head out
> **Alex Harrison:** Meet in the lobby?
> **Casey Maitland:** see u down there.

He's leaning against the far wall, his legs crossed and his hands in his pockets, waiting for me like he's got nowhere to be and all the time in the world to get there. His eyes track me as I make my way toward him. Looking like a goddamn Calvin Klein model in his slacks and loafers and crisply pressed button-down—an outfit that seems boring on everyone else but somehow groundbreaking on Alex Harrison.

Three feet away, I stop. There's a flash of something dark and curious in his eyes, and with a jolt, what he said to me yesterday comes rushing back: *You'll look just as pretty tomorrow as you did the day we met.*

Alex swallows. "Saanvi said the footage was good enough to air."

"Was she by chance being held at gunpoint when she said it?"

Alex laughs and falls silent for a few seconds, scratching at his chin, eyes glazed. I almost say something else just to fill the silence, but then he releases a long, weary sigh and nods to himself, as if succumbing to some internal debate.

"I'm a bastard. You know, like, the illegitimate kind."

Well.

I was simply not expecting that. "Right. I mean . . . Uh, what?"

Alex's lips kick up into the beginnings of a smile, but it never fully forms. "My dad was married to someone else when he got my mom pregnant with me. Still *is* married to that same someone else, for that matter."

"Oh." I pretend (probably very badly) that I didn't read Robert and Linda's marriage announcement in a scanned *New Haven Register* that I found online last night. There was a picture, too. Robert was around the same age that Alex is now when he got married.

"My mother," Alex goes on, "was a waitress and a freelance writer. She grew up in Queens, as a first-generation Korean American of two immigrant parents. I know next to nothing about how she and my dad met, or what their relationship was like."

My eyelashes flutter, batting up a storm while I process.

Mostly, I'm processing that Alex said his mother *was*. Just like I say that my mother *was*.

"For a while, we lived in Seoul. Just her and me. She died when I was eleven, and that's when my dad moved me back here, to a boarding school in Connecticut," Alex goes on, his voice clinical, like he's reciting a speech he's been practicing. "We've never been close, but that's his fault, not mine. He gives me lots of money that I never once asked for, and absolutely nothing else. Not time. Not answers." He blinks. "Just money."

I have so many questions. First of all, how much money are we talking here? Asking for a friend. What does Alex remember about Seoul, from the first time he lived there with his mother? What's it like to have memories of her that aren't hazy, six-year-old snatches? Are those memories part of the reason he went back to Seoul when he graduated from Harvard? What was boarding school like?

But the first question that bubbles up on my tongue is "Does your dad have other children?"

Alex shakes his head. "His wife wasn't able to get pregnant, and as far as I know they never looked into adoption. I'm his only child."

I feel like a window that's been frosted over for weeks is finally melting, the flaky ice dripping away to leave behind a clear pane. Alex Harrison is on the other side of it, with a chipped heart and a handful of memories that I might be able to match.

"You were owed an explanation," he says.

"I was?"

He nods, then lifts himself off the wall. Capturing my attention with razor-sharp focus he adds, "But only you, Casey. Please."

So, basically: don't tell anyone.

He didn't broach the subject of Dougie Dawson, only told me about his father in direct relation to *him,* so I have a perfectly clear conscience when I say, "I'll keep it to myself."

And I will.

He waits to see my reaction, brow furrowed with nerves, but at the same time his shoulders relax like a weight's been lifted from them.

It dawns on me, right then: the only time we've ever touched was when he shook my hand in the cooking studio the day we met.

I mean, it makes perfect sense for two coworkers not to touch a lot, but I want to . . . hug him?

Yeah, that must be it. A nice, comforting, professional hug. But obviously, there's no such thing. So, instead—

"Want to get drunk?"

CHAPTER TEN

We wind up at Sleight of Hand, a trendy bar near Washington Square Park.

"You ever been here?" Alex asks as he holds open the door for me.

Suavely, I walk through and say, "Yeah, once or twice," even though I haven't. I've heard of it, though; this place is popular enough to always have a line down the block after dark. I was surprised Alex suggested it but intrigued enough by his taste in drinking establishments not to ask questions.

Inside, the walls are adorned with playing cards—diamonds, spades, hearts, and clubs, clustered together to form the bar's name against shiny black paint. Crushed-velvet booths in deep burgundy line the walls and freestanding gold benches are scattered around white tabletops. It's seven o'clock on a Friday; the sun has nearly set, and the place is packed.

Alex follows me inside and heads straight for the bar. He waves two fingers at the guy behind it as we slide into the only two unoccupied bar stools. At first, I assume Alex is waving to get the bartender's attention, but when he notices us, his lips pull up on one side. "You really can't get enough of me, can you?"

The bartender has blond slicked-back hair, like Leonardo Di-Caprio in almost every movie (I'm not convinced it isn't intentional), and a big face covered by a neatly trimmed beard. Wordlessly, he whips out a thick-bottomed crystal glass and starts pouring bitters and simple syrup into it.

"What if I wanted something else?" Alex grumbles.

"You didn't." Dupe Leo grabs the Angel's Envy from the shelf behind him and tops up the makings of an old-fashioned.

"Freddy, this is Casey," Alex says.

The bartender looks at Alex, then turns his gaze on me. "Oh, you—I thought you just walked in at the same time. Sorry." He reaches out a sticky, orange-scented hand for me to shake. I push my palm against his, and Freddy's eyes dance.

"I do have other friends besides you, Frederick," Alex says.

"You really don't."

I look at Alex. "We're friends?"

I meant that as a genuine question—Are we? Friends?—but Freddy laughs like I'm the funniest thing since Andy Samberg. "What would you like to drink, Casey?"

I lean forward on my elbows, considering my options. "Um-mmm," I mumble, stalling. God, I'm so indecisive. Why can't I have a "drink" like Alex apparently has a "drink"? And seriously, Angel's Envy? In this economy?

"Should I make something up?" Freddy suggests.

"Can you make it nut-allergen-friendly and less than eleven dollars?"

He shrugs. "Sure."

"Go for it."

The hum of voices coupled with Shwayze music fill the silence between us as Freddy whips up my drink. He pulls apart a grape-fruit, and the spray of citrus tickles my nose. I wrap my hands around my elbows and take a deep breath, relaxing into the bar stool. Beside me, ice clinks in Alex's glass while he shakes it.

It's starting to settle in—how novel this is. The two of us together outside of work hours, and on my suggestion, at that.

I really, really need to apologize to Alex.

I really, really need to find the right words.

"This a date?" Freddy asks, as if he can sense my inner turmoil. "Did you finally download Hinge, Alex?"

He spits onto the counter. "Fuck's sake, dude—"

"We're coworkers!" I squeak, blushing.

"Oh, thank God." Freddy shakes his head. "Alex, I was going to throw hands if you brought a date to this bar so you could force me to third wheel."

Completely against every rational thought telling me not to, I am *dying* to sneak off to the bathroom and redownload Hinge to see if he's . . . found me.

Yes, I have a profile. Yes, I download, use, and delete the app (in that order) every couple of months. It has led to bad sex, good sex, chlamydia (now expelled from my body), an adorable picnic in Central Park with a guy who was sweet but told me at the end of the date he was only practicing so he could ask out his childhood crush when he moved home next month, and a guy I went on three dates with before realizing he was my Subway Nemesis's roommate.

When it comes to dating in New York, my policy has always been: I'm not looking, and I'm not *not* looking. Miriam once phrased it as window-shopping. *Try before you buy.* It's what I wished I had done in college, but when a handsome older student basically picks you out of a lineup and makes you feel chosen, you don't ever pause to consider you never really chose him back.

I'm not making that mistake again. Clawing your way out of the wrong relationship is *always* harder than waiting for the right one.

Alex pinches the bridge of his nose and exhales. "It's been a long week, that's all. We're just . . . commemorating it with booze."

"Uh-huh." Freddy strains the freshly squeezed juice into a shaker, narrowing his eyes at Alex. "You run into your dad or something?"

Alex glares.

Freddy just smiles innocently. "You should have led with that, Al. I could have made yours a double."

"It's fine," Alex says, waving a hand. "Nothing to write home about." But then he takes a big slurp of his drink.

"Right, because you getting a job at his own company under his own nose is soooo not a thing."

"I didn't do it under his nose," Alex retorts.

"Uh-huh." Freddy passes my drink across the bar.

I take a careful sip, savoring the flavors on my tongue. Freddy throws a towel over his shoulder as my face lights up. "Hey, that's great!"

He winks at me. "If you're being forced to hang out with Alexander, it needed to be."

Alex rolls his eyes and turns to me. "Freddy and I went to boarding school together for eight years. We've known each other since puberty."

"Did you go to Harvard, too?"

Freddy pulls a face. "Hell no. I took my high school diploma and brought it straight to the New York City bar scene, where it belonged. Been here seven years now, but Alex and I stayed in touch. We both had those fractured families to keep us close."

Alex traces the rim of his glass with his middle finger and shakes his head in exasperation, but he's smiling down at the bar top. Freddy wanders down to the other end to check on the rest of his patrons, and I sip my grapefruit-brown-sugar-basil-bourbon drink, which is quickly becoming the best alcoholic beverage I've ever had.

I tilt my head at Alex. "So, before boarding school?"

He grimaces, palming the back of his neck. "International

school, in a city outside of Seoul. I lived there with my mom from the ages of three to eleven."

Every time he answers one of my questions, I come up with five more. It's becoming a problem. But I don't know if I can ask them because I'm not sure if the answers fall under Alex's definition of my "owed explanation." Freddy offering up details is one thing. Me seeking them out on my own is entirely different.

Maybe now would be a good time to start my line of inquiry about Dougie. I almost do it, but it just feels . . .

Wrong.

"What about you?" Alex asks. I blink, meeting his eyes. He's watching me with exacting, focused attention.

"What *about* me?" I repeat.

"You said you're from Tennessee?"

"Oh. Yeah, I'm from Nashville."

"Are you a fan of country music?"

I tilt my head from side to side in consideration. "Middle of the road, I'd say. My dad's a songwriter. He's done some Billboard hits for a few big-name country artists, but lately he's been into writing folk and bluegrass."

"And your mom?"

"Died when I was six."

His shoulders point toward me, and I catch a whiff of his cologne. His lips part in careful hesitation before he says, softly, "Mine too, when I was eleven."

"Cancer?" I guess, my heart pinching for him.

"Yeah. Ovarian."

"Lung."

Alex smiles, just a little. "There it is."

"What?"

"Our thing in common."

I snort. "How maudlin."

Alex shrugs. "So it goes."

"Got any allergies?" I ask. "That's a much less depressing thing to have in common."

"None."

"Must be nice," I growl.

Alex smirks. "Tell me them."

"You got three hours?"

"Then make me a copy of your spreadsheet," Alex says. "I know you have one. It's probably color coordinated, each allergen listed by category and subcategory, cross-referenced against level of severity."

My mouth opens and closes like a guppy fish. "You're . . . not wrong."

He laughs deeply, tilting his head back. There are two buttons undone at the top of his shirt. (I'm pretty sure only one of them was unbuttoned when we left work, but anyway.) Beneath it, I catch a glimpse of his chest. "Come on. I need to know, or I might accidentally kill you, which would be a travesty, because then who would approve my expense reports?"

"I'm allergic to your expense reports."

"Impossible. I annotate everything, follow protocol to the letter. All for you, Casey."

The way Alex says my name, in that clear New England accent, is different than I grew up being used to. Most people from home lazily roll the vowels in my name, but Alex says them like he's doing it on purpose.

"Yeah, well," I grumble. "You once handed me a file folder that kind of smelled like peanut butter."

His smile falters. "Seriously, have I ever triggered anything?"

I debate joking that his very presence gives me hives, but I spare him the played-out sarcasm and admit, "I'm allergic to most fragrances, but we'd have to be practically necking for your cologne to have any effect on me."

Necking? Good Lord.

"Oh." Alex winces. "I don't have to wear it. I don't even like the smell, to be honest. I dated a girl once who got it for me and kept it around for when I wanted to feel put together."

"It's really not that big of—oh, *fuck.*"

I swivel on my bar stool, facing forward and putting a hand over the side of my face to block it from the front door.

Based on social media, I already knew Jack and Jill were in New York this weekend for the Jets game on Sunday, but seriously? Out of all the bars in all the neighborhoods, they had to walk into this one?

Panic blooms in my chest, pumping college memories and boyfriend insecurity and alcohol-induced blood thinning through my veins at hyperspeed. Freddy catches my eye, back from the other end of the bar, and then he peeks behind me like he's some kind of mind reader.

To be fair, I'm not acting very subtle.

"You hiding from that couple that just walked in?"

"Yes," I groan quietly.

"Who is it?" Alex asks. He starts to turn, but I grab the loose cotton of his sleeve and yank him still. He lets out a tiny grunt. "*Ow.* Rug burn."

"That your ex?" Freddy guesses.

"My ex's best friend and his fiancée."

Fuck, fuck, fuck, fuck, *fuck.* Okay, it could be worse.

It could be Lance.

"Who's the other couple with them?" Freddy asks.

My stomach drops out of my asshole.

"The . . ." I gulp. "The couple . . . Describe them."

"The girl is wearing seven pounds of St. Tropez fake tan, and the guy she's with is a short king."

"Oh my fuck, it's him."

Of course it's him. In college, the four of us—Jack, Jill, me, and Lance—spent uncountable weekends together, and looking back, it's probably a red flag Lance and I didn't hang out one-on-one very often. But he's got the worst FOMO of anyone I've ever met, and frankly, he and Jack are more codependent than Timothée Chalamet and Saoirse Ronan.

Freddy tsks. "That's rough, kiddo. I hate to break this to you, but your hair is, like, incredibly distinctive."

And it's down today. Thick, wavy, and golden brown with dyed strawberry highlights, perpetually trying to run away.

"I bet Alex would kiss you."

"What?" Alex and I say together.

Freddy holds up his palms. "I don't know, just trying to help! If it were *my* ex, I'd want to look desirable, that's all."

Freddy . . . has a point?

I mean, they're *going* to see me, it's a freaking guarantee. Chaos theory, et cetera. As soon as Jill spots me with her expertly shadowed Charlotte Tilbury hawk eyes, she's not going to *consider* walking out of this bar until we chat, reunite, clear the air. Jill is polite like that. She 100 percent was the star pupil during seventh-grade cotillion, and of course, she just *had* to go inviting me to her wedding. Like, *Please, watch your ex-boyfriend stand beside my groom at the altar while you sit in the pew alone!*

I can practically hear Jack and Lance recounting this whole experience later. It'll go down in one of two ways:

So, she hangs out with coworkers on the weekend.

Or. OR—

So, she's dating someone.

"They're looking for tables," Freddy says. He is the picture of entertained ease, twirling a strainer around his index finger. "Not finding much. We're very popular, which I'm sure they know. I bet at least one of them follows our TikTok account where we make the signature cocktails. You seen our videos, Casey?"

"No."

"My hands! In every video! I'm hand famous. Oh, the first girl is pouting now. Her boyfriend wants to leave. She's gesturing at the bar—oop, they're coming in hot."

I wonder what would happen if I leapt over the counter to hide, or maybe crawled between the knees of the guy beside me.

Ugh. Actually, scratch that last one.

I hear Alex gulp. "Casey?"

"Alex, can you . . ." I trail off, unsure what to say next. All I know is I can't stand for Lance to stroll into *my* city with a shiny, orange-skinned girl on his arm and get to be right, more than two years later, about me never finding someone better than him.

I haven't been *looking* for someone like him. Lately, I haven't even been looking.

Alex doesn't answer. Instead, he grabs the front stilts underneath my bar stool and pulls it flush against his. I almost fall off backward, but his reflexes are lightning fast. He presses a hand to the small of my back, catching me, then traces it up my spine to my neck.

Second time. Second time we've ever touched.

Gentle pressure as he nudges my head toward his. I lean in, observing his damp, parted lips, his eyes trained on my mouth, lowered eyelashes, a thumb brushing my earlobe.

When his lips reach mine, I remember the sound of his voice when he called me pretty.

He kisses me soft, hardly qualifying as a kiss at all, and it's almost teasing, the way he holds his lips just barely against mine but doesn't push forward and doesn't pull back. His mouth tastes like expensive bourbon and smooth velvet.

I . . . I think I want . . .

I don't know.

Everything. Anything.

The kiss is over one fraction of a second after it began. Alex pulls away, exhaling a breath of cool, liquored fog over my skin. His thumb gives me another caress on the hollow of my neck before he drops the hand tamely into his lap and uses his other to clutch his drink.

"Casey?"

Hmm?

My head snaps up, and reality hits.

Jack and Jill are standing right in front of me and Alex, staring open-mouthed. Behind them, the other girl I've never seen, and beside her, Lance, who is making the exact same embarrassed face as the day the Vols lost to Georgia State. Both girls are in heels that'll be covered in bar tar by the time they traipse back to their midtown hotel later tonight (I was that naive once). Lance is wearing the shirt I bought him for his twenty-first birthday.

I gather all the fake surprise I can muster and say, "Oh my gosh, hi!"

Lance rolls his eyes. He whispers something to his maybe new girlfriend, and they turn, heading wordlessly for the door.

What a milksop.

Jack tries to follow them out, but Jill grips his elbow in a stay-or-find-a-new-bride choke hold. Recovered from her shock, she smiles brightly at me, leaning in for a hug. "I can't believe we ran into you! I almost texted you, but then I thought—" She gives an awkward little shake of her head. "Well, anyway, this is even better. How *are* you?" I open my mouth to say something totally cringe-worthy like, *Oh you know, just living the New York dream!* But Jill spares me by squealing, "Look at my ring!"

Dutifully, I take her hand and say, "It's beautiful." After some internal berating, I look Jack dead in the eye and say just as much to him as to her, "I'm thrilled for you two."

Jack, for his part, looks nauseous.

"Did you get our save the date?"

"Yeah, I got it."

"You're definitely coming, right?"

Funny enough, Jill, I was planning to be literally anywhere else that weekend!

"I . . ." I trail off, sensing a rebuttal on her tongue. I can't say no, and she *knows* it. "Wouldn't miss it."

"Yay!" Jill squeals. "I'll add a plus-one to the invitation for your boyfriend." She turns to Alex, going in for a hug. "What's your name?"

Well, crap. Jill assuming Alex is my boyfriend was the whole point of kissing, but still, she really just called him that.

Alex blanches as Jill throws her arms around him, but it's subtle enough that someone who doesn't know him might miss it. Cordial as ever, he puts one awkward hand on her back and pats twice. "Alex Harrison. Nice to meet you."

When Jill steps back, Alex turns to Jack and sticks out a hand. Jack eyes it like it's going to bite him, but he shakes.

"Alex isn't my boyfriend," I correct, wincing, while I simultaneously consider that if I can't even let this impromptu deception fly for longer than forty-five seconds, how am I supposed to be purposely deceptive toward Alex? "We're just, um . . ."

We're just coworkers you might see together on YouTube soon?

How did I not take that into consideration before I asked him to kiss me?! Now Jack and Jill are going to think I'm casually screwing my coworker. That is literally so cliché.

Maybe they're not YouTube people. I'm *praying* they're not YouTube people.

I catch Freddy's eye, conveying a *What now, Director?* look of helplessness. He was so quick to jump in with a suggestion before, but now he just raises a single brow at me. He's leaning on the bar top, clearly enraptured by these proceedings as they continue to unfold.

"No matter," Jill says. "The plus-one is still yours if you want it."

"Thank you," I say, then try to curtsy before realizing I'm sitting down, and also this isn't *Downton Abbey*.

Jill sighs, twisting back and forth. Her fluffy pink skirt twirls around her knees as she glances around. "Well, this was great, but I think we better go. No room at the inn!" She belts out a slightly deranged laugh.

"Oh, do you want my—" Alex starts to stand up.

"No, no!" Jill says, backing away. "You stay, we'll go."

Jack has yet to utter a word, but he couldn't look more in love with his fiancée than he does when she says they're going. Alex tries to sit back down, but he stumbles slightly, his butt missing the bar stool, and he nearly busts it seconds before he catches himself on the countertop. I do my best to ignore him, focusing on waving goodbye to my college ex-buddies. "Have a great time at the game on Sunday, and good luck with wedding planning!"

"Thanks! Good luck with . . . Um." Jill gestures vaguely at Alex, who is engaged in an intense, nonverbal conversation with Freddy. "Everything."

I shift forward again when they turn toward the door. My eyes flutter closed.

"Going," Freddy says. "Go-iiiiing." I count off one second. Two. Three. "Gone."

My breath finally spills out, for the first time since they walked in, just as two shot glasses hit the counter with a *clink*.

"That was more stressful than a third-round interview," Alex huffs.

I laugh. It starts off awkward, almost like a coping mechanism, but a few seconds later I'm really laughing, clutching my stomach, heaving breaths of air that aren't nearly enough. I snort, covering my mouth with my hands. Then Alex is laughing, too, the sound deep and amused, and when I meet his eyes, there's no regret in them. He shakes his head at me, and I think, *Yeah, we're friends now. Kissing for cover makes us friends now.*

"I never even got their names." Laugh lines crinkle the corners of his eyes.

"Jack and Jill."

There's a beat of silence. "You're kidding."

"I'm not."

Freddy pours Patrón into our shot glasses, then dresses them up with salt and a lime wedge. "This one's on me." He sets them in front of us. "Because that was immaculate entertainment. I love my job."

CHAPTER ELEVEN

The drunker and more loose lipped we become, the shinier and foggier the room gets, the deeper Alex's voice goes—it all equates directly to the matrix of work talk versus personal talk.

Every few seconds, I'm learning things that are tilting the axis of my world.

At the office, Alex is full of charisma and charm, always at the center of the kind of attention that never feels undeserved. But now, it's clear he can sustain that behavior only in spurts. I've never spent such a long stretch of time around him before, and it's obvious the way his mind ebbs and flows, his attention switching as often as his mood. One minute, he'll be laughing at the girl down the bar screaming at Freddy, "A blow job shot, can you make me a blow job shot?" Then, two minutes later, he's nodding with quiet, steady attention as I explain the situation with my parents, because he abruptly changed course and asked.

"Do you consider Jerry a parent?" Alex asks me.

I nod. "Jerry would have settled for just being my dad's husband in my eyes. He let me make all the calls about our relationship. But he's too nurturing a person to be anything but a parent to me. And I think he always wanted to help raise a kid."

It feels greedy. Two living dads who love me, when Alex's father has kept him at arm's length all his life. But he only nods softly at my words, brushing a hand through his hair, and orders another old-fashioned.

"So, what about holidays? Summer breaks?" I ask. "Did your dad . . ."

"No," he says, voice flat. "Linda, my dad's wife, loathes any time that she's forced to acknowledge my existence, so my mom's sister took care of me. She still lives in their parents' place in Queens. My aunt was never my legal guardian, but I mostly went between her place and boarding school. She and my dad had some kind of arrangement they never asked my opinion about." Alex blinks, coming out of a trance. When he catches my expression, he smiles easily. "My cousins are the coolest. When we were younger, they were like my brother and sister. Still are. One lives in LA, and the other lives in Seoul."

My breath eases, now that I know he has living family who love him.

"Cooler than Freddy?"

He blanches. "Freddy is my lamest acquaintance."

"And yet." I smile just a little, tracing the rim of my newly topped-up cocktail. "He's what you led with."

The way Alex looks at me then, his eyes sparkling, it's almost like he's thinking, *Finally, you're playing with me.*

Some unfathomable amount of time later, only measured by the drinks I consume—conspiratorially nicknamed the Jack and Jill and advertised as Sleight of Hand's drink of the night—there's a tap on my shoulder. When I turn around, Brijesh is standing there.

He's the last person I'm expecting to see.

"Brijy!"

I fling myself into his arms, but he doesn't hug me back. He pulls away and puts his palms on either side of my face. My cheeks get pushed together.

"I've been trying to reach you for *three hours,* Case. You were supposed to meet me at the restaurant at eight o'clock. I literally had to track you down on Find My Friends to make sure you were okay."

I cringe away from him. "I—I forgot."

Brijesh blinks. "Casey Maitland doesn't forget things. You once wrote out thirty-three decimals of pi to win a drinking game."

"We were just . . ." On reflex, I point my thumb at Alex, but I don't know how to finish that sentence.

Brijesh follows my finger, and when he sees Alex, his whole body visibly relaxes. "Oh, hey, man. I didn't realize that was—" Brijesh shifts. Scratches his head. "Okay, so this is, um—I'm sorry."

"Why are *you* sorry?" I ask. "This is perfect. Are we still getting dinner? I'm starving."

"Casey." Brijesh pinches the bridge of his nose. "It's ten o'clock. I literally found a stray gay walking past and invited him inside the restaurant because I couldn't bear to cancel the reservation and lose my opportunity to review the chef first."

"You could have just eaten alone?"

His nose wrinkles. "Fuck no. I am way too narcissistic to eat a nice meal without someone I can explain the dish to."

Outside, the daylight is completely gone. In a mad scramble, I reach for my purse hooked under the bar and fumble for my phone. Missed calls. Dozens of texts from Sasha and Brijesh. When I turn back around, Brijesh is on the phone, one hand on his hip in a fatherly fashion.

"Yeah, I found her. She's fine." There's a pause, and then Brijesh says, "Alex Harrison, the guy from—yeah."

"Who is that?"

"Sasha. She's meeting us later."

"Hi, Sasha!" I shout at Brijesh's face, stumbling a little bit.

When he hangs up, Alex stands. "I'm sorry. I didn't mean to get in the middle of—"

"No, it's not his fault!" I jump in. "Put all the blame on me, Brij."

He holds up a hand. "You're both grown-ups. It's just that we're all each other has on this island, you know? Better safe than sorry."

Alex nods, setting his mouth into a firm line. "I get that."

"Anyway." Brijesh peeks into my cocktail. "What are we drinking?"

I hold up the Jack and Jill for him to taste. He sips it, then passes it to the guy behind him, who I didn't realize was *with* Brijesh until now. The dude is huge, well over six feet tall, wearing dark jeans and a plain white muscle tee.

"This is delicious," the giant groans, handing my glass back to Brijesh. "So delicately balanced."

"Thank you!" Freddy shouts from behind the bar. "I'll make you one!"

Brijesh leans toward me. "The CrossFit buff is my backup Casey. Convincing, no?"

"I'm irreplaceable," I retort, grabbing for my drink.

"First, remind me what it is I always say about lateness."

I roll my eyes. "Being late all the time isn't a cute personality trait, it's just rude."

He smiles. "You're forgiven. But I'm keeping the drink."

Freddy whips up another round, and then before I know it, he's clocking out, shouting the recipe for the J&J into the late-night bartender's ear. I sign a tab. It's less money than I thought—exactly eleven dollars. I think there's only one drink on it, but I'm not sober enough to question anything.

We pour out of the bar in a tumble of drunken stupor, and Brijesh is humming, "Casey and the boys, Casey and the boys." Alex and I find street hot dogs to devour while Brijesh describes in intimate detail the meal I missed.

"Tantalizingly tender tamales—"

"Shut up."

"The huitlacoche was to die for—"

"I said I was sorry, didn't I?"

"And the *pozole*."

"You really screwed up," Alex tells me. "This hot dog's only descriptor is average."

Still, the food sobers me up a little, and I chug a bottle of water for good measure. Then all five of us head toward Miriam's favorite karaoke bar. (It took next to no convincing to get everyone on board.)

Halfway there, Freddy sidles up between me and Alex. "Want to know a song that Alex knows every single word of?"

"Don't tell her that!"

"Hips. Don't. Lie."

It is obviously the first song I request when we arrive.

The bar is a grungy basement haunt, but there's still a waitlist, and we have to get through Dolly Parton's "9 to 5," sung by a bachelorette party in purple feather tutus, and then Ariana Grande's "Santa Tell Me," performed by an Australian woman in all black. All five of us line the sticky, overrun bar as we watch.

"Dude." Alex pushes away my elbow, knocking half the liquor out of the shot I just ordered to get him primed for his performance. "This smells like rubbing alcohol."

"Welcome to the bourgeoisie." I fix him with a stern look.

Alex narrows his eyes, then takes the shot from me and drinks it straight. "For the record, I've never spent a dime of my dad's money he didn't force on me. I just have more respect for my body than this."

I'm about to retort that I treat my body like a debauched temple, thank you very much, but then Sasha barrels up to me, her boyfriend, Miguel, in tow. We all make hazy introductions, and Sasha gives me a pointed look she should have saved for a Girls' Night In,

jerking her head at Alex with a question in her eyes. He doesn't notice, too busy fangirling over Miguel, who is some famous Yankees
player or something. Figures.

"Ring of Fire" starts to play, and a smile pulls at my lips as I
remember Dad playing this song whenever we'd have a bonfire with
our neighbors. Alex notices. He pulls me close so he can shout in
my ear, and his lips graze my skin.

Since our first two touches, memorized, cataloged, I've lost
track of all the others: my feet kicking his calf, his elbow against
mine, shoulders bumping on the outside curb, knuckles scraping
as we walked.

"What's your song?" His hold on my arm loosens already.

"I go back and forth between 'Bohemian Rhapsody' and 'Pro-
miscuous'!" I shout.

"Nice range!" he shouts.

"Thanks! Tonight, though, I wrote down something to sing with
Miriam!"

The DJ calls Alex's song. He shoots me a devastating smile—
all sparkly teeth and swoopy hair and eyes that are questionably
responsible for global warming—before lifting off his chair and
heading onstage in one drunken bound. Grabbing the mic from
the MC's outstretched palm, Alex starts perfectly in sync, his voice
low, scraping out of his throat: "I never really knew that she could
dance like this."

My hand claps over my mouth.

Throughout the whole thing, I stay resolutely put on my bar
stool despite the crowd swarming, gathering around Alex, belting
out the lyrics in a cacophonous echo. He kneels like a prince, one
elbow crossing his knee, offering his mic up to a girl's eager mouth,
and she sings, "You make a woman go mad!" And I think to myself
that some days, all you can really ask for is the chance to witness a
twenty-five-year-old man in his work clothes at midnight, singing
an old-school Shakira song in a West Village basement.

Miriam materializes out of nowhere dressed in her after-work quick change of a cotton dress and tennis shoes. The moment Brijesh sees her, his expression makes it clear that she and he are tonight's endgame. Miriam goes to him after I buy her a lemon drop shot, and Brijesh's hands tangle in her hair, and hers travel underneath the sleeves of his shirt. The only time he lets her out of his arms from then on is when she's in the bathroom with Sasha or onstage singing with me ("Through the Dark" by One Direction, because we always promised we'd carry each other over fire and water).

We dance, and sing, and things get even more hazy, and then there's this point where Alex and I both just . . . stop drinking altogether. Even though we didn't talk about it, even though we don't have to. It's almost like an unspoken pact: *Okay, this is enough.*

Somewhere between "Mr. Brightside" and "Friends in Low Places," I realize half our crew has Irish exited. When I grab my phone, there's a text from Miriam: heading home. where does Alex live?

Bruh idk??? I send back.

His thigh is pressed against mine, elbows propped on the bar behind him, hand clutching a plastic cup full of ice water. When Sasha and Miguel take their leave of the stage after a truly horrendous attempt at "Before He Cheats," they call an Uber home to the Upper West Side.

On the street, Sasha pulls me in for a hug. "On a scale of one to junior-year Global Leadership Scholars semiformal, how drunk are you?"

"Third quarter of a lame football game. Against Bowling Green."

She sighs, pulling away. "That's exactly what I was hoping to hear."

Their Uber comes. Miguel and Sasha get inside. It pulls away from the curb, and then Alex and I are alone.

Like, *alone* alone.

He tucks his hands into his pockets, watching me. Again, I'm sensing the switch in his mood, having gone from the life of the party to a patient, sideline observer in the span of one song. Alex seems to be good at that. Matching your energy where you're at.

I need to get out of here as fast as possible. This is, officially, no longer just casual drinks with a coworker. Hanging out tonight was *my* suggestion. I put us into this awkward situation, and now I need to get us out of it unscathed.

I fish my phone out of my purse to call my own Uber home: *seventy-one dollars.* An involuntary squeak slips out.

"What's wrong?" His tone is concerned.

"Just expensive, that's all." I shake my head and sigh, hair falling into my face. "I'm not that drunk anymore, but I'm also not calibrated for the subway right now."

"You could . . ." Alex cuts himself off. He scratches at his neck. "It's just that I live really close, so if you wanted to stay, and take the subway in the morning . . . that would be a thing—a thing that you could do."

And in a moment of poignant, fleeting sobriety, I understand why Miriam wanted to know where Alex lives. For when she tracks me later tonight, or early tomorrow morning, because she doesn't really believe I'm going home.

I don't want to. Not only because Miriam and Brijesh will be at our place doing one of two things—loudly having sex or loudly having a talk about what they "are"—but also because . . . I don't want to leave Alex yet. I don't entirely understand it, but the alcohol thinning my blood tells me I don't *need* to understand it quite yet.

Also, I haven't gotten any closer to getting Tracy her answers about the CEO and chairman. I'm frustrated for having to think about that after such a fun evening with Alex, but the reminder still looms.

"Not very professional," I say around a smirk. "But I *am* desperate, so."

"There's only one bed," he blurts.

I blink three times. "Alex. That's not . . . Most of us mere mortals have only one bed."

He smiles at the ground and rubs a hand under his chin. "I don't have a couch yet. It's on back order. I just wanted you to know that."

One bed. No couch.

"I could sleep on the floor—"

"No!" I stick out my chin. "We're both grown-ups, right? We can handle one night of close proximity. If you're okay with it, too, that is."

He scoffs, and laughs deeply, and runs a hand through his hair. "Come on, Simba. It's this way."

CHAPTER TWELVE

The night air is as crisp as a freshly minted dollar, and my skin is peppered with goose bumps until we walk over a vent below the sidewalk that shoots warmth up my spine. New York is never quiet, but compared to the noise of the karaoke bar, the sounds of cabbies honking their horns and walk signs commanding us to cross are nearly peaceful.

"Are Brijesh and Miriam . . . ?" Alex starts.

"It's complicated."

I debate leaving it at that, but before I know it, I tell him about Miriam's college ex breaking her heart. She got dumped a month before Lance and I ended things. Jared had a habit of doing bars, and Miriam had a habit of being a nursing student, which made the drug abuse particularly difficult for her *not* to have an opinion on. In the end, it ripped them apart, but I think to this day, Miriam grieves what that relationship could have been.

"So, anyway," I tell Alex, "Brijesh is hopelessly in love with her, and she's trying to figure out how to move on from a love that broke her, and they pull each other in and then push each other away again. It's kind of a mess."

Alex nods and says nothing. I appreciate that—his ability to just nod and say nothing when the moment truly calls for it. He's a bit miraculous like that.

"Freddy is cool," I say.

"No, he isn't," Alex says, shaking his head, but his lips are fighting a grin. "Trust me. Sasha's cooler. What's her story?"

"She went to UT because she wanted to play basketball for the Lady Vols like her mom," I explain. "I love her, and so does Miriam, but she isn't a constant in our lives. Always there one minute and gone the next, like a passing ship in the night."

Alex hums. "Sounds like how people describe me."

We're at his place a couple of minutes later. It's a redbrick town house on a quiet lane right in the heart of the West Village, and at first glance—when he just vaguely *points* at it—I'm trying to understand how he's got the whole thing to himself. This multimillion-dollar, three-floor space that probably shares a real estate agent with Blake Lively and *must* be owned by his father. But when we go inside, Alex leads me up a narrow staircase to the partitioned second floor. The whole unit's been split up for renters. There is precious little space— less square footage than my and Miriam's apartment, even—but Alex has a halfway decent kitchen setup with a sink, a hot plate, and . . .

"A balcony!" I stride toward it and press my hands and nose against the glass door like a kid in an aquarium. Two canvas camping chairs are set up outside.

"You can . . . Uh."

I turn back.

Alex is looking at me with carefully concealed amusement. "You can go out there, if you want."

"Fresh air in your underwear!"

"I guess? But also, do you really want to assume the air out there is fresh?"

I ignore this valid line of inquiry and ask, "Why don't you have any plants?"

"Who would see them? That balcony faces an alleyway."

"You'd see them! Also, the critters would."

He comes up beside me and leans a shoulder on the other glass pane. "I'm not loving your sudden alignment with my *Garden Girl* enemies."

"What do you mean by sudden?" I joke.

Alex smirks. "If I get a plant, will you spare me?"

"If you promise to actually get one. This is a waste of a balcony otherwise."

"You'd have to pick it. I wouldn't know the first thing about what has a chance of surviving in New York City alleys."

I stick out my hand, and he shakes it. "Deal."

My body unleashes an unattractive, involuntary yawn. I pull out my phone to text Miriam before I forget: Staying at Alex's.

"Holy cow," I say. "Is it really three in the morning?"

The question seems to startle him. He walks into his bedroom—which doesn't have its own door and is honestly more of a nook nestled into one wall—and mumbles, "Here, let me . . ." He digs a T-shirt and a pair of sweatpants out of a dresser drawer and tosses them to me. "Will that irritate your skin? I use scented detergent."

I look down, feel the cotton beneath my finger pads. He gave me a HARVARD T-shirt. It puts me in a kind of unexplainable trance.

Harvard, Boston, snow in his black hair—

"It should be fine," I mutter quietly, touched he remembered what I'd said earlier about the fragrance allergy. Confused why I'm suddenly mesmerized by this HARVARD T-shirt. "Perfume and cologne are the real culprits," I explain.

Alex digs out a blanket from his closet and tosses it on the bed. Then he moves the fluffy comforter over to one side.

"There you go," he says. "The bathroom's right there if you need it." He points to a skinny door by a big empty space where a couch might feasibly belong. "Clean towels are in the plastic drawers under the sink, but there's no hot water, so don't bother waiting on it."

"Ever?"

"I can usually get it between six and ten A.M."

I laugh, tripping over his coffee table. "Thanks for the warning. I'll keep my clothes on." Alex bites the inside of his cheek. "I just meant—um. I can wait to shower, and . . . stuff. Until I get home."

"Okay."

I curtsy like an idiot, clearly *still* not certain if I'm on the set of *Downton Abbey.* "Thank you for your h-hospitality."

Ugh. My childhood stutter always comes back when I'm tipsy and nervous.

I flee to the bathroom to change, wash my face, and finger-brush my teeth. Alex goes in after I exit. I snuggle under the cloudy layers of his comforter, sighing in contentment, feet wiggling happily as I breathe in the scent of his spare pillow.

The door opens. "You look cozy."

I twist to find him in a T-shirt and plaid pajama bottoms, staring down at me with an unreadable expression. I've never seen this much of his arms exposed before. His muscles are gently sculpted, like a man who cares about his fitness but doesn't care about it the *most.* Again, the outline of that tattoo is visible, but it's too dark to decipher.

"I am," I say. "Thanks for this."

"Of course."

His footsteps cross the room to the door, and then the apartment goes black. I hear the turn of a lock, then more footsteps back toward the bed. The mattress groans as Alex's body sinks onto its other side.

He shuffles around, getting comfortable, and I stay absolutely still.

"Good night, Casey. Thanks for getting drunk with me."

The heat from his body is radiating off him, lulling me into a calm, dreamy slumber. "Good night, Alex," I say, and then yawn. "Thanks for kissing me."

My eyes snap back open. Good *Lord,* why is my rational decision-making on vacation?

"You—You're welcome," Alex rumbles. I tilt my head toward the sound of his voice. His figure is starting to emerge beside me in the dark. "But also, I'm welcome. Wait. *What?*"

Wait, what?

I turn fully onto my side, tuck my hands beneath my cheeks. Alex mirrors me. His eyes shine, but they look kind of glazed, too. As we lie here in the silence, watching each other, I take stock of all the things we've unearthed today.

Alex's relationship with his father. My relationship with my ex. His aunt. My parents. Miriam. Freddy. Sasha, and Brijesh. We offered up all these pieces of ourselves to each other, like the bindings of a truce.

This is it.

Now or never.

My perfect moment to push the envelope a little further.

If Tracy Garcia could see me now, I think queasily.

Beneath the comforter I shift, jittery with the conscious weight of what I'm about to do. One of my feet comes to rest against Alex's ankle by accident. He doesn't move away, and neither do I. He just dips his eyes down, then back up.

"Alex?" I ask.

"Yeah?" His voice is a ghost of what it *can* be.

"What's the deal with your father and Dougie Dawson?"

His mouth pulls into a taut line, and I instantly regret bringing it up out of the blue, or at all, if it's something that puts that sad of a look on his face.

"You don't have to tell me."

Don't tell me. Say you still think it's hilarious I would even ask.

"No, it's fine," Alex whispers. "It's not some huge secret."

"It's not?" The question comes out embarrassingly hopeful, and the relief I feel is instantaneous.

He takes a deep breath. "Dougie has a son my age who went to Choate, too. Ellis. He's cool. One night after a party, we wound up smoking a joint together. That's how I know some of Dougie and Robert's history."

I say nothing, but it's pretty telling that Alex doesn't even know the truth from his own dad; he heard it through the grapevine.

"Dougie and Robert were in the same class at Harvard," Alex starts. "Before my dad's wife married him, she dated Dougie all through college. Their senior year, Dad basically stole Linda from Dougie. So, that's how it started."

"How it *started*?" I repeat.

"It gets worse. Did you ever see *The Social Network*?"

I nod.

"Picture what happened between Zuckerberg and all the people he screwed over, but with a start-up that flopped and lost hundreds of thousands of the founders' own money. Dougie was supposedly the biggest investor, too. He's Eduardo Saverin, and my dad is Zuckerberg in this scenario. But whenever the failure gets brought up—in press, and even more so in private—each of them makes a point to blame the other."

"Damn," I whisper.

"Yeah," Alex says. "After they both finished grad school, Dougie made it his life's mission to have Robert disregarded from every job he wanted in New York. He eventually got one at LC and worked his way up the ranks, but it took him a lot longer because of Dougie."

"They both sound so ruthless," I say.

"*Were*, and still are," Alex says. "Two men intent on each other's destruction."

"Is that why Dougie became our CEO?" I ask. "To steal Robert's legacy?"

What would my mom have thought about that? Legacy was so

important to her. In her eyes, there is probably no greater sin than overwriting someone's name once they're gone.

Alex turns onto his back, puts an arm over his forehead. "Maybe. I think part of it had to do with Ellis and me," he admits. "When we were old enough to apply for Harvard ourselves, my dad started to care about my schoolwork and extracurriculars. He even came to my college counseling sessions." Alex says all this in the same clinical tone he used earlier, as if it's boring, monotonous stuff. Like he's trying to keep some unnamed emotion at bay.

"And when I got in . . . I was thrilled, of course. But I also felt like I'd finally pulled myself over the top of a cliff I'd been climbing for four years. Like it was a reward I fucking *deserved*. When I got the acceptance email, I forwarded it to my dad, and he replied with two words: 'atta boy.' Which is, objectively, the most affection he's ever shown me," Alex says, laughing dryly. "Ellis Dawson didn't get in, didn't even go to college at all. He lives in LA now and does photography. But I think Dougie viewed my acceptance and his son's rejection as some sort of loss. It revived his hatred of my dad years later, and that's why he gunned for CEO when he heard Robert was stepping down." Alex sighs. "I mean, that's my theory, anyway. But who really knows."

I hate that Alex was collateral damage in two grown men's power plays. Even worse, I hate that he knows it.

He looks tired. Not in the physical sense, which—yeah, that too. But he looks like he's finally dropped the face he wears for the world. Right here, in this bed with me.

"I'm sorry." It's all I can think to say.

Alex shrugs, sinking closer to me. "Their rivalry has never really affected my daily life, to be honest."

"No, Alex. I mean, yes, I'm sorry about all that, but I'm sorry about . . . about *me*. How short I was with you. I mean, for *weeks*, I was just, like, the worst."

Alex laughs gently, and I do, too.

"I judged you before I knew you, and I'm just really, really sorry." I hope he can hear the sincerity in my tone. For once, I hope that emotion *is* on my sleeve. "You're hardworking, and thoughtful, and good at your job. *Great.* You're *great* at your job. Please don't put in your notice. We would definitely be worse off without you."

The whites of his eyes are visible now, and they're shining with something that looks a lot like triumph. "I had a feeling you were worth waiting for. And anyway, I could have been more forthcoming. Cleared up your misconception much earlier."

"I wouldn't have, if I had been in your position," I whisper. "It takes me a while to open up to people. I should have known to be more patient with you because I need other people to be patient with me."

He nods. "Okay. Noted. I can be patient with you, Casey. Very, very patient."

I feel the ghost of his breath on my face. Moonlight is shining through the window, illuminating the hairs on his arm, standing on end. The blanket he's using doesn't even cover his feet. "You're cold," I say.

"I'm fine," he whispers.

I lift the edge of his comforter, creating a cavernous shadow of warmth between his body and mine. Wordlessly, Alex slides closer to me in the dark. My heart stumbles over itself as I let the comforter fall back on top of us both.

"Comfortable?" his voice rumbles. My eyes peek open to find his closed.

"Mm-hmm," I acknowledge.

"Night, Casey."

I yawn. "Good night, Alex."

CHAPTER THIRTEEN

Someone is pounding on the door.

At first, it's in my dream. Heavy footsteps on stairs. They beat like a drum, a prelude to foggy Shakira lyrics, and then, the pounding is here—on the other side of my skull—and I'm awake.

The crown of my head catches sharply on Alex's chin. "Oomph," I grunt. My hands fumble for purchase against his chest and I push, sliding sideways off him.

His arms pull my body back against his as he shifts onto his side. "They'll go away." His voice scrapes along my ear, blowing hair around my temples. "Promise."

This is . . . the coziest. Ultimate. Unbeatable. I feel practically drugged.

"Who is it?" I croak.

"Someone who's got the wrong apartment," he grumbles.

Surprisingly, there's no awkward morning talk, no weird adjustment between halfway-drunk-bed-buddies and mostly-sober-morning-after. I got up too many times in the middle of the night for that. Every time I woke up to pee, Alex would shift and wake up in the process, releasing me from his arms—which I'd rolled right into somewhere during the stage of falling asleep. After the *third* time I came back from the bathroom, and he wrapped me up again like a koala against a tree, he simply murmured against my neck, "You need a catheter."

Curse my kitten bladder.

There is a kind of suspension of disbelief hanging between us. I don't—*can't*—think about our physical positioning too hard right now. But also to note: why didn't my other two one-night stands want to cuddle for warmth?

Can I even classify what's happening here as a one-night stand?

Knock, knock, knock!

Alex groans. Or maybe growls. The sound vibrates through his body and into mine. And then, that *voice*—the same one from two days ago, outside the elevator in our building lobby—*booms*. "Alex, it's your father!"

His body stiffens around me.

We both shoot out of bed like guilty, horny teenagers. I scramble back on my knees, lose my balance, fall backward. My head hits the carpeted ground with an unforgiving *thunk*. The comforter is tangled around my legs. I squirm like a fish on the floor, trying to unwrap my blanket burrito, spitting out my hair and also eating it.

Like I'm no heavier than a tissue or a leaf, Alex easily lifts me onto my feet. I stand still as he unwraps me, silent as the grave. When his eyes catch mine, he points toward a murdery-looking door beside the hot plate.

"Is that where you stash your dead bodies?" I hiss.

Alex puts a finger to my lips, his eyes blown wide. "No, just my home-brewery kit."

"Alex!" his father shouts, pounding on the door.

He points again toward the closet, more insistently this time.

A flash of anger burns through me at being treated like his dirty little secret. "Are you embarrassed of me?"

He stares, expression flat. "Do you really want the chairman of the board of the company at which you are employed to find you hungover in my apartment?"

Okay, fine, he's got a point. "Right." I nod. "Right, I'll just get in the . . . in the home brewery."

I pad across the apartment in my bare feet and twist the door-knob as quietly as possible. Inside, the pantry has been converted into a beer fanatic's starter kit. A stainless steel brew pot, thermometers, and two plastic tubes feeding into white buckets sit between a few glass jars fermenting amber liquid. I shoot one last look of incredulousness at Alex before I climb between the assemblage and pull the door closed behind me. My gaze focuses on the space underneath the door—my only source of light in this black hole of fermenting yeast.

Alex opens his front door, and footsteps barrel into the room. "I've been trying to reach you all morning," Robert huffs angrily.

"It's nine o'clock on a Saturday," Alex retorts. "And do you really want to talk about ignoring phone calls? How did you find out where I live? How did you even get in the front door?"

There is a moment's pause, and then—"I got someone in HR to look up your employee profile." My jaw drops, but Robert's casual tone conveys he does cute, illegal little things like this all the time. "And then I . . . followed someone inside."

After a beat of silent disbelief, Alex says, "I'm pretty sure that's a violation of company policy, and also probably the law."

His dad sighs. "I'm heading out of town. I had to see you in person."

Alex shifts on his feet. "What is it?"

There are more footsteps. It sounds like pacing. "Monday morning, news is going to break that I'm stepping down from the board of LC."

Holy crap.

This is . . . kind of a big deal. Is Robert leaving *because of* Dougie? Can he really not stand to be associated with him to the point that he's resigning from the board entirely? Of a company he's worked for *his entire adult life*?

My thoughts jump to Tracy. She *had* to have known this was happening when we talked in the break room. She's the CFO, for crying out loud! If Tracy knew Robert was stepping down, why did she even bother tasking me with researching his feud?

And then it clicks: Even with Robert gone, she thinks Dougie still won't be a good enough CEO. She's trying to build a case against him.

"Are you doing this because of me?" Alex asks. "I'll just quit. If I'd known you would've had to—"

"No, d-don't quit!" his dad stammers, then coughs. "It's not because of you. I've been planning this for a while. The timing's right, and . . . you'll be there. I'm . . . proud of you. Son."

The shock emanating from Alex right now clogs the air, thick and overwhelming. It's only slightly less palpable than the discomfort coming off his dad.

"Two days ago, you told me to put in my notice. Now you're fucking *proud*?"

"I was taken off guard," his father protests. "I didn't know if you'd used my name to get the job—"

"Of course I didn't use your name. I've never *needed* to!" Alex bellows, furious. "It's not my fault you found out as late as you did."

"Don't raise your voice," his father growls.

Alex laughs darkly. "A scolding? That's new."

A fist hits the table, and I jerk, squeaking a little. "Just . . ." His father exhales in obvious exasperation. "Stay. Keep doing whatever it is you've been doing for the past two months. Grow *Bite the Hand* however you see fit. Spare no expense. Invest in anything you think worthy. Money is no object when it comes to that brand right now. Got it?"

I roll my eyes. Like father, like son.

"You cannot possibly think," Alex says, "that with you gone, Dougie will allow us to launch BTH as a subsidiary. He hates me almost as much as he hates you. I feel it every time we're in a room together. He'll probably try to get me fired."

"So you're going to give up without trying?"

"That's *not* what I said," Alex retorts, masculine bravado flaring. "I'm only making a prediction, and I don't even hear you denying it."

"Well." Robert clears his throat. "I guess we'll have to see what happens."

Alex says, "Guess so."

Here's the thing. Even if I weren't hiding in a closet, this would *still* be one of the weirder conversations I've been privy to. Robert sounds like he's *challenging* Alex. And Alex sounds like he's . . . accepting it.

After a beat of silence, Robert asks, "Late night?"

"Yeah."

"Sonja?"

"Dad." Alex exhales. "I dated Sonja for three weeks when I was twenty-one."

I briefly ponder how to acquire Sonja's Social Security number and least favorite way to die before I remember that Alex is just a coworker.

"Right. I guess it's been a while since we've . . . caught up."

"Twenty-five years, give or take."

"Don't be that way, Alex. You've always been independent."

Alex says nothing. But I can feel it—the way his heart is stretching outside of him, asking for a chance to be known. Maybe he doesn't *want* to be independent.

"Seeing anyone new?" Robert asks.

A chair scrapes along the floor. "No."

Footsteps cross the apartment. Seconds tick by as Alex's dad pokes around. The creaky bathroom door swings open, then closed again. I huddle deeper in my corner.

"Why won't you use your trust, Alex? This place is a shoebox."

Alex sighs. Maybe this is a conversation he's tired of having. "If you don't understand the reason by now, there's nothing I can say to make you grasp it."

"You realize, if I die first, you get half my money, and if I die after Linda does, you get everything?"

"You realize I'm going to donate it all either way?"

There is a stony silence on the other side of my barrier.

"Here," says Robert. "Take my house key in case this place gets condemned. Our Upper East Side town house will be empty through Christmas."

"Why?"

"Linda and I are going away for a few months. I'll be back in January."

"Europe?"

"Australia."

Alex hums appreciatively. "Enjoy retirement."

"It's not . . ." Robert trails off, then says, "Thank you." He heads for the front door, pulls it open. "Don't forget what I said about BTH. You're in a strong position of leverage right now. If I gave you anything besides good looks, it's the Harrison hustle."

"Says the early retiree."

His father raps his fingers on the door. "Don't be so sure about that."

As soon as it closes behind him, I pop open the pantry door and peek around the edge of it. Alex slides across the floor in black socks, flicking the front lock closed. I barrel-roll out of the pantry, and by the time I look up, he's above me, offering a hand.

"Your dad seems . . ."

Alex hauls me to my feet. "Demanding? Authoritative?"

I frown. "I was going to say it seems like he doesn't know how to act around you."

"That's because we're only one degree removed from strangers." He looks down, at the folded white envelope in his hand, the faint outline of a single key within. Eyes glazed, he shakes his head and murmurs, "He's never invited me to his home. Not the one in New Haven *or* the one on the Upper East Side. And he's certainly never called me *son* before."

I'm proud of you, son.

A small, barely there flame of hope glimmers behind Alex's eyes. It twists my stomach up in knots. Because I know the feeling, in a way.

I have my own issues with my parents. Frankly, I don't think there's ever been a child that, at some point or another, *hasn't* felt less than enough. It shows up differently for all of us, but for me, not feeling enough looks like a teenage kid staring at her parents' bodies of work—plaques and portraits and signed guitars and old refurbished cameras—and *knowing* their legacy is marked on the world. It's there. Tangible. Art they created, together, and apart.

The absolutely mortifying thing is that their biggest expression of humanity was supposed to be me—and *this* is how I turned out.

Crying in art class because I don't *get* it.

Stage fright so bad I pee a little.

And then, this strange sense of calm, of certainty, when I discovered an old book of sudoku puzzles at the recording studio. When I could calculate the exact grocery bill before the machine. When my brain started to estimate the net worth of all my parents' art—every royalty, every gallery sale—and I wondered if I'd ever see the world the way they saw it. As an expression. Not an equation.

But despite it—despite *all* of it—I've never, *ever* questioned that they love me.

Yet here Alex is, brilliant, one of a kind, misty-eyed because his dad doesn't want him to quit his job anymore, said he was proud, called him *son*, and did it all to soften the blow of leaving Alex behind to battle Robert's own worst enemy.

"I should go," I whisper, my voice thick with emotion. Suddenly everything's hitting me wrong, and my suspension of disbelief that any of this is normal has ended.

Alex's attention snaps back to me. The hand he used to pull me up, still interlaced with mine, tugs. He looks down at my body covered in *his* clothes, and his face changes into something more concentrated. "You don't have to."

"No, I really should." I look down at myself. "I'm covered in bar tar, and sweat, and fragrance-scented laundry detergent remnants."

"Shower. If you want," Alex says. "There's hot water for another hour."

I shake my head. "Thanks, but I should head out. I told Mir we'd hang today."

I pull my hand from his and cross to the bed, where my clothes, shoes, and purse got stuffed beneath the comforter before Alex opened the door for his dad. I change in the bathroom, leave the clothes he let me borrow folded neatly on the foot of his bed. Alex hovers, waiting, watching me.

"Well. Thanks for . . ." I gesture around lamely. "This."

"You're welcome anytime."

"I'm welcome to hide in your murder closet *anytime*?"

"Next time, I'll even let you taste test one of my beers while you're in there."

"But I thought we were friends now."

Alex's lips kick up, and I smile weakly in return. Three days ago, we were bickering in a conference room about the social media budget, and I couldn't wait to get out of his presence. Now I want more than fourteen hours. I want all of Alex's hours. How exactly did we get here?

I walk past him toward the door, freaking out a little bit. "See you Monday."

"Casey."

The word stops me in my tracks, reaching past my eardrums, soaking into my body until his voice is in my veins.

I freeze, looking back. His lips are parted, breath light, clothing wrinkled head to toe. Static electricity seems to run through his midnight hair. His hands are in the pockets of his pajama pants, but I can *just* see the shadow of the tattoo on his inner wrist.

The thing about Alex is, most of the time, you know you're getting only a small part of his attention because he's thinking about a million other things plus one more. Normally, I can almost see the cogs of his brain working on the next thing. Like he can't stay still. Can't look back. But lately, when he looks at me, it feels like he might be letting everything else fall away.

Hoarsely, he murmurs, "See you Monday."

On my way home, I wonder what might've happened in that bed if no one had come knocking.

CHAPTER FOURTEEN

Monday is bookended by the company-wide email at nine in the morning announcing the retirement of board chairman Robert Harrison, and a tragic afternoon hot chocolate spill on my keyboard that totally fucks with my lender proposal. Also, I forgot to bring Benny a fancy coffee like he asked for on Friday afternoon. Flawless Fari brings him a triple venti nonfat dry cappuccino all the way from DUMBO, which means I have to spend thirty minutes on the phone today talking the ex-COO missus out of hiring a skywriter to fly past our windows.

There are women who *don't* deserve their vilification as overly dramatic, scorned ex-wives, and then there is Angelica Downey.

After I finish cleaning my keyboard with makeup wipes and seltzer, Fari asks me, "Did you ever meet Robert Harrison? Back when he was our CEO?"

"No," I say. "Why?"

Also, *why* are all my succulents dying? I poke my index finger into the soil of one of my planters. Perfectly balanced, not too dry, not damp, either. My cubicle is by the window, so there's plenty of sunlight. . . .

"Casey, did you hear me?"

I poke my head up. "Huh?"

"I asked what you thought about Dougie taking over as chairman *and* CEO."

I blink. "Um. What?"

Fari rolls her eyes. "It was in the email."

I had admittedly skimmed the email.

Okay, fine, I didn't read it at all because I thought I'd already known everything there was to know. I filed it unread into a sub-folder labeled *Executives on Soap Boxes*. (I like to think the people in IT monitoring my work usage get a kick out of my subfolder nicknames, too.)

Actually, I spent the 9:00 A.M. hour reading articles from the latest issue of *Take Me There*: the travel magazine headquartered in London. There was a six-page spread *on London*—more specifically, how to be a tourist in London without acting like one—and it lit a fire inside me to get back to work on *Bite the Hand*'s income projections. The faster we launch the subsidiary, the quicker I'll get tapped for a transfer. The quicker I get tapped for a transfer, the faster I'll figure out what my own legacy is supposed to be.

But now, my nose wrinkles at the thought of Dougie Dawson being our CEO *and* the interim chairman. If a CEO is the prime minister, the board chairman is the monarchy: background noise until something drastic happens. Only then are you reminded of their divine power. It feels wrong, and frankly unethical, to have the same person doing both.

"Gross," I mutter.

"You've met him?" Fari asks. "Dougie?"

"Yeah. He's archaic, and I'm not talking about his age."

Fari sighs. "Wonderful."

She goes back to scanning emails. I grab my mouse and sift through Outlook until I find the email from this morning.

> Effective immediately, Robert Harrison will be stepping down as Chairman of Little Cooper's Board of Directors. We thank Robert for twenty-five years of service and all the roles he occupied: Financial Manager, Director of Financial Operations, VP of Finance, CEO, and Board Chairman. We wish Robert the best in his retirement.
>
> Filling Robert's shoes as interim chairman is Douglas (Dougie) Dawson, Little Cooper's own CEO. While the search is conducted for a permanent board chairman, Dougie is excited to focus more substantially on furthering Little Cooper's legacy.

Look. I'm not here to promote toxic masculinity, but isn't rule number one of the *Fuckboy Handbook: Business Edition* to hold on to your territory by any means necessary? Why would Robert retire now, knowing his adversary would inevitably step up to the plate? I mean, it's not like Dougie got that position out of the blue. Decisions like that happen behind closed doors, distributed to us underlings in the form of bite-size propaganda.

So what the heck is Robert playing at?

I don't see Alex in person until Wednesday afternoon during the weekly all-hands meeting for *Bite the Hand*. He sits across the table from me and acts very professional, talking about photo shoot arrangements for Love Letters (a column by queer writers written epistolary style) and contacting a Discord rep about We Need to Talk (a fanatical and wildly inappropriate server where people both love and hate-love our brand).

I sit across from him in a room full of people, answering questions about dollars and cents, thinking about how he's so. much. better. at this stuff than I would have ever been, and also the way he cradled me as we slept.

"Casey, can we make this work in December?" Alex asks me in regard to a podcast launch he's been orchestrating. "I know we planned the expense for next fiscal year, but the guest we want for the first episode can only do before Christmas or after Valentine's Day. Don't ask me why. I think it was something celestial."

I summon all my typical malaise when Alex asks my department for money and say, "If you absolutely must, but I'll need a new expense report."

The smirk he throws me has a devilish gleam. "Certainly."

"Casey and Alex."

I cut my gaze to Saanvi. She's sitting beside Gus, who, as usual, is ignoring everyone and typing furiously on his laptop. I can't blame him; deadlines around here are brutal, and he has the added pressure of editing every piece of copy at the fastest-growing platform in our company. I sometimes wonder if Gus knew what he was in for when he first pitched BTH as a *Frame* vertical. Could he have known a year ago what it would snowball into?

"Your video premieres Friday," Saanvi goes on, and I combust. *Friday?* That's two days from now! *Two days.*

"Andre said *two* weeks!" I exclaim. "It's been less than one week since we recorded!"

Saanvi shrugs. "My team is efficient. If you want to watch the final cut, Andre will have it ready tomorrow. Just swing by his desk."

Well. She didn't say *If you want to change anything,* so watching the final video will only triple my anxiety. I really don't need the opportunity to dissect my flaws ahead of time. "I don't need to see it," I say. "I was there."

"Same," Alex echoes. When our gazes meet, he's got a perfectly professional expression stamped on his infuriatingly handsome face.

"Could you guys maybe convince Brijesh to adopt that mindset?" Saanvi grumbles.

After the meeting, she holds Alex back to sign the same paperwork I signed before they released the "Healthed-Up Hot Chicken" video. I pack up my things and head back to ninety-eight. And the day carries on.

Perfectly professionally.

> **One Day at Work in the Magazine Industry: Casey and Alex Eat an Unrealistic Workday Lunch and Slam FiDi**

Analyst Casey's in the queue! Analyst Casey's in the queue!
Lol they stole her from the food baby channel, incredible
Wait this is so mfing wholesome
I have questions . . . about Alex's relationship status
THEY ARE SO ORDINARY AND I FINALLY FEEL SEEN.
Ha. Sailboat anatomy.
YES Alex, let us ALL continue to destigmatize ADHD in the workplace!
For sure he's an enneagram 7. She's got to be a 5 or a 3
I'm sorry but there is no way they're not boning

Thirty minutes after the video goes live, I get this text from Miriam: the day you start posting your skincare routine is the day I put a bounty on ur head.

I snort at my desk and text back, the fifteen-year-old girl you knew in high school who had to beg Marty Maitland to spring for accutane would never.

Fari pulls up the video on her computer against my will, and she, Benny, Don, and I watch the intro together. I'm cringing into Benny's shoulder, but Fari tells me my hair looks good and she's glad I went with the soft purple lipstick instead of matte red, which eases my nerves more than it has any right to.

"What are you guys watching?"

Fari hits her space key. All four of us look up to see Tracy staring at us. Our faces display guilt so obvious, we might as well be watching porn.

"C'mere, Trace!" Benny shouts. "Casey's on TV!"

Don looks at Benny like he just ordered our CFO to strip, which, understandable. Not many of us are bold enough to speak to this financial goddess with that kind of familiarity, but Tracy just raises her eyebrows and comes over, intrigued.

Andre has done an *impeccable* job editing this. There we are walking, and the sun refracts across the screen in an attractive ray of light. There are clips of the street, people's shoes, cars, buildings. The inside of the market, some ASMR-level auditory work as the pizza box scrapes our table and bottles twist open. Between it all, we talk. The editing makes the dialogue feel off-the-cuff and snappy, much more comedic than it did coming out of our mouths. It's clipped together fast, like a sports highlight reel. Alex asking me about my favorite Excel formula, and me spewing all over him, draws a real laugh out of Tracy.

The final cut is the outro: me waving to Alex as he heads home to change. Then I say to the camera, "XLOOKUP, you heard it here first," and the screen blacks out.

Benny slaps me on the back in a rare bout of positive reinforcement.

Tracy says, "Thanks for reminding me why we do all this, guys."

She smiles softly and turns to Fari. "Phenomenal job on that business proposal, by the way. Let's workshop it together, just the two of us, next week."

"I—yes," Fari says, doe-eyed. "Thank you."

I debate following Tracy when she walks away so I can expel the intel burning holes in my chest, but even though Alex told me himself that it's not a secret, passing the information along still isn't something I'm particularly eager to do.

I'm not going to seek Tracy out. She'll come to me again if and when she needs to know.

"There's really no one like her," Fari says, halfway to me, halfway to herself. "The CFO wants to mentor me one-on-one. You know I interviewed for twenty companies? *Twenty.* I got offers from more than half."

"Which did you have more of? Stoles or job offers?" I joke.

Fari rolls her eyes. "It's just, none of the rest of the offers had a Tracy Garcia. A mentor. A role model. An advocate who wants to pull us up the ladder."

I nod, looking at the corner Tracy vanished around. "Yeah," I say. "I know what you mean." I turn back to Fari. "And I'm really glad you picked LC."

"Me too."

By the time I leave work, I'm starting to panic that Alex hasn't texted me about the video.

I know I could reach out to him first. I do realize it. But every time I think about what I would send him, I feel like a fifteen-year-old girl (halfway through her Accutane regimen) with a crush on someone in the grade above her, who is also way out of her league.

I'm hopping off the subway in Brooklyn Heights when it finally happens, and something that had bunched up viciously in my chest unravels.

So you're an xlookup girl, huh?

Pushing my hair out of my eyes, I smile against the setting sun. The neighborhood is dozing right now, hovering in the doldrums between the end of a workweek for some and the start of one for others. I meander along the cracked sidewalk, now a much-loved trek toward home, and type out a reply.

> Casey: don't say it
> Alex: don't say what?
> Casey: that finding that out makes perfect sense for me
> Alex: I see what you did there
> Casey: finally watched us, did you?
> Alex: I was letting the anticipation build

I freeze on the sidewalk and quirk my head. Why does it sound like we're talking about a sex tape?

> Alex: jk, i've been in the car all day. Cape Cod for the weekend with Freddy's mom
> Casey: Does Freddy know about you two???
> Alex: cute.
> Casey: Cape Cod sounds fancy

He sends me a picture of a setting sun bleeding into the horizon over a beautiful beach, his legs and bare feet propped on a wicker table beside a can of pilsner. The wooden planks of a porch staircase spill straight into the sand.

Alex: the fanciest

Knowing he's there and not here isn't the reason I get Thai take-out and Sour Patch Kids before heading back to my apartment to watch *Notting Hill*. It also isn't the reason I make up an excuse about feeling sick when Miriam invites me to her nurse friend's art thing at DUMBO House. She doesn't buy it (because she's met me), and texts me, I'm calling you out, liar.

I am who I am, I reply. Love me or leave me, babe

She texts back four pictures: an Epi Pen, an acoustic guitar, a horticulture textbook, and the *Mean Girls* GIF of Karen coughing and saying, *I can't go out, I'm sick,* followed up with a single message: are starter packs still cool?

CHAPTER FIFTEEN

"You know," Miriam says, "we could always just take a *vacation* to London."

I turn and glare, but she's too busy sniffing autumn squash varietals to notice. We're meandering through a farmer's market, the canvas bags on our shoulders already heavy with produce we *know* without a doubt can be eaten raw, since cooking is out of the question. The market smells like flowers, raw pumpkin, and coffee. Miriam's in a bright fuchsia athletic dress, her short blond hair up in a clip, and I'm wearing ripped jeans and a LITTLE BIG TOWN T-shirt from a concert my dad took me to when I was nine.

I put my bag of produce on Miriam's free shoulder so I can braid my hair back. "That's cheating. Imagine if we'd said, '*You know, we could always just take a* vacation *to Manhattan.*'"

"What magazines are even based in London?"

"*Take Me There*, for starters!" I practically shriek. "The very best one!"

In a bored drawl, Miriam says, "That's the travel mag, right?"

I scoff. "I know that *you know* it's the travel mag, Mir."

Scooping my bag back off her shoulder, I drift toward a seller shouting the price of chrysanthemums. They're golden, ruby red, and orange, arranged in lines like a sunset.

"On a scale of one to ten, how confident are you this transfer is happening?"

Something clicks in my brain, and I spin to face her. Miriam becomes instantly fascinated with a mound of russet potatoes. But I've known this girl since we were eleven, and I've memorized all her tells. "They said it was all but guaranteed."

She grabs a potato and inspects it. "For what job?"

I am . . . honestly not quite sure about that.

"Who cares?" I reason. "It's London!"

Miriam huffs. "London's not all that."

My eyes narrow. "That's my mother's homeland you're slandering. And besides, you know Marty never took me *anywhere* when I was a kid."

Miriam flips her middle finger at me. "Cry me a river, Casey. You *also* never had to haggle on Craigslist for a resold concert ticket and avoid getting stuck with one of the dude's seven cats he was also trying to get rid of, and it shows."

We manage three full seconds of glaring before we dissolve into smirks.

I step closer and lower my voice. "What's really going on, Mir?"

She rolls her eyes and shoots me a stubborn look. "Nothing. I was just making conversation. It's a very common thing that non-antisocial people do."

"I'm not antisocial. I just hate small talk."

"It's polite."

"It's pointless. And you're trying to change the subject. Why don't you want me to go to London anymore?"

"Of course I want you to go!" Miriam growls, stalking away.

I follow her to a coffee vendor, where she orders an iced latte for herself and a cappuccino for me. While we sit and wait for our drinks on the curb, I poke her in the shoulder over and over until she snaps. "I just don't want you to never come back."

I stiffen. "What? Of course I'd come back."

"You moved here, and you haven't been home since that one Christmas when you acted super weird the whole time," she reasons. "You've hardly left the city. Will that be any different when you hop the pond?" Miriam rakes her fingers through her hair. "You've got this, like, tunnel vision for your future, and I think it's cool you want to move to London, I really do, don't get me wrong. But I can't be a thing in your rearview, Case. I still need you." She stumbles over the last words.

I peer at my best friend, understanding so completely what she's trying to say. "I needed you when I moved here," I tell her. "When Lance and I broke up, he accused me of following you here. Making a decision that wasn't truly mine."

Miriam's forehead wrinkles. "That's dumb."

"Yeah, but he was right," I admit. "You were a safety net for a really big leap. The biggest of my whole life. But moving to London—because it's *my* idea, because it's the life experience *I* want for myself—it's the only way to know what kind of pluckiness I'm made of."

"Pluckiness," Miriam repeats, smirking, and I groan.

One of the greatest loves of my life is a platinum blond, foul-mouthed short girl who once pushed Ronnie Wilson off a literal bridge and into a literal creek for making fun of my speech impediment on the fourth-grade trip to the Nature Conservancy. When we were sixteen, on the playground of our elementary school, we sat side by side on the swing set and shared one warm Miller Lite we stole from her older brother. Every year on Mother's Day, her parents send my family flowers. I have done her taxes twice now.

I throw my arm over her shoulder and set my temple against hers. There's a quaver in my voice when I say, "Look, the Nashville thing . . . that's in a separate box from New York, okay? I promise you I'm not going to vanish into thin air. Through fire and water, remember? We're tethered, and either of us can tug on the string if we need to."

I feel her shoulder sag against mine. "Good, because I'm always going to need you, like, at least *metaphorically* around. And you're always going to need me to shove a needle up your ass when the restaurant fries your chicken in peanut oil."

"Masey!" the coffee guy calls through the window of his truck. We stand up from the curb, and Miriam hands me my drink.

Our conversation makes me recall something we talked about years ago: "Hey, didn't you want to do travel nursing at some point? What ever happened to that idea?"

Miriam blushes. "Brijesh. Happened."

My lips pull up. "Remind me why you two aren't just dating?"

"Because. I'm pretty sure he's the one."

"Explain that logic to me."

"Bitch, I can't even figure it out myself," Miriam says. "I've told him not to wait around for me to stop being terrified of how much I like him—i.e., a fuckgirl—but he's determined to smoke me out."

"Sex is that good, huh?"

She punches me hard enough on the shoulder to bruise. Wincing, I turn away and rub at it. A spark of dark maroon catches my eye.

"Is that . . ."

"What?" Miriam asks.

I grin. "No way."

"What?" She steps up beside me and tracks my line of sight. "Oh. That's pretty."

Sitting there, among perennials, roses, and tulips, is a potted planter of deep jewel-toned red chocolate cosmos flowers with petals like raindrops. The Mexican flower was nearly made extinct, but it's been repopulated in recent years, though it's still considered a rarity. I've only ever seen them in botanical gardens.

The *moment* of this moment strikes me as something bigger than an overpriced flower in a Manhattan farmer's market. I pull out my phone and snap a pic for Jerry. He replies seconds later: In New York City????

Casey: Right?
Jerry: You have to buy that.

In the end, I *do* buy the chocolate cosmos, but not for me—for Alex. I promised him I would, and his apartment is close enough to our brunch spot that we can drop it right off afterward.

We've been texting *all* weekend.

It started when Alex asked for an itemized list of my shellfish allergies, which led to a shirtless photo of him and Freddy on the beach shucking clams. After that, there was some argumentative back-and-forth about whether it's recommended to remove your shirt in the northeastern October weather (I argued no, Alex argued that he would not be body-shamed under any circumstance). But then he sent me another photo, this time wearing a shirt and a curmudgeonly frown, a trail of sand stuck to one cheek, and it did precisely nothing to improve the fluttering in my belly, so really, I played myself.

The kicker, though, was when he *called* me last night. I picked up the phone halfway convinced something horrible had happened— like an internet troll photoshopping our talking heads onto naked bodies, or Alex telling me he found out I applied for his job—but instead, he said, "Hey, so I'm at the Cape Cod Target—"

"With your credit or debit card? It's an important distinction."

"And I was hoping you could tell me your favorite brand of laundry detergent?"

I was alone in Prospect Park, reading a paperback from Books Are Magic like I always do when I want to romanticize my life. (In London, I plan on frequenting the Spitalfields Libreria and taking my book to Kensington Gardens, where I will sit against a tree and look enigmatic while I read about magical teenagers.) "Um. I use Tide Free & Gentle?"

"Perfect."

"Is this a hostess gift for Freddy's mom?"

He laughed at that. "No, I got her a bottle of wine."

"Did you . . . Alex, did you take your dirty laundry to Cape Cod with you?"

There was a pause, and then he said, "They're like family, okay?"

"Were they out of detergent or something?"

"No, I just wanted—" He stopped talking then, and I froze, and across two hundred miles of rocky American coastline, past Providence, past New Haven, all the way to Brooklyn, whatever it was that *Alex just wanted* left him in an exorcism and slammed into me like a freight train. "To keep you in mind," he finished lamely.

"Thanks," I whispered.

He gulped. "Thanks for the recommendation."

"You're welcome." After a stiff silence I added, "Okay, bye."

"Okay. Bye."

And then I went back to reading, absorbing precisely zero words, thinking about Alex thinking about me in the Cape Cod Target.

After a vibey, old-school French brunch where the pot of cosmos sits in the third chair at our outdoor table, Miriam and I head to the alley behind Alex's place.

"Are you *finally* going to tell me about last weekend?" she asks as I climb up the fire escape to the second-story balconies. "You know, especially considering you guys now co-own a plant?"

I grunt as I heave myself over the flimsy rail. "Toss it up."

Miriam grabs the ruby-red flowers by the base of the plastic pot. She lowers the planter between her thighs, then granny-shots them up to me. A light dusting of soil rains down on her, and she squeaks and dodges out of the way. I set the flowers against one corner of the balcony.

Miriam holds up a hand as I make to lift myself back over the edge. "You can't come back down until you spill." Her voice echoes in the empty alley.

My elbows push against the rail as I glare down at her. Being this close to the mattress where I stayed safe and warm in his arms all night is certainly making me feel warm again, but no longer *safe*. "There's nothing to tell. It was late, I didn't want to chance the subway, and Alex's place was close. All we did was—"

"Snuggle all night like a pair of lovesick teenagers?" Miriam shifts her weight to her other hip. "Yeah, got that part. I want to know what it *means* to you, buttercup."

What it *means* to me? What the eleven-dollar bar tab at Sleight of Hand and the Tide Free & Gentle in a Cape Cod Target and the BYO pizza at Eataly means to me? What it means when Alex calls me pretty, says he'd be lost without me? What it means to me that he could have—he really could have—lorded *I told you so* over my head when I discovered how wrong I was about him, and instead he gave me the comforter to his bed and an old T-shirt?

It means *everything*, I finally admit, the truth breaking free from a cage in my mind. But I don't know if it means everything to *him*, and if it means even a single drop less than everything to him, the all-or-nothing heart on my sleeve won't be able to take it.

I breathe out a sigh, shaking my head. "Nothing."

"Liar."

For the second time today, Miriam and I stare each other down.

"I'm attracted to him," I say, picturing the line of sand stuck to his cheek. "Is that what you want me to admit?"

"We already established that," Miriam says.

"We did?"

"Yes, Case, Jesus." Miriam makes an exasperated grunt. "I want to know if you *like* him. If you want to cuddle him *again*. If you want to *kiss* him."

"I . . ." How do I admit that I want to see Alex Harrison in his glasses, that I want to know what kind of couch he ordered, that I could sit for hours and listen to him talk about foreign exchange rates or, like, fuck, *even sailboat anatomy* without getting bored?

"I'm waiting, Juliet." She's enjoying this way too much.

My fingers clench around the rusty metal. "It's not a no."

Miriam narrows her eyes. "It's not . . . a no."

"Yes."

"Yes?" she repeats.

"Yes," I say again. "It's not a no."

She makes a disbelieving face. "That's it? He was public enemy number one two weeks ago! You didn't just decide to start ignoring all the things you hated about him for a sexually PG good time, I know you didn't."

"He's different than I told you at first." I explain to Miriam about Alex getting the job on his own merit, but I leave out the stuff about his father he asked me not to share. "He's good at his job, too. It's weird." My head shakes gently as I haul myself back onto the fire escape. "In some ways he's a total trust fund kid, and in other ways he's not like that at all."

"Look. Cool if he's got family money, cool if he doesn't. All I'm saying is, statistically, one of you is going to catch feelings."

"I'm moving to London next summer," I grumble.

"Right, because seven months is just too short of a window to have an epic New York love affair." Miriam looks up at the balcony. "Do whatever you want, Casey. But just know I'll be consulting your horoscopes a *little* more regularly from now on."

"Creep," I mutter. Then, a lightbulb goes off in my head. "Wait, that's it!"

"What?"

I grin at her. "Your starter pack. K-pop, earring collection, Italian food, and the zodiac."

Miriam laughs and puts her hands on her hips. "Fuck. You're fucking right."

CHAPTER SIXTEEN

Ten days after Tracy charged me with my mission, seven days after Robert Harrison's resignation is announced, she pulls me into her office for an update.

I recount for her most of what Alex told me about Robert and Dougie's history when we were in bed together, half asleep. What I *don't* do is divulge how I got the information, and Tracy doesn't ask. She just listens patiently, nodding to herself like she's agreeing that it all makes sense, the stories line up with the behavior she's witnessed. When I'm done, she doesn't say anything and keeps staring with a listless expression into space.

"You knew Robert was stepping down when you asked me to do this, didn't you?"

Tracy nods. "Robert stepping down is *why* I asked you to do this."

"You're suspicious of him," I guess.

After a moment, she admits, "I think he left because he knew things were about to get ugly."

The same sinking feeling in my gut returns in full force. "What do you mean?"

She looks at me for a long time, maybe ten full seconds, and finally says, "Little Cooper has received an offer of purchase."

I freeze. "We're going to be . . . *acquired*?"

"It's not ideal." Tracy reclines in her chair and crosses her fingers in her lap. "An acquisition would tear the heart and soul of this company apart. We'd have redundancies. Some of our magazines would remain unaffected, but others . . . Well, their company already has their own version."

"Wait." I hold up a hand. "Those redundant magazines would just . . . cease to exist?"

"Eventually. We'd attempt to mesh our assets, but a large portion of our staff would get laid off. I'm predicting a little less than half."

"A little less than half?"

Brijesh. What if *Food Baby* is a redundancy and Brijesh gets laid off? What if *I* get laid off? Or Fari, or Don? And Benny—surely the acquiring company already has their own Benny. Plus, if *Take Me There* gets dissolved, what the fuck am I even working toward in London? Will they close that office completely?

Little Cooper isn't just a place I work. Certainly, it has its own set of corporate problems I won't ignore, but still, I'm *partial* to it. I *believe* in it. And so does Fari, because she chose this place out of a dozen, and so does Alex, because he said the scope of what he's doing here feels endless.

When my mom was twenty-four and fleeing London in the eighties, she was partly running from a receptionist position at her father's wealth advisory firm. (Alex's trust fund is undoubtedly somewhere very similar.) And even though I love numbers, and even though I work in finance, I have always, *always* understood why Mom couldn't be there anymore. Dad says she described it as soulless.

Visions fill my head: getting to London only to be laid off right away, while I've fallen so hopelessly in love with the city that I'd do anything not to leave yet. Crawling to Notting Hill, the front door of Gran's—a pinched-up woman I haven't seen since Mom's funeral—and asking her meekly if that receptionist position at Grandfather's old business is still available.

"Is the acquisition Dougie Dawson's idea?" I ask Tracy.

She shakes her head. "The offer came to us. We didn't seek it out."

"Who's it from?"

"Can't tell you that. I'm crossing a line as it is."

"Are you going to say yes?" I ask.

"We have a fiduciary duty to consider it. The offer is *high*. Much higher than our company is worth. I have to decide on the best financial solution and present it to the board, emotions and people and personal feelings aside." Tracy shrugs.

I'm angry at her, even though I *know* I have no right to be. Last we talked, Tracy admitted she didn't think Dougie was fulfilling his own fiduciary duty, so I can hardly blame her for stepping up to the plate now. But I literally don't know how to process this, and I don't understand how it ties back to Robert Harrison. Did he leave so he wouldn't have to witness the fallout? Did he not want the association of another failed company after his Harvard start-up flopped? And why did Robert challenge his son to see the BTH launch through if he *knew* this was a possible outcome? For Christ's sake, Dougie now has a personal *and* a professional reason to obliterate Alex's whole purpose here.

"Why are you telling me this?" I ask.

"I know you'll keep it to yourself." Tracy leans forward, lowers her voice. "Also, I'm kind of hoping someone in the weeds of our numbers might spot a solution I can't."

Challenge accepted. I'll do anything possible to keep this acquisition from happening. I don't want the heart and soul of our company to be torn apart. I want *Bite the Hand* to launch. I want my friends to keep their jobs. And I want to go to London on my own terms, no one else's.

But if I go to London without Little Cooper, there won't be a single familiar thing.

I'm sitting outside Saanvi's office when Alex sprints around the corner, bottled tea in one hand, his notebook in the other, dressed in an Orvis half-zip and gray slacks. He's panting just a little, lips parted, and when our eyes catch, all the nerves in my body concentrate in suspect places.

"Hey," he says.

"Hi," I say back, and my heart *thump-thump-thump*s. Definitely not because I *wanted* to see him. More likely, it's because I was dreading it. My conversation with Tracy has been following me like Eeyore's dreary rain cloud since yesterday, and the sight of his trusting face might as well be a stab in the heart.

I want to warn him that his odds of a successful launch for *Bite the Hand* have gotten even slimmer. I want to apologize for using him for information when I'm not even sure what purpose it served Tracy at all.

I want to kiss him. Like, really badly, I want that.

Alex deposits his things on the table and sits down beside me in the other waiting chair. He peers through Saanvi's glass walls where she's speaking with Andre, Eric, and another salt-and-pepper-haired man I've never met.

"How was your weekend?" he asks.

"Lamer than yours. I'd give anything to experience the Cape Cod Target."

"Be that as it may, we did eat enough seafood to kill you."

"Charming."

"Freddy's mom lives in Cape Cod full-time," Alex explains. "Before I moved to Seoul after college, I used to spend all my Thanksgivings with them."

"Not with your aunt and cousins?"

Alex shakes his head. "Sometimes I felt like my aunt wanted some family stuff to be just her, her husband, and her kids. So, I asked Freddy one year if I could go with him. And it became a tradition."

His father was probably only ever a couple of hours away, deep-frying a turkey with Linda in a country club they bought just for the occasion. I feel for her, too—spending Thanksgiving with the breathing reminder of your husband's infidelity would probably suck—but Alex was *just a kid*.

He turns his body in the chair to face me. "You know," he says, voice deep. "When I asked you to pick a plant for my balcony, I assumed it was going to be a later, through-the-front-door situation."

I smirk, rapping my fingers on the computer in my lap. "The fire escape was more convenient. I didn't want to drag the cosmos around until I saw you next."

"Yes, dragging around a galaxy. A bit unwieldy."

Saanvi's door pushes open, and Alex and I rip our eyes off each other. We stand up, and Saanvi gestures for us to come in. Andre and Eric say a quick hello before leaving, but the other man stays seated as Saanvi closes the door and tells us to sit.

"This is Andrew. He's with Legal."

Andrew, who looks like he was born for the predestined purpose of Being With Legal, nods and hands us each a stack of papers clipped together.

"So," Saanvi says, sitting down across from us, "as far as debuts go, your video did pretty well. We typically mark a new face on the BTH channel as a success if they get eight thousand views in the first twenty-four hours, and you guys did ten. Last I checked, it was up to fifty, and that was over the weekend when people are busy, so we should see that number double in a week's time."

I let out a tiny squeak. "One hundred thousand views?"

"Yes. So, obviously I'd love to do this again," Saanvi goes on. "A 2.0 version of the segment, so to speak. It would be more like a vlog, a day in the life here at the office. Actually, it was a suggestion in the comments section—which was colorful, and um, overall, very warmhearted regarding you both. And then after that, I thought we could try out the best coffee in the building idea, for a third video. Do those concepts work?"

I look over at Alex to find him nodding, his eyes tracking the document in his hands. "What's this?" he asks. "I thought we got the standard rate for employee appearances."

"There is no standard rate; there's a base rate. It's part of my process that if I ask you to return, we can negotiate it."

Wow, money! I forgot about that part.

"This is a unique situation," Saanvi informs us. "Most contracts are negotiated separately, but then again, most YouTube segments Little Cooper runs only have one anchor. In the interest of equity, I thought it was best for you two to be in the same room for this conversation."

I am totally here for Saanvi's pay equity agenda, particularly because negotiating isn't my strong suit. When I was offered my job with LC, they gave me the salary I'd written down as my minimum on my application (which was a ballpark shot in the dark based on NYC's cost of living, my student loan payment plan, and some entry-level salary research). I knew LC giving me that number was strategic on their part, but I was just so happy I'd gotten the offer at all to ask for a penny more.

And when it comes to *this* stuff, Saanvi could propose anything she wanted, and I wouldn't know the difference. But Alex does. He throws out a number that makes my jaw want to unhinge and follows it up with a single word: "Each."

I realize something stark in that moment. Even though Alex and I both have a degree in business, I went to a state school and he went to Harvard, and the differences between the whole learned cultures behind our educations show up in the space between what words are exchanged in that room. I just sit there and try not to look like a complete idiot.

Where does that kind of confidence come from? Is there a class at Harvard for it?

There is some negotiating, paper signing, and schedule wrangling, and then we are dismissed. Outside Saanvi's office, we slow our walk to let Andrew From Legal get ahead of us.

"You were quiet in there," Alex says. "I hope I wasn't being too . . . presumptuous."

I shake my head, hitching my bag higher onto my shoulder. "I'm not good at that kind of stuff. I'm glad you knew what you were talking about."

"I know a guy with similar experience."

"It tracks that you know a guy."

Alex laughs. "Saanvi's great, but not everyone's like her. I had to learn to protect myself early on."

I nod. "I get that."

Outside the floor-length glass windows, the sun's last dregs are dripping into the horizon, casting the office in a golden-hour glow. Alex and I reach the end of the hallway, and I turn, heading for the elevators.

"Casey." He swallows thickly. "Tomorrow is Wednesday."

"Yes, very good. You can stop showing off now."

Alex bites the inside of his cheek. "I spent all last night trying to forecast revenue for *Bite the Hand*'s first six months. Gus wants me to distribute packets in tomorrow's meeting."

I think I know where this is going, but I want him to squirm for it. "And?"

He steps toward me. Today, he smells like soap and linen. "And I think my numbers are garbage because I'm trash at this kind of stuff. Can you please take a look?"

"Why didn't you ask me for help earlier, Alex? That is literally what I'm here for."

His eyes are pinned to mine. "Honestly?"

"Um. Sure, why not?"

"I was trying to impress you." His voice comes out rough at the admission.

And that's when I see it: Behind the humor on his face, there's a sort of desperation. A hunger that makes me feel so desired, I could bottle that shit and sell it as an aphrodisiac.

"So . . . ," he goes on, "since that obviously flopped. If I go grab my stuff, and I buy you dinner in exchange for thirty minutes of your analytical brilliance . . . will you leave with me?"

I clutch my computer tight to my chest and say, "Sure."

CHAPTER SEVENTEEN

We settle into a table with a rickety leg at a quiet restaurant in SoHo, split the second-cheapest bottle of red wine, and order a couple of appetizers to share. Twenty minutes after we've finished grazing on the food, we pore over his spreadsheet, shoulders touching, working out the kinks.

The waitress comes by to clear our plates, and Alex closes the laptop and puts it back in his leather Herschel backpack. "So, Brijesh told me you play guitar."

My lips pull up. "I'm not positive you could call what I do to a guitar *playing* it, but yeah, a little. My dad taught me."

"What was the first song you learned?"

I conjure a snapshot of me and Dad sitting on our porch. A tiny house on a huge acre of unkept land. The association is pre-Jerry, because he basically transformed the landscaping of our place when he moved in, but for a few years there, Dad and I lived among the proper brush, two people healing together while nothing else mattered. When I was *really* young, Dad would strum for me as I held down the strings with the finger pads of both of my hands, working to build up calluses and memorize chords.

"It was one of my dad's songs. 'Road to Heartbreak.' He wanted to teach me songs like 'Smoke on the Water,' 'Dust on the Bottle,' and 'American Pie,' but I just wanted to learn all his stuff first."

Alex sets his elbows on the table and leans forward, causing the muscles of his shoulders to strain. "Did you ever . . . I don't know, like, perform?"

What I will absolutely *not* be telling Alex Harrison about is the talent show fiasco. "I'm sort of allergic to strangers."

"Yes," he rasps. "I've noticed." When I glance up, he's watching me thoughtfully. "I'm sensing an ellipsis."

I bite my bottom lip. Rolling over how honest he's been with me. Thinking I can tell him *something* honest, at least.

I can be patient with you, Casey.

"I had a stutter as a kid. It was Jerry who first suggested I try singing along while I played guitar. I still have no idea why it worked better than speech therapy, but somehow, music was the thing that helped."

He holds my gaze and nods. "Sure did. You slayed karaoke like a champ."

"Well, all credits to my Hello Kitty boom box and Miriam's One Direction phase."

He laughs and empties the wine between each of our glasses. Something about the angle, the lighting, makes him look like his father's son right now.

"Alex?"

"Hmm?"

"Is there a chance your father telling you to put in your notice was his way of trying to protect you?"

The corner of his mouth pulls down. "Protect me from what?"

From a layoff.

"From Dougie. From failure." I shrug. "I don't know. I was just wondering if you thought there was a fatherly instinct to it."

Alex rubs at his jaw. "It's hard to know," he says. "There have been moments throughout my life when Robert showed his fatherly instincts. When I was eight, living in Seoul, attending the international school, I was bullied by this kid who loved to say that I didn't have a father. A few days after I told my mom about it was the first time I consciously remember meeting Robert. He appeared in our apartment, knelt down in front of me, and said, 'Your last name is Harrison, because you're my son. You have a father, and that man is me.' Then I asked him why he didn't live with us, and he said it was because his wife wouldn't let him. I'm sure you can imagine how confusing that was for me."

I nod. "I bet you had so many questions."

"Did, and do. There's a lot about my parents' relationship that I'll never know. That nobody knows, except for them. Aunt Jane has pieces, but even she never got the full picture. She seemed surprised when I told her that sometimes Robert appeared in Seoul, at our apartment or at the park, sometimes at a restaurant. I don't know if my parents loved each other, but I think they might have."

"Did you ever ask your dad? When you got older?"

Alex nods. "Once. I was told that it wasn't my business," he growls. "So, to answer your question, yes, Robert does have fatherly instincts. He just doesn't have enough of them."

"Tell me something happy," I say. "About your mom."

His lips kick up, and he reaches his arm toward me. My gaze tracks to his forearms, and his tattoo—the one I've only ever glimpsed peeks of—is displayed proudly now on his skin.

"What is that?"

"Roses of Sharon. The national flower of Korea."

The femininity of the design, and his frank explanation, is a startling turn-on. The tattoo is delicate with dark branches that span Alex's upper wrist and an inch or so of his forearm, covered in soft white and pink flowers.

The wine is warming the tips of my ears, and Alex's hot eyes watching me across the candlelit table are making me squirm.

"My mom loved them. We'd go on adventures all the time to find as many trees as we could with the flowers in bloom."

"That sounds adorably aesthetic. And happy."

"It was," he murmurs. "Also . . ." Alex drifts off, peering at me through thick eyelashes. "It means *eternal blossom that never fades.* Which is supposed to be a reminder for me when I look at it. I've always thought of myself as rootless and untethered. I don't have much in my life that's permanent, let alone eternal. But this tattoo is, which means other things can be, too. Plus, it always reminds me of Mom."

His words are gentle, almost a confession, but they make a pit open up in my gut.

I have a crush on someone who thinks of himself as a rootless, untethered person.

It's like Alex is giving me a *warning.*

My body starts to lock up, and I realize how close I came to falling for someone who might be incapable of falling back.

"I . . . bathroom," I mutter, jerking up from my chair.

"Wait, are you—" But I'm already too far gone to hear the rest.

I barge into the single-person bathroom, clicking the lock closed on the door behind me. My reflection stares back through the mirror above the sink. I'm flushed, my cheeks rosy. My eyes look as wild as the hair spilling over my shoulders.

"You're going to London," I tell myself. "In seven months."

What was I *thinking*? Alex doesn't want a relationship, and neither should I.

I press my eyes closed and breathe deeply. I can get this under control. It's just a crush. He doesn't know. I can make it go away. Because if I fall for him, I'll really get *stuck* this time, almost like I did before, but worse, because it's *Alex,* and he's just so . . . and if he leaves, I'll be too heartbroken to go anywhere, and then I'll never figure out what I'm supposed to—

Someone knocks loudly, *rudely* on the door.

Giving myself a stern look in the mirror, I say, "Don't tether yourself to him." Then I open the door and step back into the dim hallway.

"Casey, are you okay?" Alex grabs me by my shoulders.

"Fine," I grumble. "Just really had to pee."

He sighs. "You scared the shit out of me, Case. I thought you were having an allergic reaction."

A broken, deranged laugh escapes me. "Not today, but I appreciate your worst-case-scenario mindset."

He shakes his head, smiling softly.

Almost like it's instinctual, one of his hands travels up my neck. A soft gasp slips out of me at the light pressure of his fingertips.

He looks just as surprised as I am as he stares at my throat. Through hooded lashes, his focus travels to my mouth. One of his thumbs scrapes along my neck.

The way he wants me is written into the bend in his body. It's in the charged space between us, the rasp of his voice. There is palpable desire looping back and forth, him to me, me to him, and no, we can't playact like it's not exactly what it is for one more second. I think, maybe, this was a foregone conclusion the minute I crawled into bed with him. And I think I knew it then, and Alex knew it, too.

And bought detergent accordingly.

"Remember when you called me pretty?"

"Beautiful." He gulps. Takes a step forward, pushing me lightly with his hands until my body presses against the wall. "I remember. And what I meant to say is that when I first saw you, I thought you were so fucking beautiful that I would have razed Manhattan to see you smile."

Light-headed, half-delirious, I blurt out, "I've never been out of the country."

Wow, I am really all over the board right now. Got to find the plot.

To Alex's credit, all he says is, "No?"

I shake my head, hair spilling into my face. His hand lifts from my other shoulder to tuck it behind my ear. "It just never happened for me," I whisper. "My dad is terrified of planes, so it was out of the question when I was a kid. And I never studied abroad because I was just . . . scared of the idea of it back then, I guess." Alex is watching me with rapt attention, like these stumbled-over half sentences coming out of my mouth are the most interesting thing he's ever heard. "Anyway, I'm desperate to go explore."

Another caress of his thumb on my jawline. Alex clears his throat. "I bet you'd love it."

"I think so, too. Which is why I'm getting transferred to Little Cooper's London office next summer."

There is a moment of hesitation, just one moment, and then Alex says, "That's great."

Yes. It's great. Get this under control, Casey. Make it mean less. Make it meaningless. That's your solution. Set the terms.

"But also . . . I've been thinking about how you and me . . . We aren't in the same department."

His lips part softly. "Definitely not."

"So . . ."

"So," he repeats. "If we wanted to . . ."

"Kiss again, for example. Or, you know, do other things that, um, consensually follow kissing, on occasion."

Alex is still staring at my mouth. "There wouldn't be any problem with that. Professionally."

Except for the fact that we do work together pretty damn closely, and also, we've got this whole YouTube gig—

"And it wouldn't have to be awkward," I say. "Or even a big deal at all, because—"

"Because of London," Alex whispers. "Works for me. Can I kiss you now?"

"Okay."

His lips reach mine, and when they do, I realize there was no. way. we could have avoided this for much longer.

He does it again, that *thing,* the gentle tease where his mouth *just* brushes mine and hovers there, savoring, but somehow it's the most intense thing I've ever felt, slow and intentional, a swallow of wine before the full glass is poured. But this time, it lasts only the span of an exhale, and then his mouth slants fully against mine in crushing, burning heat. Our noses kiss, too, and Alex's lips are impossibly soft like clouds, and they're wet, like rain.

If this moment is a blind slope, Alex and I are about to stumble over it, incapable now of retracing our steps back to safety.

And outside, the sky thunders like the universe *knows* what we've just done.

Alex's fingers ghost across my neck, into my hair, tugging, and I grab a fistful of his shirt to pull him closer. Like a drug, I want more. I don't understand it, don't get what makes this different from any other kiss I've ever participated in, but it just . . . *is.*

I make a small, frustrated noise when his hand skates down my side and palms at my butt, and then a much louder noise of turmoil when he pulls his lips off me a split second later and sets his palms on the wall, bracketing my head. He's panting heavily, staring at the floor, and I'm panting heavily, staring at him.

"Alex?" I squeak.

"Just give me a minute," he groans miserably. I let my head fall against the wall and watch him out of half-closed eyes.

Eventually, he looks up at me and says, still mostly breathless, "The flowers."

I blink. "The flowers?"

"Cosmos, you called them." His voice is hoarse.

"Chocolate cosmos."

"Right." Alex nods. I think he's the one who's lost the plot this time. "I hate to break this to you, but they're looking a little worse for wear. You should probably come over right away and water them."

I bite my lip. Humor is dancing in his dark, stormy eyes.

"Alex, even you are perfectly capable of watering flowers."

He shakes his head. "I'd do it wrong. It's got to be you."

"On a school night?" I stage-whisper.

His voice *scalds* me. "Don't make me beg, Casey."

I'm nodding before I even make a conscious decision to do it.

CHAPTER EIGHTEEN

The second I walk through Alex's door his lips catch mine, his hips *kiss* mine, and there's another wall behind my back, every thought floating out of my head except for *Holy crap this is so good how is this so good.* It's pouring rain outside, and my skin is damp with dewy drops. A crack of thunder makes me shiver, and Alex just laughs, pressing closer.

One of his hands is on my waist, the other skating across my cheek. I'm overwhelmed by his touch, the way it's both *achingly* gentle and a contained kind of pressure. Every place he touches me starts a mini-inferno, and I make a noise of surprise as he kisses me hungrier, then hungrier. His mouth slides against mine, warm, firm, purposeful. I feel like I'm getting devoured.

"For the record." Small kiss, big kiss. "I've barely gotten a *thing* done at work since I learned what it's like to sleep next to you."

"No?" I pant.

"*No.* You are quickly becoming the best distraction I've ever encountered."

"I'm sorry."

He sucks on the side of my neck and mumbles, "I'm not."

I start to unbutton his shirt. He smells clean and cottony and perfect, like a rainy vacation rental on your first day.

"Can you describe to me," Alex rasps, "in a bit more detail." He's looking down at my fingers working his shirt open. "What exactly you meant when you said, *Other things that follow kissing, on occasion?*"

I pause and look up at him. "I meant that I want to have sex with you."

He nods, staring at my swollen lips. "Thank you for clarifying."

The next thing I know, I'm being carried to his bed. We land on his sheets in a heap of half-torn-off clothes and newly formed love bites.

More kissing, which Alex seems content to prolong more than any guy I've ever hooked up with. Probably because he's *better* at it than any guy I've ever hooked up with. The way Alex is kissing me puts all other experiences of foreplay to shame, using his teeth and tongue to mark my skin.

"Beautiful," he sighs, his capable hands rubbing at my waist, gripping it in his palms, moving my body this way and that. Clothes are removed, slowly, lazily, and I feel practically strung out, high off the arousal he's already managed to induce. My silk pants and small cotton T-shirt are discarded. Alex watches my eyes, waiting for some signal to stop, slow down, speed up, or just kiss me again.

"Kiss me again," I say.

He smiles easily, his lips a cherry-red color, and obliges for only a moment before he starts kissing down the length of my stomach. I lie there, staring at the ceiling, feeling like I'm the center of his whole universe. Every kiss he presses against me is reverent, every word like a prayer, and I wonder to myself, *Is this hotter than it should be because we're coworkers, or is it really just that hot?*

The groan I hear when his lips push against my thigh makes me gasp. His thumb traces the inside of my knee, and it's everything. There's a greedy look in his dark eyes I can't describe as anything other than the most flattering feeling I have ever, *ever* felt. It flips a switch of confidence inside me; I yank him up and turn us sideways. Biting my lip, I work up the courage to put my hands on him.

This whole experience feels better since we're sober, but it's scarier for that reason, too. My knuckles trail down his body, rubbing at his chest, dipping into his waistband. Alex unleashes a strangled huff against my neck. I haven't touched anyone like this in years. His lashes are stark against his cheekbones as his eyes flutter closed, which I take as a good sign, and he mumbles something that sounds suspiciously like *Imagined this.*

I blush, freezing up. Alex's eyes snap open to reveal large black pupils, a wicked challenge in them. But then he kisses me hard, ending it for both of us, and I mumble something about *Can we please have sex now,* and Alex mumbles something like *Hell fucking yes.* He grabs a condom from his nightstand, and our foreheads rest against each other as he slips it on. He palms my butt, pushes into me, and kisses me at the same time.

For a moment, it's still, his thumbs brushing my cheeks. My legs wrap around his waist. I try and fail to do much of anything helpful as he slowly, *slowly* begins to work himself against me in a delirious kind of perfection.

One thrust. Two. By the third, we're both shaking. He pushes all the way inside, and a fleeting thought burns through me—there and then gone—that this feels better and more important, more vital, more permanent, than any sex I've ever had.

But also, now really isn't the time to get in my head about it.

My fingers grasp at his back. Every thrust is punctuated with a dreamy sigh in my ear. I'm shivering and melting at the same time, and Alex is paying careful attention to it, figuring out what I like and how he can do more of it.

"This." His voice is disjointed. He's looking down at me with hooded eyes. "Is so, so good for me, Casey." As if he really, truly needs me to know.

"Me too," I pant, my vocabulary debased.

"It was all worth it," he jerkily mumbles, his head dropping beside mine until his mouth is at my ear. "I *knew* you'd be worth it. Every email, every glare."

"How do you know I wasn't working you up?" I try to joke.

"Don't think I'd have minded," he replies. "What do you need?"

"Nothing."

"Tell me," he demands.

"Just this."

We are so close, and his body is landing against mine just right, and I've already been worked up by him for half an hour plus seven whole weeks, and it shows. I come undone seconds later, and Alex kisses me through it, hips still working. Based on his expression as he watches me, I think he's in awe at how little it took me to get there, and yep, I am, too.

I hold his head against my neck when he collapses on top of me, spent. He swears against my skin, and *that* noise, combined with *this* feeling, morphs into something permanent that lodges beneath my rib cage.

At that inconvenient moment, I ruin all sexual aftershocks with this thought: *Holy crap, I just had mind-blowing sex with Elevator Man! The playacting we spun for Jack and Jill came true after all, which means we're a living, breathing cliché, and I'm not mad about it?*

I start to laugh. It's quiet, lacking the oxygen it truly needs, but the laugh still works its way out of me against my will. I'm embarrassed about it for all of two seconds before Alex is laughing with me, kissing along my ear and throat.

He rolls onto his back and pulls me halfway on top of him, grabbing my leg and hiking it up across his stomach. We lie there, catching our breath and finding our bearings, and I let myself bask in the comfortable bliss of it all before the inevitable departure that follows casual sex ruins it.

After a few minutes of me thinking Alex *actually* fell asleep, he says, "I just need to state, for the record, that we can do that again, Casey Maitland, whenever you want, however often you want, until the day you leave for London."

A noise between a hum and a sigh works its way out of me. "Okay. Let's go again."

"Okay." He pushes my leg off his stomach.

"Alex, I was just jo—"

But he rolls back on top of me and kisses me quiet.

CHAPTER NINETEEN

The thing about sex is, it's great until it ends (honestly, they should put that on the abstinence pamphlets we always got handed on campus, which would later get defaced with dick drawings and left on classroom desks). But here's the other thing about sex: afterward, things get really awkward, really fast, and half the time, the only way to stifle it is to just leave, bucking up and putting on your walk-of-shame face as you head out the door.

I worry my lip between my teeth as Alex sits up, tugging on his boxers. Mentally, I'm preparing my casual "Wow, it's getting so late!"

But Alex goes completely off script and says, "Want a drink? I'm parched."

"Um." I start gathering up my clothes. "That's okay."

"I've got raspberry lime seltzer," he calls, heading to his wannabe kitchen. "Diet Coke, bottled tea, and beer. What's calling to you?"

I hesitate for a second before I decide he's genuinely asking. I, too, am parched from the excessive sexual intercourse. "Diet Coke."

Alex comes back holding a Diet Coke and a can of seltzer.
"Catch."

I have to drop my bra to stop the can from hitting me in the
face, but I catch it, setting it beside me in the bed. I grab my bra
from my lap and try to put it on.

The sinking of the mattress only makes my hands tremble with
urgency, but half a breath later, his hands are gently tugging my bra
away. Deeply he says, "Could you be naked for, like, thirty more
seconds, please? As a personal favor?"

The shock is obvious on my face. I'm unable to disguise it, considering I've never heard any line like that before. Alex grins at my
expression, hair falling over his eyes, and he turns his gaze on my
body, slowly but deliberately cataloging.

Though I wouldn't consider myself fair skinned, I do flush head
to toe at the slightest provocation, and right now, I'm on fire.

Let's put it this way: I'm not ashamed of my body by any stretch,
but I'd also *never* walk naked around a guy's place on purpose.

He settles beside me, a finger trailing across my stomach. "I've
thought of you like this more often than I should admit," he whispers. I gulp, feeling heat bloom in my core again. "The fact that I
infuriated you only made me want you more desperately."

Want. It's a very deliberate way for him to phrase it. My body
gets dunked in a metaphorical ice bath when I consider that, to
Alex, maybe this was all one big chase.

The girl he couldn't get. The one who, for so long, wouldn't
bend.

He *wants* me. Physically. I'm an accomplishment, a win. But he
also told me point-blank he understands why I think I'm nobody's
dream girl.

I want it stated for the record that I *do* have the thought *End
this now, before it starts to hurt.* It blips across my mind at the speed
of light, but his breath warming my ear erases it.

Completely.

"Case?"

Through my brain fog, I try to pick up the last thread of our conversation. "You still infuriate me," I say, just to be contrary.

He frowns, attention focused on a cluster of freckles on my shoulder. "How so?"

A sigh I try to feign as exhaustion slips out, but it's more a response to his fingers on my body. "To be honest, you can be just as much of a distraction for me."

He smirks. "Really."

"Not like that." *Yes, like that.* "Your and Gus's grand plans for BTH take up all my energy. Do you even know how much money launching a subsidiary company costs?"

"A lot?"

"A lot."

"It's worth it, Simba," Alex says. "A social news and entertainment platform is *exactly* what LC needs to stay contemporary. Tell me, have you *ever* gotten a bonus?"

"No," I admit.

"Are print subscribers not shrinking?"

"Yes."

"Is *BuzzFeed* not a popular concept?"

"*Alex,*" I groan.

He laughs, reclining. "We're *so* close to being ready to pitch our growth strategy. We'd get staff expansion, and Gus will probably be promoted to editor in chief." Alex looks at me. "Maybe we'll even get *you,* in a more permanent capacity." I'm kind of distracted by his hands tracing circles on my skin, so I nearly miss the way his face changes when he says, "Well. Until London, that is."

"Right. London."

I have no clue whether *Bite the Hand*—and Alex's job by extension—would stay safe through an acquisition. On one hand, there's not much like it on the market, which makes the concept desirable. On the other, it's an expensive new venture that might get put on a back burner for years.

The shine in his eyes has me arching toward him, a sunflower straining toward its light source. He's so beautiful. Always, but especially now, lit up from the inside out as he talks about all the plans he has for BTH, all the big, bright ideas.

He'd make a good CEO.

"Alex," I whisper. "What if something terrible happens?"

His eyes flick down to mine, and they gutter a little at my expression. "What terrible thing is going to happen?" he murmurs. It's an unassuming question. He's not hunting for intel, but I think he finds some anyway. "Hey," he says. "At the end of the day, we can romanticize our jobs all we want, but we're just selling magazines. When you think about it like that, the stakes are embarrassingly low."

But what if the stakes were actually that we might not have jobs to romanticize?

I push the thought out and shake my head. "You're right." My fingers pull at the tab of my soda, and it erupts, spewing froth all over me. "Crap! You really had to throw it."

Wordlessly, Alex leans down and *slurps* Diet Coke off my stomach.

"Alex!" I shriek.

He sits back up. "I acknowledge that that was weird, but I don't want to wash my sheets yet. The laundromat near my building is . . . *not* near my building." He grins as I shake my head and take a sip of my drink. Then, seconds later, he gives me a straight command: "Tell me what's got you so interested in London."

I raise my eyebrows. "Can I tell you with my clothes on?"

His face falls, which makes me giggle. "I guess."

I re-dress and sit on the edge of the bed, and Alex reclines, one hand behind his head as he waits patiently for my answer. I fight an irrational urge to climb into his lap, but the inked reminder of his tattoo spread across his forearm catches my eye.

"My mom was from London," I start. "Notting Hill, actually. But her parents were the stereotypical type of British stuffy that's more obtuse than it is endearing, and she moved to the US as a band's photographer-slash-groupie when she was my age. She and my dad met at a music festival, fell in love, and she never moved back to the UK."

"Wow," Alex says. "That's, like, a whole movie plot."

"Yeah." I laugh.

"So, you want to move to London to feel connected to her?"

I consider this. "Yes and no," I say, twiddling my thumbs. "I mean, yes, part of me wants to go specifically there because she was from there. But in a broader sense, I just . . . I just have this urge to drop everything and *go*. I've spent a lot of my life scared of change—I mean, I've never traveled anywhere except the Florida Panhandle and one trip out west in an RV—and then, I moved to New York, which was objectively terrifying, and I could have crashed and burned. But instead, my whole world opened up, and I just crave that feeling now. I want more of it. I can't just *settle* anymore, not now that I know there's another option. And London makes sense because Little Cooper has a branch there, which means I could afford to live abroad, and I think working for *Take Me There* would be the coolest. So, really, it just seems like a job and a life that's been waiting for me to want it."

When I'm finished talking, slightly winded, retroactively disentangling the absolute word vomit I just expelled, Alex's lips are pulled up faintly into the ghost of a smile. "Those are all really great reasons."

"Have you been? To London?"

"I studied abroad there for a summer."

I roll my eyes. "Of course you did. I should have known."

He laughs. "How'd you wind up majoring in finance?"

I cock my head, trying to keep up with his train of thought. "What?"

"It's just that after hearing all that, I don't see your parents pushing you toward it."

"Fluke." I shrug. "I meant to circle printmaking on my college applications."

He throws me a look.

"I'm good with numbers, that's why."

"But do you *like* it?"

"Yes." I start fiddling with my nails. "I know it's dorky and, like, also kind of masochistic when you take Finance Bro Culture into account—"

"Sorry, I'm not—I'm not judging you, I promise." His voice is soft. "I was just wondering."

But comments like that—no matter how offhanded or meaningless they're supposed to come across—are why I always feel so *wrong, wrong, wrong.*

When I first started at LC, there was this guy named Wilfred Honeycutt. He studied at Columbia, majored in finance, and absolutely loathed his job. Then he got famous on TikTok with food-based splatter art—his true passion—and started making enough money from sponsorships to quit.

"You'll get out of here, too, someday" was the last thing Wilfred Honeycutt ever said to me—a twenty-two-year-old who'd just upheaved her whole life to pursue the thing he was running from. Wilfred said it like I was in hell, even though I'd never thought of it that way, and ever since, part of me has been trying to get out of the hell he told me I was in. Maybe it's this industry, stuffed to the brink with writers and designers who are, honestly, *obsessed* with using "creative" as a noun, but maybe it's also just that people are snobs, because I know Miriam deals with it, too: *Why would you want to only be a nurse?* Even Wilfred's parents forced him to major in something practical like finance, when all along, he just wanted to crush up berries and splatter it on canvas.

I slip off the bed. "I'm going to water the flowers."

"Oh—thanks." Alex follows me to the sink, then out to the balcony as I pour water from a cup into the lip of the planter. "You should do this in the morning, if you can remember," I say quietly. "That's the best time of day to water flowers because the soil is cool from the night before and the plants can absorb it best."

"I, too, am thirsty in the morning. How do you know all this stuff?"

"My stepdad is a florist," I say. "It was our big bonding activity when I was a kid."

I recall this one day when I was eleven. I was sitting outside on our front porch steps, rubbing Pirate's belly. The sound of the musical chords Dad was plucking at random—testing out the tone of a new song—drifted toward me from inside, but the memory's vision is trained on Jerry, knee-deep in our flower beds.

I'd met Miriam that fall of fifth grade, and together, the two of us were growing into our personalities. We'd both gotten cut from the soccer team after spending all of tryouts screaming at the flying ball and laughing at each other. Miriam decided to do our middle school's dance program, but that had sounded as anxiety-inducing as reliving the talent show that wasn't.

Instead, I'd opted for an after-school volunteer club. We did everything from park cleanups to elementary school math tutoring, and I was actually enjoying it. But the more I figured out what activities I liked, the less time I had to practice guitar with Dad. Miriam said she was trying to turn me into a joiner, but I still felt guilty. Mostly because the older I got, the more I realized that music was just something Dad had lent to me. It was never going to belong to me the way it belonged to him.

"How does he make songs out of nothing?" I asked Jerry,

frustrated. "I've heard him do it a million times, and it still doesn't make sense to me. I'd just end up copying someone."

"Well," Jerry said, yanking up a weed, "it's not really from nothing. There are chords that are already known, and it's just about making up a new order for them to go in."

"Still," I grumbled, and Jerry laughed. "And the lyrics! How do you decide what's good enough? How can you know if people will like what you made?"

"You prefer a sure thing," he said.

"Maybe," I answered, wrapping myself in my own arms. Pirate whined forlornly.

"Come here," Jerry said. I hopped up and went over to his work section, and Jerry handed me a spade and a pansy out of a plant tray. "There's very little guesswork when it comes to making flowers grow," he told me. "They need soil, sunlight, water, and air. Every day, again and again. It's as sure a thing as any."

And in that moment, while I speared the earth and carefully loosened the root bulb, Jerry became a second father to me. I'd spent a lot of my childhood feeling unsteady—the passing of Mom, shyness around strangers, trouble speaking, and frankly, a little bit of confusion over Jerry not being a woman—but in the span of a single conversation, he identified something about me I'd never been able to name, *and* offered a solution: *When you're feeling lost, do what makes you calm, and sure-footed.* I've been beholden to him ever since.

It's pitch-black, I note vaguely as I stand. I should really head home. We're approaching sleep time, which, last I checked, was *not* included on most fuckbuddy agendas.

Alex is blocking the doorway, all broad chested and rumpled hair and expressive eyes. He's looking at me like he's searching for something, worry lines between his brows, and I try to smile, but I'm sure it must come across the same way I feel inside: tired.

"Shoo." I flick my fingers at him. "I must be going."

He stiffens but steps aside to let me through. I find my workbag, yanked from my arms and thrown onto the countertop as I came through the door earlier.

"Thanks for . . . for . . ." I can't meet his eyes.

"The sex?"

I wince. "Yep. The sex."

Loosely, he grabs my elbow. "Casey. About before. I'm sorry if I hurt your feelings again."

"*That* sounds like an apology that's lost its efficacy," I try to joke. "But lucky for you, you didn't hurt anything."

He tilts my chin up with his finger, forcing me to look at him, burnt-sugar eyes swallowing me. "Okay. If you say so."

"I do," I insist.

"*Okay,*" he says again.

I head for the door, but there's a yank on my wrist, and then we're lip-locked.

It's wildly different from our first kiss at Sleight of Hand, twice as intense as the one in the restaurant. This one's hungry, an act of pure relish. Alex's teeth scrape against my bottom lip as I wrap my hands behind his neck. One of his arms brackets my hips, pulling me up, up, *up* off the floor, and my toes settle on top of his. He wraps his free hand around my hair and lets the kisses get softer, tugging on my bottom lip, tugging on my hair. I steal gulps of breath in between each one, flushed and undone.

His touches reignite something I could've sworn was supposed to be dimmer now, less mystical. But it isn't. If anything, every press of his lips to mine leaves me just slightly more addicted to the sensation than the last.

Eventually, he lifts me off him and presses one more kiss to my jaw. I stumble back, lashes batting so ferociously they could induce a small tornado. When my eyes refocus, Alex is watching me with his hands loosely fisted at his hips, biting the inside of his cheek.

His boxers are decorated with corgis in Christmas sweaters, and yet he still manages to look like sex got dressed up for a night of revelry.

"Goodbye." His voice is so scratchy, I want to ask if he needs a cough drop.

I jerk out two nods like a marionette. "Goodbye," I repeat.

The door shuts between us, and at eight thirty on a Tuesday evening, I do my first ever hangover-free walk of shame.

CHAPTER TWENTY

A week passes in a haze of pumpkin spice lattes, Oktoberfest beers, and a pumpkin-carving contest that leaves me with a bandaged thumb. I find out over the stretch of it that Alex has an absurdly busy social calendar, made even more so thanks to (*a*) his three-year absence from the US and (*b*) his personality getting him an automatic yes whenever people are curating guest lists. It's disgusting and obnoxious, and honestly, extroverts should be studied in a lab.

The weekend after our hookup, he flies to California, where a friend from college is launching a start-up and hosting an extravagant party to celebrate. (But of course.) The Tuesday after that, he attends a notable alumni dinner at the Harvard Club in midtown (Dougie apparently declined the invitation, but only after inquiring who'd be in attendance). Alex tells me he's positive he's never done anything notable besides *existing* as the whispered-about bastard child of fabled businessman Robert Harrison—neither hidden away and kept secret nor bandied about like Robert's pride and joy.

Alex is just sort of there, always has been, and people know who he is, but nobody talks about it much to his face.

The day after the Harvard dinner, Alex recaps it for me in a slew of texts we exchange between meetings.

> **Casey:** I have to agree I can't fathom a single notable thing about you
> **Alex:** In between blood rituals, we went around the circle and bragged about our most notable contribution to high society. The best I could come up with was "ability to infuriate"
> **Casey:** and how are the pagan gods of ivy league education
> **Alex:** up to their usual. Ruminations on northeastern weather, Stanford smack talk, organizing a protest against student loan forgiveness
> **Casey:** that last one sounds like something you wouldn't know a thing about
> **Alex:** point taken. Do you have loans?
> **Casey:** yes, but v manageable. Dad was in tight spot for a while after mom's uninsured cancer treatments, but I got a couple of scholarships, plus I was a waitress for like seven years
> **Alex:** thanks, now I'm sweating in front of gus while he drones on about SEO
> **Casey:** a waitress kink?
> **Alex:** it's news to me too.

I smile at my phone screen as I wait in line at Pret to order my sandwich.

> **Casey:** tonight's the book event, right?
> **Alex:** Right.

From what I've gathered about Harvard grads, they all like to have *something* going on—a new business venture, a book debut, a humanitarian fundraiser for a nonprofit they're chairing. They always invite each other, too. Alex says it's veiled in camaraderie, but he thinks it's mostly a flex.

His social calendar doesn't surprise me, considering I've long been aware he's the type of person that's good to have in any room. But it *also* means we haven't gotten another chance to see each other outside of work, and neither of us has been brave enough to fire off a late-night booty call. Meanwhile, Alex's texts are getting more quietly randy—vaguely disguised behind his growing concern over the chocolate cosmos or a casual mention that he's craving Diet Coke. He's even starting to explain his obligations as though they're sandwiched between unspoken apologies. And almost by accident, the less we see each other, the more we talk.

> **Casey:** did you always want to go to Harvard, or was it more of an assumption with your father that you just would?
> **Alex:** both. my dad offered to pay for Harvard the same way he offers to pay for everything. Pretty much announcing it as a done deal. I liked the idea of having that thing in common with him. But it was ignorant of me to think it would change anything

I place my order at the register and sit at a table, completely absorbed.

> **Casey:** What exactly did you want to change?
> **Alex:** His desire to be included in my life. I know how desperate that sounds but it's just the reality of how I felt. I wanted him to be there, and to think I was

a good son. I wanted him to sometimes choose my
feelings over Linda's.

    Casey: How often do you see him?

Alex: once every few years, by necessity or fate. I ran
into him and Linda one Christmas in new haven, when
I was visiting my girlfriend at the time. He came to
both of my graduations. We email sometimes, but I
know more about him from the internet than his own
mouth

    Casey: that blows. He's never tried to get to know
    you?

Alex: nope. As a kid, I held on to this idea of him as a
real father for a lot longer than I should have, reaching
out all the time when he clearly didn't want to be
contacted. It was honestly embarrassing on my part. I
got the picture eventually.

Sometimes, Alex's honesty is so disarming, it scares me. He
doesn't have walls anymore. He wants me to know him. I'm not
sure what to do with that, because even though my emotions play
out on my face whether I want them to or not, I do my best to keep
everything inside.

My fingers are moving of their own accord in the Instagram
search bar, typing Alex's username, hitting his tagged photos, scroll-
ing to the one that started all this. @harvardalumni: A photo of
Alex in his graduation gown, his smile genuine. Robert is smiling,
too, his arm thrown over his son's shoulder.

How much of the distance he puts between himself and Alex is
dictated by Linda, and how much of it comes from Robert alone? It
feels wrong to blame her for anything, but it's easier than thinking
Robert truly doesn't care. I can't imagine Alex would have sought
his dad's attention and approval so desperately over the course of

his life unless Robert was giving him reasons to. I heard one reason myself, just the other day: *I'm proud of you, son.*

I twirl my finger around my braid. Briefly, I consider my next text. I type it and hit SEND before I can chicken out on the invitation.

> **Casey:** Are you doing anything Friday night?
>
> **Alex:** Yes

I groan louder than I mean to, and a guy standing near me gives me the side-eye.

Seriously, what could Alex possibly have to do now? Another video game marathon with Freddy? Skype call with his cousins? I need downtime like I need rain to fall, or the egg sandwich from Thai Diner, or a solo day trip to the Rockaways with an audiobook and a D8 gummy: as a matter of absolute necessity.

I can't imagine if the two of us were in a real relationship. It would *never* work out. Between his schedule and my aversion to strangers, we'd set off a fire alarm.

I wait Alex out, watching his type bubbles appear again.

> **Alex:** I've got this birthday party for a girl I know. It's themed. I have to wear a costume.

I blink, looking up.

My birthday is Friday.

But I never told Alex that, and I'm not having a themed birthday party. I was only planning to get dinner with Miriam and Brijesh. Sasha's not even in town this weekend.

A scowl breaks across my face at the thought of Alex going to some other girl's costume party on *my* birthday. Then I scowl even harder, because *why* am I so worked up about this? Wasn't I just making internal arguments *against* getting worked up about this?

> **Casey:** you should hire Benny to coordinate ur
> calendar. Maybe then you'd have a day off once
> every few months
> **Alex:** I miss you too, simba

A scoff lurches out of me. I didn't . . . That's not what I— Ugh!

I eat an embarrassed, petulant lunch, followed by an elevator ride to thirty-seven, because of course it's a *Wednesday* and the BTH all-hands meeting is today. When Alex sees me sweep past him in the conference room, he winks at me. I shove down my weird feelings and try to focus on work for the next hour. But every time I look up, I catch him watching me with carefully concealed amusement, like he knows he got under my skin and considers it a *notable* achievement.

Well, screw him, and screw that girl. I hope her party theme is silly, and I hope Alex feels absolutely ridiculous.

Halfway through the meeting, Gus slides a single pink Starburst over to me, like a secret, and says nothing. Five minutes later, I watch him slide a yellow one to Amanda, just as secretly.

He's so weird. And fiscally irresponsible.

Oddly, the taste of the Starburst on my tongue makes me feel calmer.

After the meeting, I make a beeline for the elevator. Alex is either heading up to my floor for a genuine reason or just wants to work me up a little more, because he sticks an arm in between the closing doors and follows me inside.

His eyes flick up and down and his voice drops lower, more weighted than how he talked in front of the others. "Hey."

"Hey."

He frowns. "What's wrong?"

"Why would you assume something's wrong?"

He presses his lips together and steps closer. "Heart. Sleeve. We've been through this."

I take a steadying breath and fight back tears that have no business breaching my ducts right now. My mind is working overtime, doing that thing where it rationalizes for me. The thought I had in Alex's bedroom comes again, more insistent this time: *End. This. Now.*

Obviously, I wasn't clearheaded when I suggested he and I could have something casual. Nothing about my personality is casual. I'm the type of girl who visits the dentist every six months without fail, who makes pros and cons lists for each travel points credit card before she ever goes anywhere, who will *never* sleep with her makeup on no matter how drunk. I will figure out why the balance sheet is off by one dollar and eighty-three cents if it's the last thing I do. And the people I care about—I do not casually care about.

I have to end things with Alex before it hurts even worse. If we cut this off now, there's no harm done, and the only thing I'll lose is a tiny bit of my sanity between two and four o'clock on a Wednesday afternoon.

"I think we should call an audible," I blurt. "You're busy, and I'm busy, and this is honestly getting to be more trouble than it's worth."

The ghost of something acerbic and bitter crosses Alex's face. He breathes a tiny laugh out of his nose and mutters at the ceiling, "Clockwork."

"What?"

His hands pass over his forehead. "Nothing."

We're nearly to the top of the beanstalk, and I feel the elevator slow to a halt. "Have fun this weekend," I force out. "At the party."

Alex shifts, the soles of his shoes squeaking against the floor. "Am I not . . . uninvited?"

I turn, catching the tense roll of his jaw. He looks confused and . . . hurt.

"Wait, you were . . . You were talking about *my* birthday?"

Alex searches my face like he's trying to decide whether I'm lucid. "Yes." He takes another step forward. "Did you think I meant someone else?"

"Yes!" My voice is semi-hysterical. "I'm not having a themed birthday party. I'm not having a birthday party at all."

We both get there about two and a half seconds later.

"Fuck," Alex grumbles. "I'm going to kill Brijesh."

"Miriam is going to kill you, and I'm going to kill her. I hate surprises. Those are for people with chill personalities only."

The doors open. I walk toward Benny's deserted desk. Warmth stains my cheeks as I replay the way I acted over the past hour.

I am a mortifyingly emotional person.

Alex's fingertips graze my forearm, and I turn to face him. "Do you want me to come? Or did you really mean that you . . . you think this is more trouble than it's worth?"

It sounds terrible, hearing those same words back. I can't believe I said them.

I tug on my braid. "No, I didn't mean it, and of *course* I want you to come. I'm sorry for saying that. I was just feeling—"

"Jealous."

My eyes flick up to his. He looks down, daring me to contradict him, but I don't have the energy for it. Alex lifts his hand and rubs his fingers against a runaway lock of my hair. "It's okay," he says softly. "I get jealous, too."

I shake my head in disbelief even though his admission thrills me. "Alex, I haven't given you any reason to be jealous."

"I know you haven't. I still find plenty." He smiles softly, an apology, like it's something he's working on. "But for my part, Casey . . . you should know." He steps closer, and all I see are dark lashes and hooded, caramel eyes. "For the time being, you're it. When I'm with someone, I'm *with* them."

His words pummel me to pieces just as much as they bind me

back together. I don't know how to process the emotions battling for dominance inside me.

For the time being, you're it.

I want all of you until the day I don't want any of you.

"What's the theme?" I ask.

"I am obviously not going to tell you that."

"Please?"

"I already might get murdered by your best friend for saying what I have so far."

"Exactly. What's the harm now?"

Alex walks backward, shaking his head. "No chance."

He pushes the button for the elevator, and I gape. "Did you follow me up here?"

"Yes." He arches an eyebrow. "You were trying to telepathically communicate with me in that meeting, but I haven't learned all your faces yet, so I had to inquire in person. But now I've got *jealousy* down, so that's progress."

"Screw you," I say, but the words lose their bite when I laugh.

He grins, rubs his jaw with a palm, and shakes his head at the floor. Quietly he says, more to himself than to me, "You really scared me for a second there."

He's gone before I can utter a word.

I walk toward the Hive in a daze, my inner chaos from the past few hours simmering down. Benny is leaning over Fari's desk when I approach.

"Oh, Casey!" He straightens. "Perfect timing. Fari and I are scouring Amazon for costumes. Can you clarify—since it's a murder mystery party but, like, only a few days before Halloween—are we supposed to be dead-*looking* seventies icons, or just seventies icons who happen to be dead?"

CHAPTER TWENTY-ONE

Half the people didn't know it was a surprise, and half the people didn't know it was a birthday, and well more than half thought Miriam meant the Halloweeny kind of murder, with fake blood and zombie eyes and gashes in your flare jeans. Brijesh *swears* he never heard her say "surprise" over the phone, but it all works out when everyone shows up to Sasha's swanky Upper West Side apartment in their disco best.

By everyone, read: exactly fourteen people, because that's the number of character cards in the murder mystery party kit Miriam ordered. Even after all the plus-ones she gave out (Benny brought his boyfriend and Fari brought a thirty-three-year-old insurance agent she's seeing), Miriam still had to invite three nursing friends to meet the quota.

When I walk in the door, the first thing I spot is a bowl of sherbet fizz, plus a pitcher of a premixed Tom Collins cocktail. A sign hanging over the front entryway reads THE NIGHT DISCO DIED. Star confetti pieces are strewn all over the floor. An electric disco ball is projecting colored lights onto each wall and, incongruously, "Lucy in the Sky with Diamonds" is blasting from a soundbar.

"John Lennon, I must apologize," I mutter under my breath.

"Surprise!" Ellie 1 shouts at me as I walk in.

Ellie 2 hisses at her, "It's not a surprise anymore, dumbass."

Miriam has two nursing friends named Ellie. One has red hair and green eyes. The other is so petite, half the hospital must think she's a runaway sick kid who found scrubs in the bathroom. They're matching tonight, dressed up alongside Miriam as Charlie's Angels, but the Ellies also have fake blood splattered on their skin. At least, I hope it's fake. They work in a hospital, but . . . I really hope it's fake.

The third nurse, Hector, is dressed as a cop. (He scored that character card because he has a real mustache.)

All three of them greet me at the door while Miriam rushes off to change. We just came from dinner as planned but gave up on the surprise element days ago.

Sasha is leaning against her kitchen counter in flares and platforms. "What a shock to see you're in town after all," I deadpan.

She rolls her eyes. "I told Mir you hate surprises."

"And I told Casey that sometimes she doesn't know what's good for her!" Miriam shouts from the half bath. She emerges seconds later in full costume—black crop top, shiny leggings, finger pistols to boot.

"How was that going to work, anyway?" Miguel asks. "You guys coming to our place when we were supposedly out of town?"

"What the fuck do you mean, *our place*?" Sasha asks him.

Miguel, dressed as some ambiguous movie star, blushes and grumbles something before he walks into the living room.

"I admit, the plan could have used some fine-tuning," Miriam says. "Problem is, Casey's always the one who does that shit."

"It's the thought that counts," I say cheerily.

Sasha pulls me into her bedroom so I can change into my outfit:

a chrome-white dress, flower crown, and sash that says BIRTHDAY BITCH.

"Can I talk to you?" Benny asks when I make it back to the living room. "Tracy asked for a copy of my résumé today. Completely out of the blue, zero context given. I was scared to ask, and now I'm freaking out about why she'd want—"

"Casey!" Jude says, hugging me. Saving me. My stomach bottoms out when I spot Alex over Jude's shoulder. He smiles, but every atom in my body has stuttered to a standstill. Is Tracy already job hunting for Benny?

I've met Jude, Benny's boyfriend, exactly once, at a brunch drag show Benny invited me to before he banned me from coming to any more. (He said it gave him cross-pollination career panic.) "Can you please tell Benny to chill, and that Tracy loves him, and she's probably just putting him up for a pay raise or something?" I am spared from lying through my teeth when Jude turns to Sasha, eyeing her drink. "Are you drinking Fireball out of a Healthy Habits water bottle?"

"It's Jack Fire," Sasha says.

Jude laughs. "You're violent. I like you."

That's when Fari walks in with the insurance agent. She introduces him to us as Alfred, and he starts an ill-timed thirty-minute conversation with me like this: "So, Casey, what are your career goals for twenty-five?"

To have one, I think. When I look over at Benny fifteen minutes later, he's half-drunk and jovial, but I can't get rid of the protectiveness for him swelling in my gut.

Spot a solution Tracy can't.

There's still time. I'm not going to solve anything tonight, but there's time.

When I manage to get within five feet of Alex, I've already gone through a drink and a half. He follows me over to the punch bowl, where I'm topping myself off.

"Hi." His fingers brush mine as I pass over the drink ladle. He's wearing a tie-dye T-shirt, light-wash jeans, and boots.

"Hi." I bite my lip, stifling a giggle. "Where did you acquire *that* outfit?"

"Would you believe it? This is what I wore to Lollapalooza in high school."

"Nice try, but I've already seen how sparse your closet is."

"Which is why I had to procure the ensemble from Aunt Jane's," Alex says. "Are the cowboy boots doing it for you?"

Kind of. "In your dreams."

He leans closer, looming over me. "Has anyone ever told you you're a terrible liar? You better hope for the sake of this game's longevity that you aren't the killer. We'd collectively out you in seconds."

"I can be deceptive when I have to be," I say, frowning. Almost like I'm trying to convince myself that it's true.

Alex looks across the room. "Am I meant to stay away from you tonight?"

My mind tumbles over itself. "What?"

He clears his throat. "Fari and Benny are here."

Oh. I look over at the coworkers in question. They're laughing with Miriam and Sasha, who are no doubt telling them my most mortifying college stories.

I guess it wouldn't matter if . . .

No. Bad idea.

It doesn't matter, Devil Casey says. *The people they're screwing are here, too, and Brijesh already knows.*

"Your face is doing somersaults," Alex says. "I wish you could see it."

I roll my eyes at him. "Only stay away from me if you're the murderer."

Freddy Rollerblades up to us, catching himself on the table. He's wearing a white jumpsuit, his chest on full display. "Hello, lovebirds."

"Your chest hair looks great," I say.

"That's not going to convince me to look the other way while you commit murder."

"Gather up, you drunk hoes!" Miriam shouts from the coffee table.

Sasha swats at her. "Bro, get *off*, this isn't the Phi Sig basement."

Miriam hops down, scowling but unperturbed. "Benny, want to narrate? I feel like as a performer, you're the natural pick to narrate."

The fourteen of us gather in a circle, and Sasha passes around a hat with slips of paper inside. "If your paper has an 'X' on it, you're the killer!"

Alex is beside me, and when he pulls his paper out of the bowl, he twists away so I can't see. I grab mine and do the same; sadly, I am not the killer.

Next, Miriam hands out our character cards, which have lines that we're supposed to playact with every other character.

"Does everyone have a beverage?" Benny shouts. "I'm going to get started."

"Wait, dim the lights!"

"I need more vodka!"

"I'm still confused. None of us are dead."

"The death is an omnipresent human manifestation."

"What the literal fuck does that mean?"

"Disco is a *person*. Disco is dead."

"Everyone shut up!" Benny shouts.

We quiet down, settle onto chairs and against walls. Benny dims the lights, then strolls back in front of the TV. There's a performative smirk on his face as he holds our unwavering attention. His script is nowhere nearby, and I wouldn't be surprised if he already memorized it.

"This," he says, tone low and dramatic, "is everything we know so far about the night disco died."

An hour later, I'm certain I've got the killer.

"I know it's you, Freddy."

He props his feet on the ottoman and smiles at me. "Did you get what you wanted for your birthday, Casey?"

"My name isn't Casey. It's Gloria. And what I want is to put you away for murder."

"You watched a lot of *CSI* growing up, didn't you?"

I narrow my eyes. "I did, actually."

Freddy laughs. Across the room, Ellie 2 shouts at Alfred, "If you had just *told* me you like to dress up as a woman, then none of this would have happened!"

Alfred blushes, fumbling for his script.

"I think someone assigned the character cards wrong," Benny grumbles.

Miriam throws up her hands in exasperation. "It was mostly random!"

Cop Hector strolls past. His detective notepad is taking a bath in his cocktail glass. "You're all under arrest," he slurs.

I point my finger at Freddy. "I need another drink, but when I get back, I *will* get you to admit that someone who has had, say, thirty perms in their life would know showering risks deactivating the ammonium thioglycolate."

"Please." Freddy winks. "Everybody knows that."

Alex comes out of the bathroom right as I reenter the hallway. I scoot up to him and slap the wall beside his head. He freezes, amused.

"Is it true you stand to inherit the club now that Doctor Disco is dead?" I ask.

"Disco was like a brother to me," Alex says. "Sure, we were business partners, but I'd never off him. You, on the other hand . . ."

"What?"

"The bouncers overheard you and Disco fighting."

I gasp theatrically. "We never fought!"

Alex consults his script, then goes rogue. "You were mad he wasn't giving you enough stage time. Disco said you were pitchy."

"He did not. That's not on the script!"

He rasps out a laugh and grabs me by my waist, pulling me against him. "I guess you'll have to sing something to prove you're not the killer."

"Alex, the stakes are too high, you have to take this seriously!" I cry.

But this feeling—this giddiness I can say with 100 percent confidence I've never felt so intensely—swallows us both up in a feedback loop of wanting and being wanted. The days apart are demanding an end, and my free hand comes up behind his neck, and I let him tip me back a little, and—

"Ha!"

My drink tilts, sloshing out of the glass. Alex and I both twist to see Benny staring at us, mouth agape.

"Fari, you owe me five bucks!" he shouts, running off.

I groan in exasperation, and Alex hums against my throat, "You said I didn't have to stay away from you if I wasn't the murderer."

"Did you just give yourself away so you could kiss me?"

"Yes," he says, tilting my face toward his, and rumbles, "I'm done with games."

We slip away when the party winds down—the murderer still at large due to an admittedly botched investigation—and head back to the West Village, where cold air and wind and lights revive us from the edge of sleep the Uber ride sank us into.

"When's *your* birthday?" I ask Alex when he comes out of a bodega and hands me a Gatorade. "And why didn't you get the nipple-top bottles? They taste better."

He slants his head, looking down at me with amusement. The blue lights of the neon sign above us paint his face a dreamy glow. "They definitely taste better, but they were out. And my birthday is Christmas Eve."

"What?"

"For real."

"What are your Christmases like?" I ask, then bite my tongue. If Alex doesn't even spend Thanksgiving with family . . .

"When I was a kid," he says, putting a hand against my waist to steer me in the direction of his street, "they were full of *miyeok-guk* and experimental skin-care products my cousins would invent. They've upgraded since then and now co-own a skin-care line that they operate out of LA and Seoul, where each of them lives. I think I have some of their face masks at home, if you want to try one."

I chew on my lip, peering up with pure intrigue at the man beside me. "Were your aunt and your mom close?"

He nods. "They were best friends growing up. Aunt Jane has tons of old stories about my mom she tells me whenever I stay with her," Alex says, smiling. "Just yesterday, I went to dinner with her, and we spent three hours talking. She was sad when my mom decided to move us to Seoul, but apparently, she also thought it was the right call for my mother's happiness."

"To get her away from Robert's vicinity?" I ask.

Alex frowns. "I guess so. Though Aunt Jane doesn't think Robert is so bad, mainly because her own husband was worse. He bailed on his wife and kids about eight years ago and never looked back. At least Robert didn't vanish."

"That's true," I say. "Robert did not vanish."

Alex's hand on my waist slips to my free hand, and he doesn't let go as we climb the stairs of his place. Still doesn't let go as we stroll silently toward his bed. He puts both of our bottles on the dresser and pulls me close. Tilts my head back with the tip of his finger.

"Tell me what you want for your birthday," he whispers. "And I'll give it to you."

I kiss him. I ache for this now. The feeling of his lips on mine. *All the time.*

He tugs on my bottom lip with his teeth, traces the marks he left behind with his tongue. I lift myself toward him, pressing our bodies flush. We kiss, and kiss, and kiss. Just standing there.

He's hard against me, and I make him sit so I can straddle him. Alex moves my body against his, and we just keep kissing, like neither of us can stand to move on from this. My dress rides up eventually, and he lifts it over my head. I peel off his shirt, let my hands roam over the contours of his chest. He massages my breasts, thumbing over the fabric of my bra. Under it.

Mouth. His mouth is on my breast. It's warm and dark and flooding me with a sensation that I have honestly, without a doubt, never felt before in my life.

I'm making noises that I've never *heard* from myself in my life.

He lays me out and strips off the rest of my clothes. I'm dizzy, my vision blurring, my body humming. Hot breath tickles my thighs. Alex pushes my legs up to bent and spreads them wide. "Is this okay?" he whispers.

"I've been checked recently!" I blurt. Then, mortified, I shut my eyes and squeeze my lips shut.

"Good to know." He chuckles. "Not what I meant, but thanks for the safety check."

I shake my head, looking down. "I just meant that I went to the doctor more recently than I was with someone else."

He exhales against me. "Me too. For the record. I scheduled an appointment the week after you slept in my bed."

"That's almost presumptuous," I say lightly.

"It was incredibly presumptuous, and also a desperate attempt at wish fulfillment."

He puts his mouth on me with no further preamble, and I spend the next few minutes cursing and gasping and thinking this is the best birthday anyone's had, ever. I fall off a cliff one minute later, having completely lost any sense of control over my own body's pleasure. It's in his hands now. Which is just as terrifying as it is beguiling.

Afterward, Alex crawls up beside me. In between kisses brushed along my jawline, he has the audacity to ask, verbatim, "Want another?"

I am so stunned that all I can think to say is, "Are you running a deal?"

He rumbles out a laugh. "Well, it is your birthday." He reaches for his nightstand and grabs a condom out of the drawer.

"Alex?" I ask softly as he puts it on.

"Yeah?" he half groans.

"I want to use the condom, but I also wanted you to know I have an IUD."

He looks back up at me, leaning most of his weight on one elbow, searching my face. "Okay," he whispers hoarsely. "Thanks for telling me."

"And—I'm sorry I didn't say this the other day, but I'm not going to sleep with anybody else while we're . . . while this is . . ."

He settles back against me and murmurs, "I'm not going to sleep with anyone else, either. And condoms are great." My spine arches and I gasp faintly as his teeth slip against my earlobe. "It's just you and me, Casey. We can make it be however you want."

Oddly, that might be the most romantic thing anyone's ever said to me.

The spaces between our bodies shrink, and Alex wraps me up, memorizing the shape of me under his hands. He kisses me until

I'm gasping for breath. His scratchy voice rumbles against my jaw. "Though, you still have to *tell* me what you want."

"I can show you."

I roll myself on top of him, push against his chest, and let our bodies join. Alex mutters something unintelligible under his breath as the whole of me sinks onto him. His thumbs hook onto my waist and his fingers spread across my back. We watch each other beneath half-closed eyes as I find a rhythm.

I marvel over the way his lashes flutter when my hips finally still.

CHAPTER TWENTY-TWO

"Um. Do you want to grab some breakfast?" Alex asks the next morning, only once my stomach finishes its growling marathon. It's the first either of us have spoken today. We've been lazily awake for twenty minutes, drowsy eyed and spooning, shifting every few minutes to tug our bodies closer, burrow deeper into the sheets and each other. But we stayed silent the whole time, as if we both knew our first words would break the spell.

Lying there, bracketed by Alex's arms and legs, shivering under his warm breath tickling my neck, I can't think of a single reason why I shouldn't say yes to breakfast. So, I do.

After we get up, I change into the clothes I wore to dinner last night. Alex slips on jeans and a dark blue sweatshirt from a cancer fundraiser 5K in Boston.

I point at it. "You run?"

He grabs his On Clouds, slips them on. "Every morning, if I can."

"So, you literally wake up and choose violence."

Alex makes a show of stretching. He props one foot on his nightstand and bends his hands toward it. "McBurney YMCA before breakfast to work up our appetites?"

I throw a pillow at his head, and he laughs as he ducks into the bathroom.

I spend my unobserved moments surveying his apartment. From what I gather, Alex is utilitarian, like an army guy or a mini-malist, his furniture sparse but high-end. The couch he had on back order has finally appeared; it looks like it came from Pottery Barn or Restoration Hardware. Same vibe with his kitchenette; there's a Le Creuset Dutch oven sitting on his electric hot plate. Even his bedding is linen. It's so comfortable, I'd put money on the whole set being an Italian import.

It's like Alex doesn't have a clue how *not* to shop rich, even when the things he's buying are in complete dissonance with the rest of his lifestyle. He's living in a tiny apartment in the heart of the city, where everyone's existence is transient, held together by tape and tomorrow's paycheck. But Alex is out here buying the type of ex-travagant home goods that feel like he's putting down roots.

Two framed photos sit on the dresser in his bedroom. The first is Alex as a kid, maybe ten or so years old, standing between two Korean kids, one girl and one boy, both a few years older than him. The second is clearly Alex as a baby in his mother's arms; she's sitting in a wicker chair on a small apartment porch, smiling softly at the camera.

His mother is gorgeous—just like Alex—but to me he looks more like his father.

A minute later, he comes out of the bathroom wearing his glasses, and my brain short-circuits.

This . . . is going to be a problem.

I point at his face. "Glasses."

The corner of his mouth pulls up on one side. He pushes the glasses in question up the bridge of his nose—OH MY GOD,

CUT IT OUT WITH THE EROTICA—and says, "I slept in my contacts last night and my eyes were hurting."

I nod. Stand. "I wouldn't want you to be in pain."

I'm in pain. He's so hot. Must find a way to break his glasses in the interest of my personal sanity.

If Alex knows what I'm thinking, the only indication he gives me is in his smirk. "Need to pee before we leave?" he asks. "I'm not sure you got up enough times last night to take care of that."

"I have a small bladder, okay?"

Alex grins. "Okay. Want to check on the state of the cosmos?"

"Sure thing, Skywalker."

He follows me to the balcony, and I kneel down to poke at the soil. It rained yesterday morning, so we don't water the flowers. I'm actually impressed with how well they're faring, considering it's almost November and this alley gets only a few hours of sunlight per day.

"Have you smelled them?" I ask.

"No."

I nod toward the flowers. Alex kneels and leans in, taking a big, purposeful whiff. He smiles and laughs a little. "They smell like chocolate."

"Don't be fooled. They're toxic to eat."

He looks at me and raises an eyebrow. "Up until this very moment, I wasn't convinced you weren't in league with the *Garden Girl* editor in chief."

"Don't rule it out yet. I'm wooing you into trusting me."

He stands back up, and I follow suit. "When I go to LA for that conference, can you take it to your place?"

I roll my eyes even though the way he's fussing over this plant is endearing. "Alex, it's not a puppy. It might dry out a little, but it'll be fine."

He frowns. "You can't force me to get a living thing and then tell me it'll be fine if it sort of dies. I'm leaving you with a key."

When we head downstairs, a gust of fall weather threads into my hair. We walk to a bakery two blocks over that Alex promises me is to die for. "They have twice-baked almond croissants," he tells me as we're led to our table.

I brighten up as we sit down. "Hey, I'm not allergic to almonds!"

Alex unwraps his silverware. "Thank God. I would have had to cart you out of here. They're that good."

We peruse the menu and order a carafe of coffee to share. I don't miss the way our waitress eyes Alex appreciatively. He's got the weekend look nailed, projecting a well-rested but disheveled air that makes you want to know how he's spending his Saturday so you can re-create it for yourself, or even ask if he'd like some company and maybe a blow job on the house.

"One check or two?"

"Two," I say at the same time Alex says, "One."

He holds up a finger when I start to protest. "Let me pick up your tab as a birthday gift?"

There's a genuine question in his eyes, like he's really asking me if I'm okay with it and not demanding me to agree.

"Thank you," I murmur softly.

The waitress leaves, and Alex picks up his menu, hiding behind it. I grasp the table on either side, look out the window—sidebar: Is that @dudewithsign who just walked past with a stack of blank cardboard?—and take a moment to gather my bearings.

Because the truth is . . .

The truth. Is. Even though I've been ignoring it, I'm not so delusional as to think there isn't a word for what's going on here.

"Dating." The word is "dating."

Hooking up, exclusively. Hanging out one-on-one. Taking care of someone's plants when they're out of town. Asking questions about each other's past. Offering to pick up the tab.

This is what *dating* is like.

But Alex and I . . . We're not dating.

Are we?

I know dating can mean about a million different things. Some people do it with an endgame in mind, dating with the intent to be in a relationship. To have a life partner, build a future, sacrifice things for the sake of each other's happiness and all that jazz. But others date to stay entertained. It's just a hobby to pass your time until the tide of either of your lives takes a turn. You don't ever break up, but at some point, you're just not dating the other person anymore.

I'm starting to wonder, as I sit in this gorgeous café with this gorgeous male specimen on this gorgeous Saturday morning, mildly hungover, mascara under my eyes, teeth unbrushed, and unbothered by it all—if this is what's happening between Alex and me. If we're dating by the second definition of the word. It would make sense, considering that's pretty much how dating has operated for me since I moved to New York. Alex is likely in the same boat.

"I'll have the breakfast sandwich," he says, putting down his menu. He must catch my far-off expression because he waves two fingers at me. "Case? You there?"

"Sorry." I give my head a small jerk. That's when I notice our waitress is back, pen and pad in her hand, our coffee on the table. "Oh! The omelet, please."

When she leaves, Alex leans forward. "You okay?" he asks.

I nod and grab the carafe to busy my hands. "Mm-hmm. Just, thoughts."

His eyes narrow. "What thoughts?"

"Erm. Work stuff."

Alex looks unconvinced. He grabs the cream and dumps an overwhelming amount into his mug, followed by a heap of sugar. "Let me guess. You're deciding how to spend your Q3 bonus. Cosmos tea or dried oleander powder? It's a tough call."

"The fact that you know oleander can kill you means you

definitely researched what plants to avoid. And anyway, a bonus? You're funny."

He smirks. "Is it my fault we're not getting them? All those sunk costs you keep complaining about?"

I sigh. "Honestly, I wish that's all it was, but the financial misses are much bigger."

Alex frowns. "Really? How bad is it?"

The muscles of my stomach tighten as the truth pulses nightmarishly behind my skull. I feel powerless, knowing the decision to stay independent or sell to another company is out of my hands. But I can't change our financials, and isn't that what I always loved about numbers to begin with? They are immutable. They do not lie.

"Casey." I look up. Alex is watching me, expression thoughtful. "Whatever it is, you can tell me. I mean, as long as it wouldn't get you into trouble, you can tell me."

But I can't, Alex, because Tracy asked me to keep it to myself. And before that, she asked me to use you so I could give her a history lesson. And I'm still not sure what one has to do with the other, and I don't like keeping things from you when I want to tell you every secret I've ever known while you rub circles on my wrist, just like you did this morning in bed.

"We're in some trouble," I say, knowing that if I flat-out lie, he'll be able to tell.

Alex blows on his coffee, seemingly unflustered by my admission. "It'll pass. We just have to wait the launch out," he says, too confidently.

But there's no time. Alex doesn't realize Tracy and the others are making decisions *right now.* "How do you know launching one subsidiary company will be enough?" I ask.

"Because you believe it will," he says, instantly, automatically.

My eyes narrow, but my chest warms. "You're giving my judgment too much credit."

"I'm not. You wouldn't be working so hard on this if you didn't think it was a smart idea, and I trust your instincts more than just about anyone."

"You took this job before we'd even met," I argue.

"So maybe knowing you makes me even more inspired than I was before."

"'Inspired'?" I reply. "That's the word you're going with?"

"Why not?" Alex asks, leaning back.

"I'm not trying to be self-deprecating. But really, out of all the words my coworkers would use to describe me, 'inspirational' is definitely not one of them. 'Analytical,' maybe, or even 'meticulous,' but definitely not—"

"That's bullshit."

I snap my gaze to him in surprise. "What?"

Alex looks back at me, his expression perfectly serious. "Casey, I think you're inspiring as hell. Do you have any idea what people at work think of you?"

"Um. I mean, I'm pretty sure I come off rude at first. I'm not great with strangers."

Alex starts to say something but cuts himself off and says, "That's true, actually, but beside the point. Once people get to know you, anyone with half a brain can tell you're special. You take raw potential and turn it into something real. You figure out how to make things happen."

"No," I argue. "That's what *you* do."

Alex laughs and leans forward. "My follow-through is terrible, and we both know it. I suck at long-term commitment because I get distracted by the next thing."

Yeah, *definitely* the second definition of dating. If that. I move my foot underneath the table away from where it was resting against his.

"I don't really understand what you mean," I say softly.

"I can start a million projects at once, but you're the reason they get pushed over the finish line, Case. If you get on board with an idea, that's how I know it's a good one. I wasn't joking when I said I'd be lost without you. Half the time, Gus is too busy to be any real help, but you—you're like a North Star." The intensity in his voice has me mesmerized. I process his words slowly, trying to figure out how on earth he could think of me like that.

"I do numbers," I say, feeling tired all of a sudden. "All I do is numbers."

"There's more to you than just that. I hope they offer you an incredible job in London, because right now, you're running circles around the rest of us."

I hope, I hope, I hope.

"Just, please, Casey." He's leaning forward, voice dropping low. "Don't go around thinking you aren't remarkable. Or inspiring," he adds, grinning—completely unaware that in one sitting, he's found my deepest insecurity, ripped it out of my chest, flayed it open on the table between us, and told it to fuck off.

I was in high school when I decided that statistics were boring but that I really liked learning about economics and money, pretty much around the time *The Big Short* was released. I was *obsessed*. Completely, utterly enchanted by the idea that a bunch of brilliant outcasts everybody else in the industry thought had a screw loose could predict something like the housing crisis of 2008. The fall of my senior year, I put finance as my major on my college applications. "Just for now," I told Dad.

He looked at me and shrugged, smiling in this privately amused way I didn't understand, and said, "You know something, kiddo? You're the total opposite of your mom. But her parents would certainly be proud." After everything Dad told me over the years about Mom's relationship with her parents, he may as well have said I was betraying her ghost.

As an underclassman, I told my college adviser *twice* that I wanted to change my major. But whenever she asked me what I'd rather do instead, I never had an answer.

"Thank you," I say softly to Alex right when our food appears. He nods once and turns to his plate. Always reading me, knowing just what to say, and when to say nothing more.

Later, after a stroll around the neighborhood while we let our stomachs settle, plus a chrysanthemum purchase "to keep the cosmos company," we're heading back in the direction of Alex's apartment when I catch sight of a subway station.

My steps falter on the street corner.

I could . . . I *should* probably go home. I've got all my belongings with me, and it's two o'clock at this point.

Alex keeps walking, but he stops and turns when he notices I'm not with him anymore. He has the chrysanthemum in one hand, and his other slips into his pocket as his gaze cuts to the station across the street, then back to me.

I should head out, I try to say, *because you're not great with long-term commitment and I'm moving to London, and even if neither of those things were true, every time I look at you, I want to break my promise to Tracy because keeping secrets from you is starting to hurt me inside.* But the words get lost somewhere in the ether. Instead, we just look at each other for a couple long seconds, separated by five feet and at least eight cigarette butts.

Then, Alex gives a tiny, almost nonexistent shake of his head.

Standing there under the landscaped trees dotting the length of the sidewalk, burnished golden leaves under my feet and cool air on my skin, I can't think of a single reason why I shouldn't spend the entire day with Alex Harrison.

So, I do.

CHAPTER TWENTY-THREE

Alex heads to LA the next weekend for the Hermosa Beach Digital Creator Conference with Gus, Saanvi, and Social Media Amanda. It lasts until the following Wednesday (I visit his place once to water the cosmos and chrysanthemum, affectionately dubbed Cleopatra and Calliope), but then Freddy convinces Alex to stay out west for a few more days so they can road-trip up the Pacific Coast Highway like a couple of Barbour-wearing, Amex-carrying surf boy wannabes. I laugh out loud at the mental image; their anything-is-possible attitudes coupled with that northeastern boyish naivety seems a little cataclysmic.

Call me ambitious, but if I'd known at the time that I wouldn't be alone with Alex for over two weeks, I probably would have pushed for a fourth round of sex that Saturday we spent at his apartment together. When we got back from breakfast, we fucked in the bed, slow and drawn out, taking an exquisitely long time to get ourselves there. Then again two hours later, on the couch between episodes of *The Marvelous Mrs. Maisel*, spurred on by his hands on my thighs and my ass in his lap and a quarrel over Abe's funniest lines. Around six, right when I summoned up the willpower to leave and responded to a very hangry Miriam that I'd be home with chicken tenders forthwith, we had sex *again*. Frantic, frenzied, against the front door. A goodbye christening on my way out of it.

Alex is good at sex. *Really* good at it. So good, in fact, that I have to assume he's had copious amounts of it with a copious number of (probably) women. All of whom, like me, dated him by the second definition of the word, with the understanding that he's not good with long-term commitment but makes up for that fault with orgasms.

I wish I could say it was an equitable arrangement, but my body's starting to feel like it's *his,* and sex is starting to feel like something that'll only be good with *him,* and I wonder if he might be ruining me, just a little bit.

We spent last night in this camper van, he texts me, followed by a photo of a van painted with a terrifying hawk clawing at a mouse on the passenger door, but Freddy broke down trying to do his hair this morning, and I think I swallowed fifteen bugs last night, so we ended up renting a king-sized bed at a five-star hotel on the edge of a sea cliff.

Bugs are a great source of protein! I reply.

And lyme disease! Alex replies, followed by a picture of Pebble Beach in Monterey. The coast is rocky and wet, and the mid-November chill hangs heavy in the beach air, almost palpable from the ninety-eighth-floor break room.

The sight of him traveling does funny things to my insides, and I get weirdly excited every time he sends me a photo. A meal he loved, a shot of the van, a selfie of him reading a thriller on the beach. He'll send voice notes over text, recounting a story of how surreal it was that someone from the conference recognized him from YouTube, or how he accidentally slammed Freddy's finger in the van door and they had to visit an emergency clinic for a splint.

You'd love this: a photo of a plant nursery on the side of the road.

Rate on a scale of 1/10: a video of a guy at a bar singing George Strait and playing guitar.

By the time he's on a red-eye home Sunday night, I almost feel like he took me on the whole vacation with him.

I avoid Alex until Wednesday on principle. Just because he's back doesn't mean I need to see him, and he's busy anyway, judging by the radio silence the minute he got back to the city. But as the all-hands meeting creeps up, the minutes slipping closer and closer to 2:30, I start to fidget restlessly, smooth out the pleats of my Rent the Runway maxi skirt. Ruffle my hair. Ask Fari for a piece of gum.

"Oh, right. It's Wednesday," she says, handing it over the wall between our cubicles with a smirk.

At 2:27, I gather my belongings and stand up.

"Casey?" I step around the wall to see Fari wringing her hands.

"What's up?" I ask.

"Have you talked to Tracy lately?"

I freeze. *What does Fari know?*

"Not for a couple weeks," I get out. "Why?"

Fari bites her lip. "Remember that business proposal I created that Don sent to her? She never scheduled time with me to workshop it like she said. My first performance review is next week, and I wanted to mention it because . . . because when I accepted this job, I thought the bonuses were part of our regular pay, and since they're clearly not, I really need a raise."

My heart stretches outside my chest and gets tangled there, out in the open. Maybe that's why Alex is always saying it's pinned to my sleeve. "What did Benny say?" I ask softly.

"He said Tracy hasn't asked him to schedule anything."

"She didn't forget," I promise, with no real confidence. "She wouldn't have. She's probably just"—I wince—"busy, or stressed about . . . something."

Fari nods. "Yeah. The other day, I saw that the purple dip on one fingernail was missing."

"Oh my God," I whisper. "Tracy Garcia came to work without a flawless manicure?" *This is even worse than my most fatalistic nightmares.*

"It was unnerving," Fari says, and shudders.

"If I see her, I'll try to bring up your proposal without actually bringing it up. And about the bonus, I know it probably won't cut it, but they usually give something out over the holidays whether we hit our targets or not."

Fari nods and exhales. "Hopefully enough to reimburse myself for my surprise flight home for Thanksgiving."

Oh, *fuck*. I forgot to book my flight!

Also—"Oh, fuck, I'm late!"

"Sorry!" Fari shouts at me as I dash toward the elevator. My fingers fly over my phone screen, typing out a message to Dad and Jerry: booking my flight home for thxgiving TODAY!

Dad's response comes right as I'm stepping through the elevator doors: NO CASEY DON'T! We decided to come to you instead!

Oh . . .

Oh my God. Marty Maitland and Jerry Abrams loose in New York City.

For the first time ever.

What??? I reply.

Sorry, we meant to tell you, but we must have forgotten. (At least that makes two of us.) You can come to Nashville for Christmas instead!

Don's hand slips through the elevator doors right as they start to close. "Joining you for the all-hands today," he mutters, stepping inside. "Gus says there's big news."

"Big news?" I repeat. "From the conference, maybe?"

"No clue." Don shrugs. "But if he's being hyperbolic, I'm going to throttle him. I haven't eaten lunch in four days."

Regardless, if Gus wants Don there, it means his *big news* has a financial impact above my pay grade. My mind jumps to worst-case scenarios, anxious worry clawing at my rib cage all the way down to thirty-seven.

But when I walk into the conference room, Alex is there, and my vision goes to Portrait mode. The frame is focused only on him.

He's holding a stack of pamphlets, distributing them in front of each seat, and when he spots me, his gaze sweeps up and down my person, a heated look breaking across his features that turns me into a puddle of liquid gold. His eyes are warm and soft and open and basically screaming *Come here, immediately.*

"Don!" Gus says. "Thanks for joining us today."

"Happy to," Don says, sounding a little shy of happy. "Something specific you pulled me in for?"

Gus places both of his palms on the tabletop, holding everyone's attention as we settle into our seats. He usually spends these meetings typing furiously on his laptop, present in body but absent in mind. Not today, though. Today, Gus Moskowitz looks practically wolfish.

Reading his feverish expression—and then Alex's when he matches it—I predict what Gus is going to say about two seconds before he starts talking.

"I'm sorry for the short timeline on this, but a bunch of lights turned green at once, and when it rains in this industry, it pours. I just received word from Tracy Garcia that in four weeks, we're presenting a business proposal to the board to officially launch *Bite the Hand* as the first digital media company in Little Cooper's portfolio."

Beside me, Don freezes, a deer in headlights, his hesitation sweeping over me like something almost palpable. Saanvi and Amanda congratulate Gus, clap their hands, exchange exclamatory praise before immediately jumping into their thoughts on the presentation. To them, this is good news, exactly what they've all been working toward. But to me, and apparently to Don, too . . . the timing couldn't be more suspicious.

Thanksgiving is next week, cutting down on our prep time, and the presentation is scheduled in between Hanukkah and Christmas. That is objectively a *horrible* time of year to be making important business decisions.

Tracy's not thoughtless. What are the odds she genuinely thinks this is a good plan?

What are the odds she *knows* it's a bad one, but she's out of time?

What if a shiny *Bite the Hand* business proposal is her last-ditch attempt at convincing the board this company is worth saving?

When my eyes cut to Don, he's watching me with a frown, and that's when I realize we're both in on the same secret. We might even be having the same thought: This presentation isn't going to decide whether or not to launch a subsidiary. It'll decide whether LC stays independent or gets sold for parts.

"You're coming with me to Tracy's office," Don says on our way back up to ninety-eight. "I know you know. We need to talk about how to handle this with the others."

I nod mutely, fully embodying a child who's gotten in over her head.

I couldn't even look Alex in the eye for the rest of the meeting. It felt like a betrayal not to celebrate this step forward with him, but an even bigger betrayal to act like I thought everything would work out the way he wants it to.

But he *must* know something is wrong with me.

"Short timeline?" I probe, repeating Gus's words from earlier.

Don sighs. "The terms of the other company's offer expire in two months. I have a feeling one plus one equals two here."

Don looks . . . *mad.* I've never seen him like this. He's usually so docile, but as he storms toward Tracy's office and barges in, I'm fully aware he's about to go to bat for something he believes in.

"We need to talk," he says, and Tracy's mouth falls open before she hits the END CALL button on her desk phone. "Whose idea was it to present a BTH launch plan in *four weeks*?"

"It was mine." She reclines in her chair, perfectly at ease.

Don crosses his arms over his chest. "Does this mean what I think it means? Is the presentation supposed to be some sort of signal about LC's ability to stay solvent?"

"To be perfectly honest," Tracy says, "it's less about whether BTH can make money and more about whether it's exciting enough to rally the board to our side."

Don rubs at his forehead. "If the entire company's future is riding on the back of one team's ability to deliver an exciting presentation, they should at least be allowed to know it."

"No," Tracy says. *"Nobody tells anyone anything."* She looks right at me, like she knows I'm the weak link. "This is privileged. I mean it."

I have no idea where my bravery comes from, but I match Don's aggressive attitude and say, "On one condition."

Tracy narrows her eyes. "I can't believe I'm indulging this, but what condition?"

"Schedule that workshop with Fari. Did you know she got more than ten job offers? She chose LC because of you, and now she can barely afford to go home for Thanksgiving!"

Tracy blinks. I think my words both very much confuse and also somehow land with her, because she retreats into herself, and her voice comes out muted when she says, "Of course. Thank you for reminding me."

I nod, satisfied, and avoid the blushing face of Don, who is no doubt highly uncomfortable discussing one employee's pay with his other employee in the room.

"Why is this all happening so fast?" I ask, steering the subject back on course.

Tracy picks up a pen and twirls it through her fingertips, sighing. "Dougie wanted to accept the offer from Strauss Holdings this morning." *Strauss Holdings.* I make a mental note of Tracy's slip so I can research the company later. "At this point, he's content to get bought out of his well-endowed contract and retire, and he's even managed to convince the other board members it's the right call. Robert Harrison deserting was a huge hit to their faith. I got Dougie to postpone until the original deadline, but he needed a reason. I told him the launch plan might change his and the others' minds."

"Will it?" Don asks.

"Hope so." Tracy shrugs. "Because I, for one, am *not* ready to get bought out of my contract and retire."

Don narrows his eyes at her. "You don't seem confident he'll be persuaded."

She shoots me a pointed look, and Don turns to me. "Alex's involvement doesn't exactly help," I explain.

"Right," Don says. "The corporate warfare." He shakes his head and looks at me. "I still can't believe Gus hired that kid. It should've been you."

No, it shouldn't have.

"Look," Tracy says. "Blood in the water aside, I wouldn't have suggested this if I didn't think *Bite the Hand* was ready for it. That subsidiary launch was always coming. It's just coming a little sooner now."

CHAPTER TWENTY-FOUR

The next day, Alex comes home with me for the first time.

He wanted me to sleep over at his place last night, but I knew seeing him without a night to process my conversation with Tracy and Don would be a horrible idea.

I made dinner plans with Brijesh as a cover-up—although *that* didn't end up serving my mental state any better. After researching Strauss Holdings and concluding that *his* current job and *my* future dream job are both at risk—honestly, the only safe magazine is *Frame*, that beautiful behemoth—sitting across the table from Brijesh made me feel like a character from *Succession* with an inside scoop and no fucking loyalty.

He'll probably be fine. Brijesh is quasi-famous, and if he gets laid off, another company might find that fame attractive. But he's told me before about food media hierarchies, how long it takes to work your way up, how competitive that sector of the industry is. He'll probably be fine, but he might not be *good*, which was enough guilt to slice me in half. I was quieter than normal all night long.

Finally, he slapped a hand on the table and said, "Okay, did you get dumped, or am I about to get dumped?"

I had to remind him neither of us are in real relationships.

Yesterday, the scale was tipped like this: guilt = heavy, missing Alex = a little less heavy. Today, the scale tips in the other direction. I'm practically jonesing for him by five o'clock, when Sasha has a wardrobe malfunction and needs an emergency outfit change between a work event in Murray Hill and another in DUMBO. I meet Alex in the lobby and ask if he'd mind going to my place instead.

"Do I mind," Alex repeats. "I've been dying to see your apartment. Every day, I stare at my whiteboard and ask myself, *When will Casey invite me over?*"

I roll my eyes. "It's cramped, and far, and not remotely private if Mir's home."

"It's a window to your soul."

"Based on that logic, *your* soul is made up of expensive home goods and blank walls."

He smirks and shrugs. "I wouldn't be surprised, but I don't think I count. My living situation is too ephemeral to have a soul. I haven't had a real home since I was ten."

His tone is easy, a throwaway statement, and I don't think he knows it breaks my heart. I never considered Alex's place is so bare-bones because he's not planning to stay in it—or anywhere—for long.

Later, on the subway, out of some instinct to make sure he'll be okay, I ask, "Are you going to Freddy's mom's house next week for Thanksgiving?"

His normal energy is missing today, interrupted by a bout of quiet introspection I've begun to realize always manifests whenever there's a roadblock in Alex's head. Right now, he's playing with a lock of my hair and leaning his head against the subway wall behind us. He nods in answer to my question but doesn't elaborate further, so I let the silence stretch out comfortably, feeling his fingers in my hair and his eyes on me.

"Casey," he says eventually.

"Alex."

He leans forward and presses his nose into my hair. "I know you're worried Dougie's going to deny the launch out of spite. But I promise you, Simba, I'm going to make that presentation so damn good, even that vengeful man will love it."

I turn and smile at him a little sadly, relieved he guessed half my fears, so I don't have to lie about the other half. "Do you really promise?"

"I swear it." He kisses my hair. "Can I have Casey back now? I've been stressed out of my mind just thinking about how stressed *you* looked yesterday, and I'm usually very easygoing."

"Well, *I'm* not easygoing. And I hate mimosas."

His mouth twitches. "Do easygoing people usually like mimosas?"

"Most." I shrug. "It's linked in my mind."

"Your mind is weird," Alex says, and when the subway slows to a stop and we stand, he adds, "I'm starving. Is there any good food in Brooklyn?"

I laugh and say nothing.

Inside my place, Alex evaluates our smorgasbord of an apartment with a neutral expression. Eclectic throw pillows strewn over a couch we got for free when Miriam's sorority updated their interior design, the bar cart stacked with bottles of wine, our freestanding coatrack sentinel beside the front door. There's even a photo wall of me and Miriam—one picture from every year we've known each other.

Alex points at the picture of us covered head to toe in mud, smiling in braces and matching purple T-shirts. "Explain?"

My lips tug up at the memory. "Crud Day at our church. It was a youth group fundraising event they held every year. Mud games, tug-of-war, relay races. The year after that photo was taken, we tried turning our T-shirts into crop tops and got kicked off the premises."

Alex snorts, scanning the other pictures: backstage passes at CMA Fest in high school, general admission camping at Bonnaroo in college, standing in front of a jellyfish tank during a middle school field trip to the Chattanooga aquarium.

"You were pretty cute." Alex grins at me.

"You were, too," I echo, thinking of the two lone photos, sparse but precious, in his apartment.

There's a knock on the door, and I retreat to my room, leaving Alex to answer it while I riffle through the Ikea rack for the jumpsuit Sasha wanted to borrow. It's going to stop at her midcalf, but if anyone could make that a look it's her.

Her voice filters through all five hundred square feet of our place. "You're a life—oh, hey, Alex!"

"Hey," Alex says. "That looks nasty."

"Someone spilled three-bean chili all over me," Sasha seethes. "I was running late as it is, and I need to get to DUMBO before they start the Nets booster campaign."

I walk into the doorway and hold up the outfit. "Here. Come change in my room."

"You are the number one bitch," Sasha says.

I giggle. "What they call me."

"So. Uh," she says, closing my door and widening her eyes at me, "Alex is here."

"Is he?"

"Not that you asked, but I like him better than Lance."

"Not that *you* asked, but I like Miguel better than *all five* of the NBA players you dated senior year."

She snorts. "Glad we established that."

After she changes, we walk downstairs together, and Sasha hails a cab while Alex and I meander toward dinner, winding up at an upscale Chinese spot. We order our waiter's suggestions (minus the cashew chicken, because death trap), then spend dinner talking about *Bite the Hand* presentation plans. I can tell from his voice how ready he is for this step. Every emphatic idea that pours from his lips wraps me in a bind, tighter and tighter, suffocating until it transforms into something like hope.

He's just too infectious of a person. His smile is practically a welcome mat, and when he starts talking, everything narrows down to the sound of his voice, the shape of his words. At least for me it does. Without even trying, Alex is making me believe this launch plan will really work. Because what other possible conclusion is there?

As we head back to my apartment, the sky an inky blot and the air frigid, I wrap my scarf around my neck and breathe warm air into it. Alex turns up the collar of his coat and shoves his bare hands deep in his pockets.

On a corner waiting for a streetlight to turn, he steps up behind me, wraps his arms around my waist. Tongue in cheek, he whispers, "I'll warm you up soon." When I twist and look up at him, his eyes are both scorched and laughing.

This is dating.

This is not dating.

This is dating.

This is not dating.

"What job will you do after *Bite the Hand* launches?" I ask. *After, not if.* "Will you work for the editor in chief?" My voice is faint, half stolen by the wind.

Alex shakes his head and tugs on the belt loop of my coat to pull me across the street with him. "I technically could, but I'll probably find something else by next summer."

I frown. "Like, a different job at LC?"

"A different job, not at LC."

"Oh," I whisper.

This is not dating.

"They'll need more staff on the editorial and IT side," Alex reasons. "Which isn't my area of expertise. And I've got friends in Silicon Valley that could use the project management help."

I scoff. "You weren't kidding."

"About what?"

"About your living situation being ephemeral."

Alex looks at me, the lines between his eyebrows drawing together as we start climbing the stairs of my building. "That's not always by choice."

"This sounds like a choice. One year, and you're out the door? How long will your next job last, six months?"

"Maybe." His voice is too calm. It's unnerving. "This was a project-oriented position. Project complete, job over. And anyway, why does it matter to you? You'll be in London."

The crazy thing about it—the weirdest, most bizarre part—is that the more I learn about Alex, the more certain I am that I have to go.

He treats me like a boomerang, pulling me close to whisper against my heart about what I need to experience myself before flinging me out into the wind. I'm even surer of London now than I was sitting in that HR meeting with Molly last August, and Alex Harrison is, without a doubt, part of the reason why. But it doesn't change my confusion over why he thinks of himself as rootless, untethered, when that's not the way he wants to be. He got the rose of Sharon tattoo as a reminder that some things *can* be permanent. So why doesn't he give this city longer than ten months?

The only thing I can figure is he's chasing something that keeps slipping through his fingers.

I unlock the door to my apartment and step inside. "I just don't want you to screw yourself over, getting a reputation as a one-and-done kind of employee."

Alex shrugs off his coat and rubs at his forehead. "What you're describing is a very legitimate occupation known as freelancing."

I frown. "Is this because of your dad?" I ask. "Are you . . . disappointed he's not part of the company anymore?"

Alex pushes his hands through his hair, loosening the black strands. "Of course I'm disappointed," he says, voice like gravel. "There's no question part of me took this job with the hopes that Robert could be a different kind of role model for me, if not the father I deserved. But his resignation isn't why I'm planning to move on. That's just who I am, Case. It's in my nature to want a new diversion."

This is definitely, no mistaking it, not dating.

I put my hands on either side of his face, anyway, because like it or not, this man has burrowed his way into my bones, and even if he hears something unrequited in my voice, I don't care so long as the right message reaches him.

"You are the kind of person people should bend over backward for to keep in their lives, Alex." My fingers trace along his jawline, past his cheeks, up to the corners of his brown eyes. "Your aunt and your cousins see that, and so does Freddy, and so do I. It's a real fucking shame Robert won't bend for you, but that's *his* shame to bear, not yours."

His thumb grazes my wrist. "All I heard," he says, "was something about you bending over for me."

I laugh, and he tugs me into a hug. "Seriously, though," he nearly growls. "Thank you, Simba. Thank you for being a person I can trust with all my heartbreaking, brutal truths."

I press my lips to his neck. "I'd trust you with mine. I'll give you one right now."

"Okay," he says, voice cracking, hands grazing my waist. "Give me one heartbreaking, brutal truth of yours."

There is an acquisition on the table, and it might ruin you—

"I only like change when I get to see it coming," I admit.

"No wonder you hate surprise parties," he jokes, his voice going straight into my ear. I laugh weakly, and he tilts my head up toward his. "I can tell you with one hundred percent confidence that what's happening between us is going to change," he says. "It'll have to, at some point. But just because it's not permanent doesn't mean it's not important."

We kiss, and I feel like I'm pouring myself into him. It's been nineteen days since we last did this, but every single one was its own marathon. I drink in the taste and smell of him: butter mint on his tongue, crisp deodorant, clean linen, orange hand soap from the restaurant bathroom. Alex hauls me against his body, lifts my feet off the ground. My mouth slides against his in a harmony that carries musical chords I never learned. I don't know how I can kiss him right now and envision a future where this all stops.

"I think of you," Alex tells me. His voice is already husky against my neck. I pull him back toward my bedroom. "At work, on vacation, at home." His hands run over my chest, down my stomach. He grips my ass, groaning lightly.

"I think of you, too. All the time."

"All the time." He shakes his head. "It's a problem."

"Agreed."

Alex lifts my shirt over my head. "What's the solution?"

I yank at his belt. "This, probably."

Seconds later, he's crawling up the length of my naked body on my bed, and the sight of him like that makes my eyes roll back in my skull.

He kisses me through every thrum of pleasure between us, and I don't know how to process how *right* it all feels, how sturdy, how perfect, when I know whatever this is has an expiration date. It will end. Signed, sealed, and delivered by the very nature of who we are.

If my heart were a patched-together thing, refurbished from a relationship that chipped at it slowly, Alex is here now with glue, and later with a hammer. He is healing my heart, and he is breaking it.

A while later, while he feathers kisses over my rib cage, I say, "You think it's a good idea. Don't you."

He looks up at me through thick lashes. Asks hoarsely, "What's a good idea?"

"London," I scrape out.

He presses his lips against the hollow between my breasts. "Yes, I think it's a good idea."

I already knew the answer, because I know who Alex is and what he believes about the world, but my eyes still flutter closed hearing it. "Why?"

He lies down beside me, tucks my hair behind my ear. "Primarily," he breathes against my skin, "because I can tell you want to do it, and I think you should always go after the things you want in life, the things that make you happy." His hand grabs my thigh and hooks it up around his leg. "Secondly—"

"Secondarily," I correct. "If you're going for consistency."

Alex's nose catches on mine. "I'm going to secondarily throttle you."

I bite the inside of my cheek and whisper, "Continue."

He draws loose, lazy circles on my hip bone and stares at his fingers, entranced. "I think it'll be good for you."

My eyebrows pull up as I exhale a single breath of laughter. "Good for me how? So I can expand my uncultured, limited worldview?"

He rolls his eyes. "That's not remotely what I meant." His body moves on top of me, elbows pushing into the mattress. "You're open-minded, and curious, and hungry to explore, which is the best place to start in my opinion. Not that I'm the gatekeeper of worldliness or anything."

"Then what?" I mumble, turning my face to the side. He follows me, trying to steal a kiss. "So I can do something absurdly fucking cliché like find myself?"

Alex grins against my lips. "Maybe."

"Wait." My body stiffens. He uses the opportunity to slide his hands down my arms, loosely pinning my wrists to the mattress. "Really? You don't think I know who I am?"

"I think there are parts of yourself you don't fully know yet. Especially the part that doesn't just *let* change happen, but that *wants* it to happen. I think you're starting to realize you don't need as much safety as you used to need."

I frown, deeply disturbed by the poignancy of his psychoanalysis. "Well, who the hell are you, then?" I ask.

Alex laughs. "A guy in your bed doing his level best to worship your body. Fuck if I know the rest right now."

"Then how come *I'm* supposed to know?"

"You're *not*," Alex groans, still laughing. "Never mind. It's not that deep."

I harrumph, rolling our bodies so I land on top of him. "You're being difficult."

"Me?" His hands settle on my waist. "*You* brought this up."

It's annoying that I know what he means—about me finally wanting change to happen. Moving to New York was the most unsteady I've felt since I was little. Conquering that fear of the unknown, mastering it, unlocked something inside me I haven't been able to tamp down since. Not only that, but it's brought me this awareness—this *knowing*—of Mom and her choices. Completely of my own will, I'm making the same ones, and I think that's the reason I'm so close to cracking open what she always wanted for me.

I lay my head on Alex's chest and listen for the sound of his heartbeat. It quickens, then evens out again. His fingers stroke my hair.

"Tell me things," I say.

"What things?" he murmurs.

"Stories." I close my eyes and gulp. "Just . . . you know." I don't finish my thought.

Alex clears his throat. "What do you want to hear about?"

"Go chronologically. That's how stories work."

"Not always," he muses. The vibration in his voice hums against my cheek. "Sometimes stories happen in reverse, or they're told out of order."

His words trigger a half-formed thought: that *our* stories are happening in reverse. Maybe it was inevitable we'd cross paths eventually. It feels like we're traveling the same road from opposite ends. When Alex was born, the stuff that made up his soul had already been scattered into a million pieces. He never knew any existence but how to be everywhere at once, and only now is he figuring out what he means when he says the word "home." But I was born in a barely cracked eggshell, careful with my steps, terrified I'd falter. Taking my ever-loving time to learn how far and for how long I can bear to go.

I smile sadly, cheeks pinching up against his skin. "Okay, then. Tell me stories however you want."

"What if I want to go chronologically?"

"Now who's being difficult."

"Still you, Simba." He nestles his head deeper into the pillow. "Anyway, here's a story about the first sweet potato I ever ate from a street vendor and how it made me into the man I am today."

He paints me a picture of his childhood: waddling barefoot through a wood-floored apartment, toy in one hand, green crayon in the other. His mother, always at her desk, hair in a bun, a steaming cup of tea on the coaster, writing pieces for whoever wanted them about a single Korean American woman who grew up in Queens and saw South Korea for the first time at age twenty-eight.

"Did you ever get to read anything she wrote?" I ask.

"A few pieces my aunt hung on to before we moved to Seoul. The rest are probably recycled coffee filters by now."

Alex describes their upper-middle-class lifestyle, supplied by a father he only ever saw in sporadic bursts. He tells me he remembers his parents smiling at each other, but sometimes fighting, too. He never knew what any of it was about. What he knew was he and his mom spoke English at home and Korean in public, and he loved baked sweet potatoes so much, it became the only way his mother could console him if he was the slightest bit ornery.

Her name was Charlotte.

Alex tells me about the Korea International School where he went for elementary. How he hates to think about it because it's tainted with all the sting of his mom getting ill, of her dying. But Charlotte Yoon never let Alex see her at her sickest. She never prepared him to expect a world without her, and it still makes him angry to this day.

He tells me about her funeral in Queens. His aunt, cousins, a grandfather who isn't alive anymore, and strangers whose faces he never raised his eyes far enough to see. For years after that, he felt guilty every time he loved his aunt's cooking because his mother's had always tasted like ash.

I hear about the moment Alex got back to the States. He was at the airport being shepherded by a flight attendant when his father appeared before him just like he'd done a dozen times before, and said this:

"'I can't be the type of parent she was,'" Alex repeats for me, his eyes glazed with memory. "'But I swear I will never turn my back on you.'" He shifts beneath me. "And he lived up to it."

There are stories about boarding school. Pulling back from speaking Korean. Figuring things out about money, how much of the stuff Alex had tangential access to. Researching his father on the internet. Staring at a picture of his wife, blond and white and prim faced, and feeling confused, even disoriented, and kind of angry for her in a way that surprised him.

He tells me about his first kiss at Choate with a student who was two years older than him.

"Were you popular?" I ask.

"There were hardly enough students to know."

"So, unpopular."

Beneath me, he scoffs. "Adriana in the eleventh grade certainly didn't think so."

At some point, I nod off, lulled into the bright black nothingness of slumber between Alex's recounting of a heated classroom debate on Maine versus Connecticut lobster rolls and subsequent memories of his freshman year at Harvard. His voice bleeds into my dreams, and I'm on a plane to London, but he's there, too. I whine because my acoustic guitar doesn't fit in the overhead compartment. Alex laughs and tells me to buy the guitar its own ticket.

When I wake up, I'm tucked under my covers, head on a pillow, and Alex is gone.

CHAPTER TWENTY-FIVE

On the day before Thanksgiving, the blocks closest to Grand Central Station are more claustrophobic than a Bassnectar concert. I'm holding a bouquet of roses. Miriam's got a fir-scented candle and some peppermint chocolate in a shopping bag—welcome gifts for my parents to make their midtown hotel a little homier, since they seemed disappointed when I told them staying at our place was logistically out of the question.

My phone is empty of new messages from Jerry or Dad. I frown, feeling like an anxious parent picking my child up from summer camp. I try to track them on Find My Friends but give up once their contacts start jumping around.

"Remind me why we're meeting your folks at Grand Central?" Miriam asks me.

"They wanted to arrive in the city like people do in movies. Which is absurd, because they traveled by plane and took an Uber here from LaGuardia."

She snorts. "That's adorable."

"Get this." I throw her a grin. "At first, they assumed I was picking them up from the airport. *The* airport, as in, they didn't even know which one until they double-checked their flight itinerary."

Miriam cackles, doubling over and clutching her stomach. "Didn't you sell your car before you moved here?"

"Yep," I confirm, popping my consonant for emphasis. "I had to shoot their plan down on account of the fact that hell will freeze over before I take a one-hundred-dollar Uber just to meet someone at baggage claim. Walking to their hotel from here was their next suggestion."

Miriam shakes her head. "The drama."

"Gotta love 'em."

"You realize your dad's going to write a country song about New York City."

I groan. She's right. Holding my hands up in prayer, I mutter, "Lord, have mercy on the country music industry. Preserve the sanctity of its lyrics about dirt roads and summer nights and cold beers in the truck bed of a Chevy. This might sound sarcastic, heavenly father, but I couldn't be more sincere. Don't let Marty Maitland ruin a good thing."

"Amen!" Miriam shouts, pumping a fist in the air.

Inside the terminal, we dart like minnows between New York's railway-inclined holiday travelers. "Jerry!" I shout when he picks up the phone. "Where are you?"

"Heading in! Sorry we're late, I had to yank your dad away from a busker with an extra guitar on the sidewalk outside."

I laugh, grabbing Miriam's hand as we push through the throng. My eyes smart the closer we get, and then I don't just hear Jerry's voice on the phone. I see him.

He's grinning ear to ear, and Dad is behind him, and I have a full-on breakdown right there in Grand Central Station during the chaos of holiday rush hour. Dad's hair has more salt than pepper now. Jerry got new glasses. I haven't laid my eyes on them in almost two years, and the time apart hits me in the chest right now, asking me to pay the toll of time and distance and whatever self-preserving walls I constructed from a half-assed belief that I had to be who I was without them.

Tears stream down my face as I get swallowed into a hug. Dad ruffles my hair. All southern twang and long vowels, he says, "Hey, honey!"

He and Jerry smell like old leather and I breathe it in like a balm.

When I turn around, Miriam's crying, too (fourteen years of friendship will do that to you). She and I hug, because why the fuck not, and then she and Jerry and Dad hug.

"Your father did really well on the plane," Jerry tells me. "He only cut off my circulation three times and yelled at a very small flight attendant once!"

We all four walk to the hotel where they're staying, just a handful of blocks away, near Bryant Park. They both gape in audible wonder at the Chrysler Building, and I can't even find it in me to make fun of them because my first trip to New York was magical, too. While they settle in and freshen up, Miriam and I have a drink at the hotel bar. When they come back down, Dad's wearing his cowboy boots and Jerry has on plaid. They're adorable.

There's a round of shots, something made in Kentucky, and then we're off in a cab, cruising toward SoHo for the prix fixe menu at Balthazar.

"Thanks for letting me tag along," Miriam says.

"Are you working tomorrow?" Jerry asks her.

"Yes, and let me tell you, there's no place more interesting than the emergency room on Thanksgiving Day."

At Balthazar, Dad makes a disgruntled comment about how close all the tables are, and why must he be subjected to the neighbors' conversations about French conservatism and skin boils, left to right respectively? But that's the only hitch in our otherwise perfect evening. We drain several bottles of wine, devour our soups du jour and birds du domestique and pies du pumpkin, catching up about life up here, life down there, the past, the present, and yes—the future.

"Sorry," Dad says, shaking his head. "You want to move to *London*? Christ, Casey, is this not far enough already?"

"Um," Miriam says, standing. "Bathroom."

I can see how this comes across to him—me avoiding Nashville for two years, then moving to another continent. "Dad, it's not like that. I'm not running away from my family forever like Mom."

The hurt is etched between his brows. "Then what's it like, Case? Help me understand this so I don't spiral into thinking I've chased you away."

"You *haven't*," I say, grabbing his hand. "I just . . . I just *want* to, you know? And, like, I'm surprised as shit that I want to, don't get me wrong. I'm still the same kid who made you pick me up halfway through sleepaway camp. But also, I'm scared this feeling will leave if I don't just . . . act on it. And it's different than Mom moving here, because I swear to you, I will be just as excited to come home again, every single time."

He leans forward and narrows his eyes at me. After what feels like the familiar prelude to all my childhood scoldings, Dad says, "When you visit your gran—which you *will* do, because she is your mother's mother—you will not let that tiresome woman change a single thing about you."

Gran's never been Dad's biggest fan. Back when my grandfather was still alive, they refused to attend my parents' wedding, then spent years trying to convince Mom to leave Dad and bring me back to London so they could raise me "right." I have this memory of Gran at the funeral accusing Dad of failing Mom, even though I know for a fact he bent over backward to get her the healthcare she needed. That was pretty much the last time either of us heard from Gran. The only reason I know she's still kicking is because I check to make sure on Grandfather's firm's website now and then.

"I promise," I tell Dad. "That I'll visit, and that I won't let her change me."

"I mean it, Casey, you better come back to me exactly like this. No High Street Burberry, no shit-talking Meghan Markle—"

"Okay, but what if it's vintage Burberry?"

He laughs, and Jerry makes a motion with his hand, and then Miriam reappears, sitting back down. "If you got anything from your mother, kid, it's the clothes."

I cock my head. "I thought you said I was her total opposite."

The glass of red wine pauses halfway to his mouth. "Did I? Hmm. That's not true at all." He sips and looks at me. "She knew her own mind, and so do you. I think she'd be proud of you right now. And I think she'd also be touched."

"Well." Jerry grabs the bottle of wine to top off his glass. "When does this London excursion begin?"

"Summer," I declare firmly, speaking it into existence. Since I spoke with Alex about the BTH presentation last week, my confidence in both our futures has been renewed. "That's all I really know so far."

"And you've decided on this?"

"Unless she falls in love!" Miriam jumps in.

I shoot her a dirty look. "The only girl at this table who's *in love* is—"

"Me," Miriam sighs. "With this pie." She shoves a huge scoop of pumpkin and whipped cream into her mouth.

"I love you, Casey," Dad says. "But my love falls *just* short of flying across the Atlantic for the holidays."

"I know, Dad."

"You remember how I feel about the open ocean."

"I remember, Dad."

"It's too deep. I don't trust what's down there, and I don't trust what secrets the water breathers are keeping."

"I can't tell if you're being sarcastic or not," Miriam says.

"He's dead serious," I tell her. "It's Marty Maitland's fatal flaw."

"We prayed for Greta Thunberg every night of her sea voyage," Jerry notes.

"Good name for a song," Dad says, stroking his beard. "Marty Maitland's fatal flaw."

A half laugh, half groan spills out of me. "If you really believe that, you're already jonesing. Check, please."

Miriam goes to the hospital after breakfast in a flurry of scrubs and scarves. Dad, Jerry, and I bundle up in an equal number of layers, heading toward the madhouse that is the Macy's Thanksgiving Day Parade. We traipse about Manhattan, guzzling Irish coffees between mittened fingertips, huffing excitedly under our breath as we walk, watching our words frost into the air. When we find the perfect spot near Central Park, we ooh and aah appreciatively at all our favorite floats.

"Did you do this last year?" Dad asks me.

"Fuck no."

There are baton-twirling, leotard-wearing people who leave a trail of red glitter on the pavement: "They've *got* to be cold," Dad mutters. There is a giant Olaf balloon smiling down at us that's more frightening than it is endearing: "That the joker who likes warm hugs?" I laugh and snap a picture of Olaf to send to Alex, who promptly tells me he sometimes watches *Frozen* just to feel something.

"Is that Zack Travis?" Jerry asks, catching the low tenor of a country singer as the next float comes into earshot.

Dad bursts out laughing. "I think it is."

"Oh my God." I touch my mittens to my mouth. "Is he singing . . ."

The lyrics float toward us, clearer now. *Rollin', tumblin', stumblin' down that wretched road, the road to heartbreak, I'm not sure I'll ever wake up again, but I don't mind—*

"She can break my heart anytime!" I scream. "Oh my God, he would be singing your least favorite song—"

"Ridiculous lyrics," Dad mutters. "Repetitive chords. Someone should have a word with Zack's songwriter."

I take a video of him smiling awkwardly as Zack's float passes by, post it to my Instagram story with the caption *IYKYK*. Thirty minutes later, I've got a handful of replies from friends, a handful more from confused strangers who follow me only because of YouTube, and a DM from Alex: *WTF, even I know that song and I've never even been to the South!*

In a state of utter confusion, I call him immediately.

"Casey?"

"You've never been to the South?!" I screech.

"Um." There's shuffling on the other end of the line. Someone's dog barking. "No?"

"What the fuck, Alex?"

"Who's Alex?" Jerry asks. I duck away, pressing a mitten to my opposite ear so I can hear Alex better.

"Miami?" I ask. "New Orleans? Austin?"

"No, no, and no," Alex says. "To quote Casey Maitland, it just never happened for me."

"Charleston. Atlanta."

"Wait, I've been to the Atlanta airport!"

I smack a hand to my forehead. "All right. This is a thing I need time to process. Goodbye, Alex."

He laughs, and I want to capture the sound, steal it from my speaker and put it in my pocket for later. "Goodbye, Casey. Happy Thanksgiving."

We go shopping at Hudson Yards on Black Friday, which is a logistic disaster, but Dad gets a new leather satchel from an obscure kiosk in the mall, and Jerry thinks the Vessel is the coolest, so I count it as a win. Saturday, we museum-hop—MoMA, the Met, the Museum of Natural History—flying through them at rapid speed, the only apparent way to keep three successive museums interesting. It's my first time visiting any of them, and although I was skeptical at first, I've come around to the idea that maybe there's something to be said for a tourist's approach to the island.

On Sunday we visit Times Square, then hole up in the M&M's store while we wait out the frozen sleet pouring down on the city. When Dad lines up to buy our selection of treats, Jerry asks to take my picture in front of the rainbow M&M wall. Not *our* picture, *my* picture. I balefully agree, standing in front of it during a break in children, hands stiffly by my sides, feeling like a world-class idiot.

When Jerry lowers his cell phone, he says, "You look happier."

"Of course I do," I retort. "Five minutes ago, I was slipping on ice and trying to dodge someone who wanted to sell me a walking tour, and now I'm literally smiling for your camera."

Jerry shakes his head. "Happier than you were in college. I couldn't tell then, which I'm loath to admit, but I can tell now because the difference is kind of astounding."

My eyebrows draw together. "Am I really that easy to read?"

Jerry smiles softly. "Yes, darling."

Still a thing I need to work on. Must get that into my bullet journal. *Learn to be more mysterious. Don't shout your emotions through facial expressions!*

"Is it because of the city, or the job, or the boy named Alex?" Jerry asks.

All of the above, my mind supplies. But really, those are just inputs, variables for an equation that adds up to the sum total of whatever's in my eyes Jerry noticed when I smile. I'm the one who made the decision to include them—the job, the city, the boy named Alex.

I push my damp hair out of my face and smile again. "Honestly, Jer . . . I think it's because of me."

CHAPTER TWENTY-SIX

I manage to spend all of Thanksgiving break carefree, but the following three weeks are indomitably overtaken by presentation prep. Don blocks off a four-hour chunk every afternoon on my calendar so we can fine-tune the financial components of the presentation. Most days, we go until seven at night or later, and sometimes Fari helps, too. She understands *some* of the urgency, but only because I told her what Molly said, about the success of this project correlating to what role I'd be a good fit for in London.

That's not even to say how much Alex's career is riding on it. For all the work I'm doing, he has me beat a hundred times over. He stays at the office late into the night, collaborating with Gus and the rest of their team to hammer out the bulk of the presentation: advertising hopefuls, lead contributor profiles, social media statistics, brand identity, graphic design, marketing pushes, growth strategies. The list goes on.

The convivial, outgoing, could-talk-to-a-wall Alex shuts off completely. Whenever I visit him on thirty-seven (under the guise of a financial question, but really so I can check on his mental health), he's all business, wrapped up in a fog of caffeine, Adderall, and a wrinkled shirt he likely slept in.

The night before the presentation, we're together in his war room cleaning everything up when a ding from his phone catches both of our attention. Out of the corner of my eye I spot the name *Robert Harrison* visible, signaling a new email.

"He's . . ." I blink. "Emailing you?"

Alex glances at his phone and nods. "Yeah. He's helping with . . . this." He gestures around the war room vaguely: notes on his whiteboard, the posters pinned to each wall. "He loved your slides, by the way. You did a great job designing that."

"You—you *showed* him the presentation?" I ask.

He stiffens at my expression. "Yeah."

"On your work email?" I all but cry. I'm more *worried* than I am *angry*. I know this girl who leaked her company's private sales data, and now she can't get a job in the whole industry because IT outed her.

"No, my personal email. Alex-loves-soccer-at-gmail-dot-com," he says with a smirk.

But that's even worse, because it means he *knew* he was doing something wrong. Alarm bells are going off in my head, which means they're going off on my face, too.

"What's the big deal?" Alex asks. "Robert offered to help, and I figured, why not?"

"Because he's not an employee anymore, Alex, that's why not. It's privileged information. It's *valuable* information."

He chuckles, but it sounds strained. "I get how it looks when you put it like that, but . . . this company is in his *blood*, Case. He's not just any old ex-employee. He was the CEO. He was the chairman."

"Well, did you mention it to Gus?"

Alex smirks, his voice coming out placating. "Today, Gus did nothing but speed-walk in circles while he talked to his West Coast freelancers on the phone. I think we exchanged three words and two grunts. But sure, I'll tell him if you want me to."

Then he ruffles my hair and kisses my forehead and fails to corroborate my impression that there's anything to be skeptical of. In fact, he looks so . . . *hopeful* about his father's interest, I worry that if I say one more thing, it might hurt him in a way I don't want to be responsible for.

So, I drop it.

I'm walking out of the war room a few minutes later, hands full of poster-size paper headed for the recycling bin, when Alex says, "Casey?"

I turn back. "Yep?"

For a couple long seconds he doesn't say a word, just looks me up and down, letting his eyes search me for the first time in weeks.

We've seen each other just twice outside of work since Thanksgiving. Once at his place, when Alex fell asleep halfway through *Parasite*, and once at mine, when we'd both had a craving for Sour Patch Kids (berry flavor, *not* tropical), but he fell asleep before I even tore open the bag, his legs on the floor, back resting against the foot of my mattress. I lugged him under the covers and followed him into slumber, but three hours later I woke up to the feeling of him hard, of me wanting him, and we made delirious, messy love tangled in sheets at three in the morning.

There's something about being tangled up in another person's limbs, half asleep, that can feel more intimate than just about anything.

Alex's gaze shifts from the war room whiteboard to my face. "When this is over," he rasps, eyes like storm clouds fit to burst, "can I have you for, like, forty-eight uninterrupted hours?"

My cheeks flush. Alex notices. His mouth pulls up, revealing traces of amusement behind the urgency that's been driving him forward for days on end.

"I don't think I've spent forty-eight uninterrupted hours with anyone since I was a kid," I admit. "Not even Miriam or my parents."

"You like alone time," he says. Not a question.

"Sometimes," I admit. He waits, silently asking me for more words. "Did you ever go to sleepaway camp?" I ask.

"Does boarding school count?"

"Not if there was air-conditioning."

"Ah," he says. "Then no."

"Well, I did, once, when I was twelve. It was in Missouri, and it was, like, this arts and crafts camp thing? You know, decoupage and whittling and songwriting and scrapbooking classes, all interspersed with pool time that gave me an ear infection and Bible school that was pretty progressive, looking back, but anyway. I hated it."

Alex laughs hoarsely. "Why did you go to arts and crafts camp?"

"Dad thought it would be good for me." I roll my eyes. "Miriam was doing an adventure camp in Colorado, and I didn't have any other friends, which worried him, so it was either that or sports camp, and when it comes to art, I can at least *pretend* to care."

He laughs again. "How long was it?"

"It was supposed to be for a month, but I made Dad pick me up after two weeks."

"I am picturing," he says, arms stretching behind his head, straining the fabric of his shirt, the seam riding up past his stomach, "a twelve-year-old fuming silently at a picnic table under an awning, cutting up magazine pages from an old *Frame* issue to glue back together. In the background, there is a cappella, and also, someone is making a friendship bracelet."

"Okay, you definitely went to sleepaway camp."

"Swear I didn't."

I smile. "Anyway. It wasn't even the activities I hated, or the people. They were cool, and the low-stakes crafting was fine. But really, I just hated that I never got to be alone. We all slept in this giant tepee, and I never felt like I could breathe, you know? When I go on a trip, I just want to be able to breathe and relax. Otherwise I get—" I rub at my side uncomfortably. "It makes me, um, anxious."

"Okay. Noted." Alex looks at me thoughtfully. "What about forty-eight uninterrupted minutes? I'm begging."

I laugh. "No, I want to. More than forty-eight minutes, I mean. Miriam's schedule has been insane, and honestly, I've been alone a lot recently."

"Yeah." He shifts in his seat. Sighs. "Me too."

The day of the presentation, I wear a navy blazer from Chico's that Jerry's mom gave me last Hanukkah and pointy, uncomfortable black shoes. My hair is tied back in a serious-girl bun. I'm not speaking in front of the stakeholders, but I get to be in the room, and I want to look the picture of professionalism. Meanwhile, Alex is wearing a blue tie with white snowflakes, and Christmas tree socks beneath his slacks. I catch glimpses of them as he paces in the boardroom. His hair is combed, suit pressed, and other than the bags under his eyes, he looks perfect. That first-day smile is fixed on his face.

He makes his way over to me. "Nervous?" I ask.

The gold in his irises is warmed up today, almost sparkling. "Not for this. Never for stuff like this."

I want to ask what, in that case, he *does* get nervous about, but the boardroom doors swing open, and Dougie Dawson walks inside.

I'm halfway expecting him to look at Alex, grimace, and escape to the other side of the room, but when he spots us both, his eyes light up and he comes straight over.

And then he . . . smiles. *Gleefully.*

"Alex Harrison." Dougie sticks out his hand, the gruff tenor of his voice slipping over me like a warning. "I'm looking forward to seeing what you've been working on."

Bewildered, Alex accepts Dougie's handshake. "It took a village," he says—probably reminding him that if he tanks this project, it'll devastate more people than Alex.

"It really is a shame your father couldn't stick around to see this," Dougie says, his tongue running over the top row of his yellow teeth. "Guess you'll have to settle for me instead."

Alex doesn't say a word, but his shoulders square and his posture straightens. He cocks his head just slightly. The stare he aims at Dougie is so intense that Dougie is the one to blink first.

"Like I said." Dougie starts to back away. "Looking forward."

Once he's out of earshot, Alex turns his stare on me. "He didn't even acknowledge you," he grumbles. "I'm sorry."

"That is not a thing I'm going to lose sleep over."

"He can't screw with this," Alex mutters, cracking his neck. "It's a decision by majority vote, in the end." *But they're voting on something else entirely.*

I still don't know whether Dougie's enthusiasm is a good omen or the nail in our coffins. He could've had a change of heart; maybe he's looking to be persuaded. Either that, or he's indulging us as his last act as CEO.

As we settle into our seats, and the projector cues up, the secret truth vibrating around the room is also written on half the faces I read.

The presentation goes like this:

As a shoo-in for editor in chief and the original genius behind *Bite the Hand,* Gus talks first—about the brand's roots, intent, and niche. Editorial stuff, writerly stuff, contributors and content, website tech, distribution platforms and frequency.

Branching from Gus are Saanvi and Amanda, who talk about social media—to the fear and chagrin of everyone in the room who didn't understand what Gus meant when he said, "No print, ever. I wouldn't even call it a magazine. I'm not joking." And funny enough, it's not an age demarcation between the people who buy in and the people who don't, because the oldest woman in the room is the wife of the late Harold Cooper himself, a man who was one half of the original duo who founded Little Cooper. She watches YouTube, made obvious when she said hello to me at the door, followed by "I also have quite a few allergies! What part of Tennessee are you from?"

Then it's Don with the financials. Simply put, he slays.

And then there's Alex, who takes it home. He talks about meaning, purpose, how *Bite the Hand* will help give Little Cooper the edge it desperately needs.

"Be the change you want to see in the world," Alex says, strolling casually in front of the projector. "An overused platitude mainly reserved for Pinterest boards and the HomeGoods sale aisle, but if Little Cooper was a family, which I'd like to think it is, then *Bite the Hand* is your ten-year-old kid who wants to reach for the stars. And that kid deserves the best chance at success, which in this instance means an income statement, revenue stream, and editor in chief."

He says it with all the brimming confidence of a Harvard-educated young man who knows what he's talking about, who *gets* it, and it shows. By the time Alex is through, I'm speechless. And insanely turned on.

After, Tracy Garcia and Harold Cooper's wife start clapping. I sneak a glance at Dougie, and here's the thing: he looks genuinely won over. He even nods at Alex congenially, who meets his eyes, then looks away—at me—and winks.

All in all, it's a freaking grand stroke. Nobody shits the bed, and everyone important seems convinced a million times over. When us underlings walk out of that room to give the board and execs time to deliberate, a raw and dangerous hope has already started to bloom in my chest.

Maybe Dougie's gotten a second wind.

Maybe he hates Robert enough to make LC profitable again, just to prove he can.

Maybe we're all going to get what we want.

CHAPTER TWENTY-SEVEN

In the Urban Outfitters near our office building, I say to Alex, "I don't understand how you're not more anxious."

He grabs a Santa hat off the rack and fits it onto my head, pulls it down over my eyes, then adjusts it to match my hairline, tapping the white pom-pom so it jingles. I peer up at his face, which is tired but strangely serene. His eyelashes almost touch his cheekbones every time he looks down at me like this. "Nothing more I can do at this point," he answers calmly.

"That's no excuse to be mentally fucking balanced right now?"

He doesn't *understand* what's at stake, and I know why—because I'm being forced to keep it from him—but how could I ever *not* be frustrated by his blasé attitude right now? With the holidays coming up, we may not find out the board's decision for *weeks*. I'm going to be a nervous wreck until I know the outcome, and really, if I liked unknown variables, I'd be an algebra teacher.

Alex's eyelashes go lower, and his hands travel down to my hips.

"I love it when you curse. The whole sentence that brackets it gets really southern."

"I don't have an accent."

He arches an eyebrow. "You do when you're gearing up to say a curse word." After a moment of consideration, he adds, "And when you're hammered."

"You wouldn't know a southern accent if it hit you in the face."

Alex claps back by speaking a full sentence of Korean to me.

I scowl. "Point made, asshole."

He laughs and walks away.

We're buying costumes for an ugly Christmas sweater party, hosted by one of Alex's Harvard friends who is apparently an assistant art curator at MoMA (congrats to her). He texted me about it this afternoon, a non sequitur to my hours-earlier check-in about how he was feeling after this morning. I said yes to the party out of pity, thinking he'd need a distraction, but after the past half hour, I realize I've been duped.

Duped into my worst nightmare—a party where I don't know a soul except the most social person invited. He's going to leave my side immediately to catch up with his college friends, and I'm going to have to get drunk and suck it up.

He pulls a multicolored sweater vest with tinsel off the rack. "Do you like this?"

"Sure," I grumble. "Now, can you *please* tell me how you really feel about the wait?"

Something flashes in Alex's eyes—annoyance, and possibly fear—and that's when I finally get it, one sentence too late: this is him coping.

"It's out of my hands." His voice cracks harshly, resolve breaking. "I did the best I could. I can't control what other people think, how they react. I can't *make* people care, okay?"

"Okay," I whisper. "I'm sorry."

He drops the sweater and pinches the bridge of his nose. After a second, he reaches out to grab my hand and pulls me in, threading his fingers into my hair and slipping his arm under my blazer to clutch at my waist. "No, I'm sorry. I just . . ." He exhales. "I know myself. I *have* to let it go now, or it's going to ruin me later. Holding on to things I wish I could change never got me anywhere."

I get this mental flash of Alex building himself a castle. Walls of rough, impenetrable stone stacked together in a fortress to protect himself. But at the end of it all, he leaves the front door wide open. Waiting for someone to knock.

In this moment, I want to be whatever it is he needs most.

"Do you *have* to let it go like Elsa had to let it go?" I ask. "Because if so, might I recommend . . ." I step backward, out of his arms, and point to the *Frozen* costumes hanging beside the reindeer antlers.

His face twists. "I *maybe* could have fit into that dress when I was six. Isn't this a store for preteens?"

"But you love *Frozen*!" I protest. "At least get the Olaf T-shirt."

Alex rolls his eyes. "I can't believe I told you about that."

"About how you watch *Frozen* just to feel something?"

He glowers. "At least I don't compulsively order a dessert I don't actually want every time the waiter brings out a dessert menu without asking me first."

My jaw drops. "I never told you that!"

He smirks. "Brijesh told me. I asked him about your fatal flaw, and that's the answer I got."

I blanch, betrayed. "Why were you asking about my fatal flaw?"

"So I can exploit it." He rolls his eyes. "Obviously."

In the end, I get a seven-dollar pleated maroon skirt, snowy-looking knee-highs, and a green button-down sweater. Alex gets that atrocious vest and the Santa hat.

We break up our subway trip to the Upper East Side with a stop in Koreatown—a small stretch of blocks near the Empire State

Building—and go to a barbecue spot, randomly selected by Alex based on nothing other than "gut instinct and the fact that a fifteen-minute wait feels promising but not daunting."

Inside, he makes me create a shared note on my phone, where I type out all my allergies. He considers them for a moment (sesame being the trickiest culprit), and then orders for both of us.

The meat comes out raw, and our waiter tells us about each selection before he cooks it on the hot plate in the middle of our table. It's kind of awkward at first, the waiter just standing there cooking while Alex and I watch, but eventually, Alex starts telling me about Seoul dining, regional Korean foods you can't get here, and American staples harder to come by over there. I'm shocked by the list of things he'd never heard of until he moved to Connecticut. The waiter listens in, too, offering up his own opinions, and at one point they both start slipping into Korean.

Then we receive the banchan, some of which I am familiar with (read: kimchi and cucumbers), some of which I am not (read: gamja salad). Truthfully, I've only had chain-restaurant Korean food before (read: bibimbap with steak and a fried egg on top), which I admitted to Alex on the subway here. Now he's watching me try everything, face attempting to conceal his curiosity, asking me if I'm still hungry and ordering more meats and banchan accordingly. Normally when I'm anxious about something, my appetite deserts me, but the food here is so amazing that I leave the place stuffed.

When we're through with dinner, he presses an unsolicited kiss to my temple.

"Why did you want me to come tonight?" I ask on the subway up to Lexington and Eighty-First. My fingers fiddle with the hem of my cheap skirt, already unraveling. "Also, should we do some sort of feature in *Bite the Hand* about the Christmas impact on fast fashion?"

Alex looks down at my fingers picking at loose threads. "I wanted you to come because I miss you," he says, and my stupid heart acts like it just inhaled a Red Bull vodka spiked with an espresso shot.

"I am both terrible at saying no to things and selfish, so this is my solution." He smiles at me apologetically. "And about holiday-driven fast fashion—I like it. You should pitch that to Gus."

I snort. "*You* should pitch it to Gus."

Alex shifts, facing me with his body. His thumb traces the shell of my ear. "You're doing it again," he murmurs.

"Doing what?"

"Acting like you're not an inspiration for people."

That's the first moment I ever think it: *I love you.* But it's splintered apart by the very next thought, crowding in to destroy the first: *Everybody loves him, you idiot, because he makes* everybody *feel like this.*

Regardless, I want to hold his words in my pocket, take them out when I'm feeling lonely or sad or boring.

Two minutes later, we step into the bitter December cold, and nervous anticipation takes root in my gut as Alex navigates us inside an apartment complex.

It has a doorman.

It has an elevator operator.

Motherfucker.

At the door to the apartment, Alex rests his hands on the varnished golden knob. "Don't leave my side, okay?" His tone is earnest.

"That's my line," I say.

Alex opens the door a crack. His throaty voice is underscored by a thrash of Christmas music within. "I think, by now, you and I are off script."

Well. I'll have to unpack *that* later between bouts of overthinking and eggnog.

The apartment is designed with chic furniture, ambient lighting, and an aesthetically muted color palette. It has things like Pampas grass sticking out of a floor vase and honest-to-goodness wall art. A white Christmas tree stands by the window. There is a counter full of drinks boasting top-shelf liquor and a tray of cookies from

Levain. The room is littered with people in their holiday best, all of whom turn to face us when we walk in the door thanks to the jingle bells someone hung on the handle.

"Oh Mylanta!" shouts a man in a red-and-white-striped jumpsuit. He smiles at us, mouth agape. "The rumors are true!"

"What rumors?" Alex asks.

"Didn't you read your own YouTube video comments?" says a woman wearing a SANTA'S HELPER T-shirt. (Personally, no, I do not read the comments. I have a modicum of self-preservation, thank you very much.) The petite woman strolls forward. "Honestly, guys," she says, gesturing between us. "The whole internet picked up on this."

"Hmm." Alex leans in to hug her. "Oops."

I am slightly more concerned about this revelation than Alex seems to be—particularly because if HR discovers whatever's going on between us, there will be *conversations,* and also because some random girl just clearly took our photo—but I sweep it under the rug so I can survive the next few minutes.

"Casey." Alex pulls me up beside him. "This is Erica, our host."

This introduction is followed by hugs and *thank you for having me*s and questions about what she can she get me to drink.

"Um, the Ho Ho Hot Toddy?" I say, reading off the list Erica has hung by the bar.

"I definitely want the Naughty or Spice," Alex says.

Erica scurries off, and then the introductions begin anew.

"Casey, this is Josh. We studied abroad together in Spain."

My eyes narrow at Alex. "I thought you studied in London?"

Patiently he says, "That was for a summer program. Spain was during my sophomore year."

"Of course it was," I reply with just a touch of sarcasm. Alex smirks.

I am then introduced to Josh's girlfriend, who is from Birmingham. She's very easy to talk to, says she loves southern sports rivalries, and asks how on earth I ever made Tennessee orange fashionable.

"I didn't," I reply, laughing, as Erica slips my drink into my hands and then vanishes again. "Did you go to Alabama or Auburn?"

"Dartmouth," she answers.

My cheeks turn as red as my skirt.

"Casey, this is Armand."

"Casey, this is Savannah."

My head is swimming.

Alex is wearing that first-day smile, the one that melts hearts and disarms even the most curmudgeonly. He listens, makes people feel heard. This is the opposite of Alex's fatal flaw. It's his best, shining trait, and honestly, it's addictive to watch.

"Casey, this is Sonja."

Sonja.

My brain short-circuits.

The girl Alex dated for three weeks when he was twenty-one!

She's tiny, with curly black hair and doe eyes that give her the look of someone who should be protected at all costs, and even though I'm positive she's shorter than me, right now she's wearing gargantuan heels that make my pointy work flats feel like training wheels.

"Hello." Her tone is smooth. When she leans in for a hug, heady perfume overwhelms me. I scrunch up my nose, trying to avoid a sneeze.

"Nice to meet you," I say, then—because the two drinks I've already downed were heavy on the booze—add, "How do you two know each other?"

Sonja turns her gaze on Alex with a knowing glint in her eye. Lips forming into a pursed smirk, she says, "We got close over winter break junior year. Alex kept me company in New Haven while my family was abroad. I even got to meet his dad! We ran into him during Christmas Day brunch at the club."

Green, corporeal envy slithers through me. She met his father at "the club"—the day after his birthday, which he and Sonja spent together—and I was shoved in Alex's weird brewery closet when his dad came calling.

He smiles tightly and rubs his thumb over my waist. He hasn't let go of me a single time since we walked in the door. Like we're tethered. "Yes. Good times. Anyway—"

"Casey," Sonja interrupts. "Your mug is empty. Come get another drink with me?"

She doesn't wait for my answer, just grabs my free hand and pulls me away from Alex, whose grip tightens before it disengages. I trail her to the kitchen counter (where there is legitimately a hired bartender in a Santa costume making drinks). We place our orders, and then Sonja asks me, "Are you really *with* him?"

"Um." I hope no one else is listening. "We haven't put labels on anything."

"Right." Sonja nods, like I've reassured something for her. "I mean, he's hot as fuck, and a great kisser"—I am dying inside— "but like, *so* different once you get to know him, right?"

It takes me a minute to process that she's genuinely asking. Not purposely riling me up, not being mean-spirited at all. After studying her face, looking for some hint of jealousy or a clue she's trying to one-up me, but finding no inkling of either, I conclude Sonja is simply trying to get to the bottom of something.

"Yeah," I reply, smiling. "He is."

"Totally. And then it's like, this isn't the person I thought I wanted to date?"

My smile drops. "Wait, what?"

But then Hostess Erica shouts, "Flip cup!" and I don't get my answer as I'm pulled into a drinking game that should honestly be illegal when Baileys Irish Cream and peppermint schnapps are involved. I bow out after only one round, then turn to look for Alex, finding him leaning against the back of a couch talking with someone. He spots me immediately, like maybe he'd been keeping an eye out, and beckons me over. When I reach him, his arm fixes right back around my waist. Tighter this time.

Once we're alone, I say, "Sorry I left you."

"It's okay." Alex squeezes my hip. "I just know you, and I wanted you to feel good about tonight."

A cascade of affection pours from my heart *straight* to my core, and all I want is to return the favor, give Alex whatever he needs to feel good right now. Suddenly I can feel all the places we're touching, the way his fingertips have worked under my sweater to play with the skin at my waist. I can feel every hour since the last time we made love, and they are tallying up my desire all at once.

I move between his legs. "I am having fun."

"Good. That's good." His hand skates up my arm, followed by goose bumps. "I suppose that means you're not ready to leave?" He's staring at my lips.

"Ready when you are." I lean forward, brushing up against him, letting our bodies remember.

"Ready," he practically groans.

He kisses me the minute we're out the door—on my peppermint-stained lips, then my cheeks and jaw and ears. He laughs lowly and picks me up, throwing me over his shoulder fireman-style, and carries me to the elevator down the hall. By the time we're inside it, the elevator operator has retired for the evening—which is for the best, because Alex is hard. He nudges me against the wall, hikes one of my legs up around him.

"This is what I imagine every time we're in that goddamn office elevator," he rumbles. "Even the first time, beautiful."

His fingers push against my core, slipping past my underwear, feeling for himself how ready I am. He sighs softly and presses his body closer to mine.

"I don't want to wait until we get home," I pant.

"No?" Alex teases.

"No."

In my mind, I imagined this would lead to the leasing office bathroom or a storage closet, but in Alex's, it leads to his dad's town house three blocks over. We walk there frantic, kissing on every corner, and then Alex is fumbling with a single key in his wallet, tucked inside a worn white envelope. When the door opens, I clock the wrought iron staircase, the chandelier, white tile floors, a tall orchid on the entryway table—and a stack of papers. One with an embossed gray insignia in the corner that looks . . . vaguely familiar. But before I can place it, line the insignia up with an accompanying memory, Alex leads me into a sunroom and draws me down onto the softly carpeted floor with him.

"You been here before?" I mumble between kisses.

"Nope," he grinds out, working his hips against mine in an imitation of what we both want. "Wasn't even sure the key would work."

"Nice place. You think they shop at Pottery Barn, too?"

Alex rumbles out a laugh on top of me. "Hush, *jagi*. I'm trying to focus."

I have no idea what Alex just called me, but it feels kind of monumental, so I do what he says and hush, let him kiss me the way he wants.

Touch me the way he wants.

Touch *him* the way he wants.

Until we're boneless, high on each other's pleasure, a mess of sweaty limbs and peppermint schnapps breath. He kisses each of my fingertips, naked on the floor of a home he's never been inside. But he isn't peeking around, doesn't seem to care in the slightest about where we are. He's looking only at me. His eyes are hot, magnetic, enthralling.

And I still can't muster up a single word.

CHAPTER TWENTY-EIGHT

I look up *jagi* the next day: *Korean term of endearment for one's significant other. In English,* jagi *is like calling someone honey, darling, or baby.*

CHAPTER TWENTY-NINE

To: Casey Maitland (Financial Analyst)
From: Molly West (Human Resources Representative)
Meeting Subject: Quick Touchbase!
Time: Thursday, December 21, 10:00–10:15 A.M.

The meeting invite comes through on my desktop monitor while I'm hours deep into an analysis for Don. It's 9:45 A.M. Molly wants to meet in fifteen minutes.

"Fuck."

I stare at the screen for a full minute, frozen in disbelief, before I realize Fari got up at the sound of my profanity and is leaning over my shoulder. "Fuck," she repeats. "That's ominous."

I quickly scan through all the reasons this meeting could be happening. Layoffs wouldn't be starting yet; we still don't even know the results of the board's deliberation. And as much as I want to warn my friends, I've kept my mouth shut about the acquisition, so it can't be a scolding on that, either. Which just leaves . . .

"Little Cooper knows about us," I whisper.

"About you and Alex Harrison?"

I nod, thinking back to that girl at the Christmas party who snapped our photo.

Fari pats my shoulder. "At least Molly didn't leave you time to stew on it."

Small victories.

I pull out my phone and fire off a panic text to Alex: Did you get a touchbase from HR?? After five minutes of no response, I check his calendar; he's in meetings until noon.

"Fuck," I whisper again.

We filmed our second video for YouTube yesterday. It was the *Day in the Life* working vlog. Andre, who was assigned to me, met me at 7:00 A.M. at my Brooklyn subway station with a portable camera. Eric met Alex at a coffee shop in the West Village (I'm expecting artsy shots of a cappuccino and a pastry while Alex luxuriates in his work clothes, looking gently amused at life). Saanvi's vision was for Andre and Eric to each film us commuting to work. Alex rode a Citi Bike—which is apparently a thing he actually does? Even in the winter? Like, not just for the camera?—and I took the subway. Because I'm not deranged.

Once we got to the lobby, Sara-who-does-sound suited us up with professional-grade mics. We did office tours, a lunch haul to the Whole Foods hot bar and back, and a Q&A session about the magazine industry, plus the highlights of our specific workday routines. Fari, Benny, and Brijesh even got to make cameos.

It was fun, but I'm glad we got the second video out of the way. I don't think my heart would have been in it if we'd already heard back from the board with bad news.

I glance at my phone. Still no response from Alex, and it's 9:58.

I take a deep breath and stand. Fari gives me a closed-mouth salute.

In college, I was in a sorority for only one year before I dropped out of it. Between my aversion to strangers and a growing distrust of the Greek system, I called it quits before dues came around the second year and I had to suffer through recruitment again. But in the short window that I *was* Greek, I got familiarized with disciplinary standards after a drunken date function where Lance slammed an expensive statue to smithereens. And since my date was "a reflection of me," I was punished accordingly: no social functions for the rest of the semester. Philanthropy events only.

The joke was on them; I've always loved volunteer work, and the social functions scared me anyway.

I feel like I'm headed back to sorority standards right now, about to be punished for my transgressions. Only this time, I'm actually culpable.

My phone pings with a new email. I glance down, and my composure shatters.

Hey BTH project team,

Thanks for your time last Friday and an incredibly thoughtful business presentation. While I was impressed, there are external factors making your proposed timeline infeasible. We will plan to delay the subsidiary launch and reevaluate based on company circumstances in roughly six months.

Best,

Douglas Dawson

Well. That's that.

We're getting acquired, and my legs don't work anymore.

The vision in my head—me, with an Away suitcase and a map (because for some reason, I always envision myself holding an old-school paper map), jumping off a red double-decker bus and looking around at London, wonderstruck—vanishes, replaced by another vision: packing up my apartment, forced to go back home to Nashville because nobody else in Manhattan wants to hire me. I don't get what I want, and even worse, I don't get to keep what I have.

I wonder how close the voting was. Did we ever stand a chance? And would I really want to know if it had been a close call?

What do I even *do* from here? I can't tell anyone about the acquisition. Panic would undoubtedly spread among the employees, and somehow, I just *know* Tracy would trace it back to me. Plus, I'd be a hypocrite to harp on Alex for sharing privileged information if I turned around and did the same thing.

"Casey." I glance up. Molly flashes me a smile. She's round faced and sweet, the picture-perfect image of an HR businesswoman. "Come in. Please close the door behind you."

I do as she says, a new kind of dread pricking at my skin. As I sit, I realize I never bothered to check the company policy on co-worker relationships.

But after that email, it suddenly seems like the least of my concerns.

Has Alex read it yet?

"You're probably wondering what this is about," Molly says, her voice coming to me a little hazy. She clasps her fingers on the desk between us.

I gulp. Nod. What is it Jerry used to secretly whisper to me when Dad wanted to ground me? *Deny, deny, deny.*

"A job opening in the London office has just posted, and I think you'd be perfect." Molly pauses, watching me.

I don't have the capacity to hide my confusion. "I . . . You . . . What?"

"Do you know who Sinclair Austin is?" she asks.

Sinclair Austin: manager of travel cost at *Take Me There*. We've never met, obviously, but I'm aware of who she is, what she does. Sinclair is responsible for researching and analyzing the true consumer cost of travel features in the magazine. She also creates budgets for each writer and helps plan their trips.

And here is the coolest part: Sinclair Austin has a *byline.* In some of *Take Me There*'s issues, she writes budgets for readers who are interested in specific travel destinations. Sometimes she even takes the trips with the writers herself.

"Yes," I say to Molly, a little shakily. "I know who she is."

"Well, she just got promoted to director of finance for the mag, and she's looking to replace herself. It's earlier than you planned. Your start date would be the first week of February. But I think you should interview at the very least, and consider that this job may interest you more than what's available come summertime."

All the background noise in my head quiets down and reduces to what she just said, over and over and over.

London office.

First week of February.

You'd be perfect.

"Wait," I say. "I can't. It's not going to be . . ."

"Breathe, Casey," Molly says. "I know what you're thinking, but the job isn't going anywhere, not for years. The acquiring company is going to have plenty of regulatory hoops to jump through, and you're a valuable worker anyway. If I were you, this opportunity is something I'd seriously consider."

"You—you know about the acquisition?"

"Yes. I'm in HR. We know everything, all the time. I won't tell you there's no risk. But I'm telling you I think it's a risk you should take."

"February?" I repeat.

Molly nods. "February."

Here is the thing about want. Sometimes, it's a dull pulse, a tickle on the back of your neck. And other times, it pushes in on you so hard that you can think of nothing else. You just want and want and want. A person. A place. A feeling.

I tell Alex that night.

I don't *want* to talk about the London job—I *want* to talk about how he's feeling about Dougie's email—but he panicked earlier when he got my text and wouldn't drop it until I told him what the meeting with Molly was about. After work, he trailed me home by half an hour. I've been waiting for him, pacing on the carpet until now.

I wish I could read him, but when he wants to be, Alex Harrison is inscrutable. While I talk, his hands rest lightly on his hips, watching me. I'm not sure he's even breathing, he's so still.

"You had an interview this afternoon?" he asks when I'm through.

I nod. "Molly scheduled it right after our touchbase. I talked to Sinclair Austin. She—she liked me, and they scheduled four interviews for Tuesday."

The last thing I expect Alex to do is smile, the pull at each corner of his lips breaking through his stoicism, but that's exactly what happens. "You're going to get that job, Simba."

I stutter out a laugh, guarding my heart against the sureness in his tone. I've been here before. I've been stung by things I want so badly, it hurts. When I first looked up the job description, I couldn't stop grinning, my chest inflated with helium. It was like all the things I knew I was good at combined with all the things I'm desperate to try. Too good to be true.

"I'm not so sure," I admit.

His face softens with understanding, and he doesn't say anything else, doesn't make me any promises. Alex's shoulders bend forward, and his arms come around me, pulling me into a safety net of warmth.

How is he coping, with all his hard work ending in postponement? This whole day has been full of emotional whiplash.

"Enough about me. Tell me how you're doing," I whisper.

He shakes his head, his chin catching on my shoulder. "Don't worry about that. Dougie didn't say no, he said not right now. All things considered, that's a small miracle."

This is the moment I should say it: *Alex, I need to tell you something.*

It wasn't a small miracle, it was a sleeper shot.

I'm so sorry, Alex, but nothing is being reevaluated in six months.

The words are on the tip of my tongue, begging to spill over. But what stops them in the next moment is: *What's the big deal? Robert offered to help, and I figured, why not?*

I can't even get the synapses to link up in my head, can't comprehend how my desperation to tell Alex the truth at all correlates to *that* memory. But I can't make it *not* correlate, either.

I think I might be in love with Alex Harrison. And I also think I don't fully trust him.

"I'm so proud of you," he says—still talking about London—and my confusion solidifies even further, pulled right from an emotion I can't even name. I don't know whether to love him for his unconditional support or ask if I mean so little to him that it's *that* easy to let me leave.

"I could wait," I say. "I could wait until summer and take a different job."

"Absolutely fuck that," Alex says. He rubs a thumb along my jawline. "This job is, like, a novel described as *perfect for fans of finance and new adventures.* That's you. That's the book you want to read, Case."

"It is," I say, laughing.

Alex smiles. "Just lean all the way into what you like. The smile on your face right now is what's telling me it's the right move."

I try to hold it, but my smile drops eventually. If I really did what he's suggesting, I'd be leaning all the way into Alex, too. "How come you're so eager to let me go?" I whisper.

He pulls back, sets his mouth into a grim line. Eventually, he says, "It's not in me to be a tether."

"Not even a little?" I ask.

"Not even a little."

"Why not?"

Alex runs a hand through his hair, blushing at the ground. "Because nobody stays anyway," he says softly. "But I didn't want to admit that because I don't want you to feel guilty, or sorry for me. Not when I want this job for you almost as much as you want it for yourself."

Something clicks in my brain. A memory. An explanation.

Alex sinks onto the couch, and I kneel in front of him. "In the elevator, when I freaked out because I thought you were going to be with some other girl on my birthday," I remind him. "You said the word 'clockwork.'"

His eyes burn into mine. "Yeah. I thought you were giving up on us because of what we texted about earlier that day, the stuff about my dad. People always distance themselves from me at the same point. Like clockwork."

"What point?" I ask.

He scratches at his jaw. "When they start to really know me, I guess."

Another memory, another explanation: what Sonja said, about Alex not being the person she thought she wanted to date. She *thought* she was getting first-day Alex. Shiny Alex. Unbroken, world-traveling, extroverted Alex. When we started all this, I assumed he wasn't interested in long-term commitment because that's just who he was. But the truth is closer to what he's been alluding to: it's almost never his choice.

"I think some people just like me best at a distance," Alex admits.

I have a pathological need to be liked, he once told me. Because he doesn't think he's capable of being loved.

I crawl into his lap and kiss him, because my heart is breaking and I can't not. He's hesitant at first but slowly opens up to me, teeth catching on my lips, hands rubbing along my thighs and up my back, breath coming more like a pant. Even his eyes are a little possessive.

"I like you better the more I get to know you," I tell him, pushing closer the only way I know how right now. "That's how it's supposed to work. When you let the right people in, they'll love you, and they'll stay."

Love you. Right there: I basically just said it.

He unbuttons my pants. "I appreciate the sentiment, but you're leaving, so the point stands."

"That," I say, unbuttoning his, "is a technicality. I'm not *going* anywhere, not in a metaphorical sense, and I might not even get that job, which would make it in a literal sense, too."

He stands, still holding me in his arms, and carries me to my room. "That specific job is neither here nor there," he responds casually, but there's a brokenness I can still hear in the tenor of his voice. "You'll go. I know it in my bones. You're going to eat atrocious pub food and delicious ethnic cuisine, and you'll pretend to love trendy East London even though you'll like the touristy neighborhoods, too. You're going to see the White Cliffs of Dover, and then Scotland, Bath, and even Windsor."

"Talk dirty to me."

Alex laughs and lands beside me on my bed. We're both quiet for a minute, smiling at each other, and then he says, "I know you're scared, Casey. But you're more scared of not going than you are of going, and that makes you brave."

Someone needs to get this human being an award. For what I've yet to determine, but it'd be nice to have the trophy prepped for inscription.

"Your birthday is in three days," I state.

Alex nods. "Your flight leaves for Nashville tomorrow."

His cousins aren't coming home for Christmas this year; too

much holiday shipping to deal with, apparently, and his aunt Jane is already in LA, helping her son pack orders. Freddy is spending the holiday with his dad's proper and straitlaced side of the family (not his mom's, which is the side that always welcomes Alex with open arms). Freddy told me this when I texted him to confirm Alex's holiday whereabouts, gearing up for what I'm about to say:

"Come with me."

His face snaps up to mine; he's shocked out of his daze. "What?"

"Book a flight, my flight, and come to Nashville with me." I am surer of myself with every word. "We can spend your birthday at the park playing soccer in our sweatshirts. And maybe we can go on a hike. I feel like you haven't done much of that. And we'll get tickets to some expensive bar downtown on New Year's Eve." I bite my lip and exhale.

He looks shocked, but his eyes are smiling in amusement. "Is this a pity invite? I was going to be perfectly content with Cleopatra and Calliope, watching Wes Anderson films and drinking hot chocolate."

"Convincing, but no. I've been thinking about this for days. Mainly because every time I picture you spending Christmas in New Haven with Sonja, I see red, but also because I just want you with me for however long we've got."

Alex's eyes warm into a bourbon color. "Really?"

"Really. If it feels like too much pressure, you can think of it as your introductory tour to the South," I offer. "I'm your tour guide. I even accept Venmo tips."

Alex laughs. "Okay. His grin is so wide, it takes up his whole face. "The answer is yes, *jagi*. Of course I want to come home with you for the holidays."

"Famous last words," I try to joke.

Emotionally, I'm aware this is a horrible idea. Alex Harrison is not my boyfriend and certainly isn't going to be if I get good news after my interviews on Monday. He likes to move around, is interested in freelancing. Maybe that means London for him, but maybe it means New Zealand. I don't have any answers, but it doesn't feel right to demand them from him, because the launch he's been working so hard for didn't get approved, and our company is about to get acquired—which might just change everything.

Yep. Emotionally this is not a genius move. But right now, I just don't care. I'm operating on one self-imploding goal now: *make me love you enough to trust you.*

CHAPTER THIRTY

Miriam rides to LaGuardia with us. She's headed to Charleston, where her aunt and uncle live, but we planned our flights so they'd be only thirty minutes apart. In the Uber ride there, Miriam grills Alex about his Instagram aesthetic.

"You need one," Miriam says.

"It was *two YouTube videos,*" Alex retorts.

"You literally majored in digital media, Alex. I don't understand how *you* don't understand the importance of this. Take Casey, for example." She pats my head affectionately. Hair falls into my face, and I blow it back out with a grumpy exhale. "She gave me her Instagram password years ago, and now she has an aesthetic: sweet autumn child who doesn't own a hairbrush posts pictures from wherever it's cloudy or raining and filters it with moody Victorian undertones."

To this, Alex says nothing, momentarily caught out.

"I own a hairbrush."

"You should use it sometime." Miriam throws me a wink.

"I'm not sure I'm ready to hand over my Instagram password," Alex admits.

"Fair. The day will come. I'm not worried."

At the airport, chaos ensues, with long lines and oversize luggage and a single, twenty-dollar draft beer split among the three of us "for good luck and a travel buzz" before Alex and I drop Miriam off at her gate.

"Meet you at home," she tells me as she squeezes me close for a hug. She'll be in Charleston for Christmas, but she's coming to Nashville after so we can all get together with Sasha and Miguel for New Year's Eve.

She hugs Alex next, whispering something that makes him blush. He smiles sheepishly and then shoots me a guilty look.

I probably don't want to know.

Since Alex booked his flight so last-minute, his seat isn't near mine. I board first, and when he passes me in the aisle of the plane, he tugs softly on my braid and keeps walking.

On the runway—literally, as we're *about* to take off—it dawns on me that I forgot to tell my parents he's coming.

It's been a crazy twenty-four hours. After Alex and I talked last night, we double-checked that there were still seats available for this flight; he got the *last one*. Then, when Miriam came home, Alex left so he could pack and get ready for the trip.

"I was right," Miriam said to me once he was gone.

"About?"

"Feelings." She grabbed theatrically at the empty air with her fist. "You caught them. Hook, line, and sinker."

I walked over to the bar cart and started uncorking a bottle of red. Soundless flashes of his body twisting toward me, the light dappling over his hair, his tattooed arm splayed out against a bedsheet all hit me in succession. I couldn't deny it to Miriam any more than I could deny it to myself. "I . . . Yeah. But it's different with Alex.

There's not, like, a future with him. He's just a person who really makes sense for this stage of life."

"The stage of life where you are happy," Miriam deadpanned. "Why are you acting like it has to be temporary? Case, you're allowed to *want* him, okay? Hell, you're allowed to fall in love with him!" I flinched, hearing it out loud—that thing I've been questioning, which is definitely *not allowed*. Miriam spun around in a circle. "Let Alexander Harrison ruin all your plans! Let him sweep you off your fucking feet!" I am certainly, 100 percent already off my feet. "Maybe he's just *saying* he wants you to go to London. Maybe he doesn't really mean it."

"He's really not," I replied staunchly. "He really means it."

Miriam sighed, grabbing the remote and flipping on the TV. "Look, all I know is that man looks at you like you are the answer to an existential question."

I wasn't sure how to respond to that, but before I could turn the exact same observation back on her with Brijesh, she squealed, "Ooh, want to watch reruns of *Sex and the City*?"

Now I shoot off a text to my parents as the plane lifts into the sky: Bringing home a friend for Christmas who doesn't have other plans—hope that's okay?

But it's too late. The text never sends.

"Jerry!" I squeak-whisper into my phone as soon as we've touched down.

"Casey! We're at baggage claim!"

"Jer, listen." I look around at the passengers unbuckling, stretching, standing up to crowd the aisle. Lowering my voice even further—because I don't want Alex to overhear and think he's an afterthought—I say, "Alex is with me."

"Alex . . . ," Jerry repeats. I'm hoping he remembers that name from Thanksgiving and I won't have to explain. Jerry's always been easier to talk to about relationship stuff than Dad. Because at the end of the day . . . my dad is my dad. "*Oh*. He's with you *now*?"

"Yes. I forgot to tell you guys. It was a last-minute thing. But can you tell Dad, and just, like, be welcoming and not weird about it?"

"Okay," Jerry says. "You got it, sweetheart."

"And for the love of God, make Marty Maitland *promise* he will not ask about Alex's intentions with his daughter."

"He said that to Lance as a *joke,* Casey. It's not our fault your ex-boyfriend was a total boner."

"Okay, bye, see you soon!"

"Kisses!"

Ending the call, I rest my forehead against the seat back. Crisis. Averted.

Outside the gate, I wait for Alex. When I see him—hair spiking like untrimmed grass, still in his work clothes, backpack hanging off one shoulder—I let him search, his eyes tracking the crowd, waiting in anticipation for the moment he finds me. When he does, his lips part softly, and he waves a little.

"Good flight?" I ask as we head for baggage claim.

"I watched the first twenty minutes of *Across the Universe*. And then I read a thriller."

"You read . . . a whole thriller. On a two-and-a-half-hour flight."

Alex glances down at me, lips tugged up in amusement at my tone. "I don't read like most people read. I skim. If I try to read everything, I get distracted and give up. That's why I work in short-form media." He nods, like that settles it.

"Okay." *Does that even count???* But I bite my tongue in an effort not to sound judgmental. "What about audiobooks?"

"I listen to those on two times the normal talking speed," Alex says. "It's almost gibberish, but you get done in half the time."

These are the types of things that petrify me about Alex. Does he think of me as something to skim? To be finished with in half the time?

But then he grabs my hand, kisses it, and says hoarsely, "I'm nervous, Simba." And it's so damn cute.

"Alex, you've never made a bad first impression in your life."

"If you'll recall," Alex says, "I *have* made *one* bad first impression in my life."

"Well, at least I thought you were good-looking."

"It was all common ground from there," he says, winking.

At baggage claim, Jerry and Dad *really* put it on. I'm genuinely impressed with how quick they are on their feet. They're all "Hey, Alex, we're so excited to have you come stay!" and "We've been looking forward to meeting you!" and Alex is all, "I'm so thankful to be here!" and "It's great to meet you both! Casey's told me all about you!"

I just stand there exhaling.

Dad and Jerry grill Alex on the way home. By the time we get there, it's well past sunset, the dark street glowing with Christmas lights scattered across the landscaping, wreaths on the doors, icicle strands hanging off the roofs, fake reindeer beaming in the front yards. The weather is muggy but cool, the temperature a near ten-degree increase from New York, but it still feels like a classic December evening for the South.

Dad leads Alex with our luggage to my childhood bedroom (thank *God* they remodeled it last year) while Jerry and I sneakily put an extra place setting on the dinner table. Cider warming in a crockpot perfumes the room with cinnamon, orange, cloves. I ladle two mugs out before chasing Alex down. Dad has him in the guitar room, trying to run interference but coming across as a show-off.

"And this is the guitar Casey was playing when she got her first period—"

"Dad!"

"Hey, kiddo."

Alex turns to me, stifling a laugh. Seeing him *here*—in my childhood home—sends me all the way back to the beginning. What would August Casey have thought about this scene? Me, offering a mug of rum-spiked cider to Alex, letting our fingers graze, letting my focus linger while he blows away steam? She couldn't have fathomed it. But I've colored in the lines of Alex's edges over the past four months. Sometimes, he seems more real to me, more solid, than anything else I've ever touched.

The four of us sit down to Jerry's home-cooked Thanksgiving dinner (we never did have any turkey in New York), and Alex asks, "Do I get to hear you play one of those guitars?"

I grimace, dishing out mashed potatoes. "Probably not—"

"But your chances increase in direct relation to how much cider she consumes," Dad advises.

Alex gets up to pour me another drink, not missing a beat. "How did you two meet?" he asks.

Helpfully, I tell him, "They met at my mom's funeral."

"*Casey.*" Dad's tone comes out scolding, the same he used when I was a kid. Jerry balks, dropping his silverware loudly onto his plate. From the crockpot Alex looks at me, his eyes dancing, trying to figure out if this is a twisted joke or not.

"What?" I say. "It's true!"

"Okay, yes, that is *technically* true," Jerry allows, directing his words at Alex in guilty apology. "I did the flowers for Sadie's funeral. But we didn't run into each other again for *two years,* and then after *another* year, we officially got together."

Dad glares at me, his eyes vengeful. "Alex. What are your intentions with my daughter?"

"Um," Alex mumbles, sitting back down, setting the refilled mug beside my plate.

"Don't answer that," I tell him.

"Actually, I think we *all* need more alcohol," Jerry says, rising from the table. "Maybe a cocktail? Alex, Marty has this great story he's got to tell you about a Serbian child named Croissant. The child is, of course, illegitimate."

"Same," Alex says, biting back a smile.

This makes Jerry blush, which in turn makes me burst out laughing. "Tell him, Dad."

Dad tells the absurd story, and Jerry makes old-fashioneds, and over the next forty-five minutes, I get supplied with enough alcohol to play one song *only* for Alex.

"What do you want to hear?" I ask him as I poise on the living room settee, looping the strap of the Yamaha acoustic over my head. Alex is across from me on a leather pullout chair, but Jerry and Dad are still cleaning up in the kitchen—because they know me, and they know I will positively freak out if I have a whole captive audience for this.

"Whatever you want." He leans forward, elbows on his knees.

"It's been a while," I warn him, tuning the guitar. But the instrument is familiar beneath my fingertips, like the edge of an old photograph or damp beach sand. Holding one of these will always make me feel like a kid again, with a grief I didn't know where to put because I wasn't even old enough to name it. For a while, I put it here, in loving something my dad loved—the thing that bound us outside of Mom.

Alex smiles softly at me. "Then play something you know by heart."

I go with "American Honey" by Lady A. It's sweet and melodic, and I've played it so many times that the words are tattooed inside my mind. It's also the first song I ever played all the way through without stuttering.

I don't look at Alex once, just sing and play very softly, focusing on the chords my hand remembers, the words I've never forgotten. It's an indescribable kind of *good*—paying homage to my dad, this band, the song's creators, even myself. Coming back to this is fucking cathartic.

The last time I was in Nashville, I was afraid of getting stuck in the past. Miriam was right to say I had a tunnel vision for my future, and Dad was right to worry he'd chased me away. Because isn't that exactly how I was acting? Like a runaway? Like Mom? Was I trying to *be* her in that way?

I want to tell *all* of them—Dad, Jerry, Miriam, even Lance— that it was never about running away from them. I was running from the version of myself I'd backed into a corner years ago, a girl who was so insecure about everything she wasn't that she'd never bothered to learn all of what she *was*.

I'm running from *her*.

Alex is the one who figured it out for me: *I think there are parts of yourself that you don't fully know yet.* And that's probably true. But it doesn't mean I don't know who I am. And it doesn't mean I can't also love the girl I used to be.

I can love this—playing guitar for someone I brought home to meet my parents—and I can love my parents without needing to *be* them. I can love my hometown, and my job, and whatever city I choose to live in. I can drag my past into the future.

When the song ends, Alex doesn't applaud. He comes over to the settee and kneels in front of me, like I knelt in front of him last night in my apartment. When I finally let myself look at him, his eyes are twinkling back at me. His hand brushes my cheek and comes away wet with tears.

"You have literally brought me to my knees," he jokes.

I laugh snottily. "I don't know why I'm crying."

"I do," Alex murmurs. "You finally let yourself come home."

CHAPTER THIRTY-ONE

I fall the rest of the way in love with him the day after Christmas, in between my third interview and my fourth.

It doesn't hit me like a wrecking ball, or slap me in the face, or anything like that. The full weight of my love for Alexander Harrison settles over me like misty fog, a slow build. One minute I don't notice it and the next, it's more certain. The day after that, even more certain. Until the fog is everywhere, and you can't see a thing. You have no idea which way is north unless he's the one giving directions.

Two days ago, for his birthday, Jerry baked a cake and scrounged up twenty-six candles while we went to the park and played soccer in our sweatshirts. Dad played "Happy Birthday" on the guitar after dinner, and we sang, and Alex blushed furiously. He got a couple of phone calls—presumably from Freddy and his aunt and cousins—but only an email from Robert. I saw the name pop up on Alex's phone while he chewed his lip swollen, reading very seriously.

He hasn't told me how Robert reacted to the BTH news. Hasn't told me if they've communicated about it at all. But after twenty minutes of watching him listlessly read the same two-sentence email over and over, I took him into our room and got on my knees, looked up through hooded eyes and put my mouth on him while he whispered encouraging expletives.

And the whole time, I silently begged him to just love the people who love him back.

Christmas morning, when the house was rich with the scent of coffee and vanilla and pine needles, the windowpanes blurred with frost, I was still half asleep when my eyes peeked open to find him watching me from his own pillow. I yawned and blinked, tracking the muscles pulling his mouth into traces of amusement.

"There's a joke in here somewhere," I croaked, "about an older man watching his lover sleep."

"I'm eleven months older than you," Alex said, his voice raw, like it always is first thing in the morning. "Besides, do you really want to compare me to the man who supposedly climbed down half the world's chimneys last night to creep around unawares?"

My nose wrinkled. "But the presents."

"Just ask *me*," he said, his voice evening out the longer he spoke. "Fuck that old man. I'll buy you the things you want."

"Finally planning to tap into that trust fund?" I joked, because the alternative would be letting the arousal of what he just said build until I jumped him.

Alex rolled his eyes. "You mostly shop at thrift stores and Trader Joe's. I'm pretty sure I don't need to go anywhere *near* a trust fund to keep you happy."

"Alex," I said. "Did you get me Tide Free & Gentle from the Cape Cod Target for Christmas?"

"Give me a little credit, Simba." He rolled on top of me. "I did so much better than that."

Thirty minutes later, I was wrapped in a plaid flannel blanket and fuzzy socks when Alex gifted me the *entire* skin-care line from his cousins' company—which means he conspired with both his family and mine to have it rush shipped from LA, then squirreled away until Christmas Day.

In return, I gave him a shiny new home brew setup from a local brewery in Nashville, which I showed him on a piece of paper that also explained it would be shipped to his apartment in Manhattan. He said it was perfect, but in my opinion, not quite.

I wanted to get him something amazing for Christmas. On my last day in the city, I even tried to make it happen; I went to the Archives department and asked if they had anything written by Charlotte Yoon. Because I just had this feeling—her being a writer, the connection to Little Cooper through Robert—that maybe she was down there, more of her words waiting for Alex to read. But the archivist came up empty.

Now, after three interviews the day after Christmas, nursing an eggnog hangover, I'm on the couch decompressing. The last interviewer was the type to ask a short question that demands a long answer, never interjecting or redirecting the conversation. I talked so much, my mouth started to hurt, and since it was the third interview of the day, I am mentally wiped at this point. Alex is working a half day, set up in the dining room doing his least favorite task— manning the help desk inbox for BTH tech support. Jerry is at the flower shop, and Dad is out Christmas sale shopping, so the whole place is perfectly quiet.

Alex peeks his head into the living room, eyes flitting over me sprawled on the couch. I roll my head toward him, smiling tiredly.

"Good?" he asks. "A thumbs-up or thumbs-down will suffice."

I give him a thumbs-up. He disappears without another word, and that's when I know beyond a shadow of a doubt that I'm all the way in love with him. Because he so perfectly understands me.

I don't remember anything about my fourth interview other than the fact that I love Alex Harrison, I'm tired of saying words, and I need to ask Dad to please upgrade the Wi-Fi.

I'm done by noon, which is the close of business in London. Alex comes into our room and pulls me into bed, hugging me horizontally. Our legs are tangled under the covers. The heat from a floor vent is pumping into the room, cloaking the air in a hazy, metallic warmth that has my eyelids drooping. The way he's holding me, kissing my temple, both of us silent because there's too much to say, has my mind reeling, recalibrating everything I thought I knew.

Here's the truth: my feelings for Alex were *never* casual. Not even when I hated him did I do it casually. I'm as emotionally invested in him as I am with this dream job. In my head, the importance of *it* and the importance of *him* are on exactly equal footing.

I love him so much that part of me doesn't want this job. I love him so much that I'm *glad* the BTH launch got denied. Maybe he'll be forced to stay in New York longer. Maybe we both will, together. A pit of despair wells up inside me, my chest tight with something sweet and lovely that wants to morph into anger. Because I have never loved like this, and it is entirely Alex's fault.

I think I might never forgive him.

By New Year's Eve, Miriam's back in town, and Alex and I meet up with her, Sasha, and Miguel, who are fresh off a flight from Chicago and staying in a swanky hotel downtown. Miriam and I give the tourists the highlights of the city, cruising around in her family's minivan. We stop at the I BELIEVE IN NASHVILLE sign, Music Row, a hot chicken restaurant, even Bobbie's Dairy Dip.

"*Casey,*" Miriam says. "We are so close to that sketchy Mexican restaurant we used to drink margaritas at in high school. Should we go *back* there?"

"As much as I love this reminiscing for you," Sasha says from the back seat, "could we get margaritas somewhere . . . I don't know, cooler?"

"Spoilsport," Miriam grumbles.

"I want the Nashville experience!"

"That *would have been*—"

"I want the tacky tourist experience!"

"Mir," I interject. "Just head downtown. Let's beat the traffic and get this girl on a mechanical bull before sundown."

It's a disaster, if a hilarious one. The bull always wins. I tried to warn her.

At 11:59, under a space heater on the rooftop of a Broadway honky-tonk we paid a whopping $180 to access, the countdown of *Ten! Nine! Eight!* ringing out with the power of a thousand drunken voices, Alex takes my face in his hands, and I know he's in love with me when we get to *five.*

He's so gorgeous right now, the neon lights of the bar across the street painting him an inky blue. He looks almost like fiction. Like he can't be real. But he's also looking at *me* like that. Like I can't be real, either.

When we get to *four,* he says it, his eyes on mine, and in them, I see a million colors inside of one. "I love you." I can't hear his voice, but I've already memorized the shape of his lips.

On *three,* I say, "I love you, too," positive he can't hear me, either.

We kiss on *two,* letting those extra few seconds go fuck themselves.

CHAPTER THIRTY-TWO

"What do you want to do this morning?" I whisper. "On your last day in Nashville."

"The Parthenon," Alex whispers back.

We're sitting at the kitchen table, staring at each other over two mugs of coffee and one stale blueberry muffin. There's no cause for whispering, yet here we are. Because sometimes, after you admit you're in love, everything besides that admission needs to get a little quieter.

"The Parthenon," I repeat.

"Yeah. Remind me why there's a Parthenon replica in Nashville?"

"I really couldn't say."

"Can we go?" he asks. "I have so many questions." And since I'm with love with him, of course the answer is yes.

We pack up our suitcases now so we can grab them and head to the airport right after our excursion. Jerry and Dad spent New Year's Eve at Jerry's sister's lake house, and I've already bidden them farewell, no clue when I'll see them next, or where I'll be coming from when I do.

On the drive to midtown in Dad's car, Alex and I are mostly quiet. I don't know what he's thinking so hard about, but for the first time in a while, I know my own mind.

Alex is my person. You don't keep secrets from your person, especially not ones they're wrapped up in.

I have to tell him about the acquisition, today.

Other than one field trip in middle school, I've never paid much attention to the Parthenon, but now that I'm really considering it, I have to admit it's pretty cool, all sprawling and stately. When Alex and I get out of the car, we look at it, then awkwardly glance at each other, and then look back at the Parthenon. Simultaneously, we burst out laughing.

"Well." I gesture. "There it is!"

"Can you go inside?"

I check my phone. "Closed today."

Alex nods, his hand shooting out to grab me. "This Parthenon," he murmurs in my ear, still laughing, "is somehow both exceeding and falling wildly short of my expectations."

"Art *does* mirror life," I quip.

The buzz of my phone dissipates the electricity snapping between us.

"That your folks?" Alex asks.

But that ringtone isn't for a phone call; it's a corporate call through our company chat app from the recruiter assigned to my job application. Together, Alex and I look down at her name blinking across my phone screen.

"It's New Year's Day," I say, shell-shocked.

"Answer it," he whispers, letting me go.

With shaking fingers, I accept the call and press my phone to my ear. "Hello?"

"Casey? Sorry for calling so late. Or—wait, I guess it's not that late for you?" Her voice is clear and distinctly British.

"It's four thirty." I gulp. "In the afternoon."

"Oh! Great. I just *had* to let you know as soon as I got word! LC is officially offering you the travel cost manager position."

Alex overhears. He grins wide, pulling me against his chest.

"Oh." I readjust my phone, slippery in my palm. My heartbeat is *beat, beat, beat*ing against my eardrums. "That's great to hear."

"Yes! I'm sure you're busy, but I thought telling you now would be a nice holiday surprise before we all get slammed with work tomorrow. We're offering a twenty percent increase on your current salary. The start date would be the Monday of the first week of fiscal February, so I think that's, like, the last couple of days of calendar January. I know it's soon, but we're very eager to have you."

"Okay." I am numb.

One month.

One month one month one month—

"I'm going to send over an email with the offer letter, the benefits, the moving support package, work visa information, et cetera. Take a look at the documentation and we'll talk tomorrow. Okay?"

"Okay," I say again.

"Great. Happy New Year, Casey."

"Happy New Year."

The second I hang up, Alex has me off the ground. He scoops me up behind my knees and spins me around in a circle. "I fucking *knew* it! I'm so proud of you, *jagi.*"

My body isn't sure how to process this. Inside, all my tiny molecules are fusing together and fissuring apart. Again. Again. Again.

He puts me back on my feet, still holding me upright. The sturdiest, most solid thing I've ever felt. "How do you feel?" he asks gently.

Terrified. Thrilled. "I'm . . . confused," I tell him, honest as I can get.

Alex's eyes glaze with sadness, and he rests his forehead against mine. "There goes all my plotting."

"What plotting?"

Alex swallows thickly and murmurs, "How to keep you."

This is dating.

"Alex." I grasp at his hair. "What the actual *fuck* are we doing?"

He shakes his head, forehead rocking against mine, his fingers bunching into my coat like the grip will hold me there forever. "I don't know. Casey, I would . . . I would *follow* you there. I think I would follow you anywhere."

The sentence calcifies into my own bones, his words becoming a physical part of me that I couldn't get rid of unless it broke. "You would?"

"If you wanted me to, I would." He tucks my hair behind my ear, sighs, and starts talking. *Really* talking.

"I've thought about this a lot. I started thinking about it the *minute* you left my place, the time you told me about moving to London with stars in your eyes after I'd spent the best minutes of my life inside your body. I've asked myself if I would ever move back to London if I'd never met you. I've asked myself if, had you'd been interested in someplace else, would I still have tried to follow you then?"

He tilts my chin up, his irises turning flinty. "Every day, Casey, every time I'd look at you, I would play out all those what-if scenarios in my head. They always ended the same, with me thinking, *Yes.* If you were existing near me, the answer was yes. And if you weren't near me—funny enough, Case, the answer was still yes. That's the best part. It doesn't feel like a tether, it feels like a *choice,* because the stars in your eyes are fucking *why* I fell in love with you."

He wipes a tear from the corner of my eye, thumb lingering on my cheek, and his voice softens even more as he continues. "So, to me, it pretty much came down to only that. Once I figured *that* part out, the rest wasn't complicated. It wasn't difficult. If you want me—if by some miracle this is a mutual feeling—then I go where you go. I am where you are. But I don't want you to feel pressured, so if you don't want me to be in London with you, I won't, and I will completely understand. I mean, we made a deal when we started this whole thing, and I broke the rules—"

I put a finger to his lips. "Stop. Just stop right there. Alex, I *do* want you there. I want to keep you, too."

Oddly, his expression falls even further. "Are you sure? It wouldn't be for a while, what with the BTH board holdup. Maybe even six months, until they really let us launch."

The cloud bursts.

The secret bursts.

It pours out of me, sentence after splintered sentence: Tracy approaching me, asking me to uncover the truth behind Robert and Dougie's feud (during which I swear to Alex I never breathed a word to her about his relationship with his dad, which is the truth). The news of the acquisition, my being sworn to secrecy, learning the BTH presentation was just a red or green light to sell.

When I say that part, Alex's eyes gutter, and his face goes cold. He stands there mutely through my apology, stiff and frozen. I want to touch him, but I'm scared he'll flinch away. I've never seen him look like this. Not in the entire time I've known him have I seen him this . . . defeated.

I shift on my feet. The grass beneath my boots is still crunchy from frost. It's all that breaks up the silence that follows.

"Alex," I whisper. "I'm sorry. I really am so, *so* sorry. About all of it."

He rubs at his face, eyes pointed listlessly toward the sky. When he doesn't say anything for a few moments, I can't take it.

"What are you thinking?" I ask.

"I am wondering," he says, voice gravelly, "if I have any right to be mad at you for keeping a privileged secret from me that might have gotten you into serious trouble, had I not kept it to myself. And I think the answer is no. I don't have that right." His eyes drop to mine. "But I'm also wondering why you didn't trust me enough to tell me that secret anyway. Because whether we admitted it to each other or not, we were dating a month ago. I was already telling you *everything* a month ago." I can see his frustration visibly growing. "I spent *weeks* working on that presentation. *You* spent weeks. Now you're telling me the whole time, Dougie Dawson was just *waiting* for the curtain to close?"

"It wasn't like that. Tracy thought we had a chance—"

"I'm sure you can understand why Tracy's *thoughts* don't hold much weight for me right now, manipulative as she's been toward *both* of us," he mutters. "*Fuck.* That was supposed to be *it.*" Alex grabs at his hair, turning away from me.

That was supposed to be it.

Successfully launching a subsidiary company at his father's old haunt was supposed to be the thing that would make Robert care.

I think of Mom in this moment, of her obsession with legacy. I still don't know what mine is supposed to be. But Alex does. *That was supposed to be it.* Only now, it won't be. It *won't* be.

"Alex," I whisper, and he turns back. "We did everything we could. We tried our hardest."

For an instant, I deceive myself into thinking his eyes warm, but it's so brief, and they go so cold after, that I must have only seen what I wanted.

"I know, Casey," he says, his voice soft and low. "And I'll come around to that, with time. That the acquisition was beyond either of our control." His jaw flexes and he breaks hold of my gaze, looking back toward the car. "But you obviously never trusted me the way I trusted you. And that's what's really breaking my heart."

CHAPTER THIRTY-THREE

My Subway Nemesis is holding two things: his usual homemade death trap granola bar and a computer bag with a vaguely familiar insignia stitched on the front. Through puffy, swollen eyes—I haven't stopped crying all week, despite the excitement of planning my big move and Miriam's constant attempts to cheer me up—I squint at it.

I've seen that before, I've seen it, I've seen it, where have I seen that before.

It's woven with silver thread, a small spiral that braids in on itself. I stare for a few beats longer, and then, I realize—

It's the same symbol I spotted on a document in Robert's Harrison's town house.

My forehead wrinkles, and hair falls into my eyes as I lower my head into my hand, thinking. The headache I haven't been able to get rid of for days is drumming loudly, choking my thoughts the same way it's been robbing me of sleep.

Focus.

I think this is important. Because . . . even when I saw the symbol *there,* on that Upper East Side entryway table, right before Alex made urgent, desperate love to me on the sunroom floor—*fuck,* I miss him so much and it's only been a week—but even then, it was familiar.

So, where did I see it the *first* time?

My Subway Nemesis is talking with someone he recognized a few minutes ago. They're having a slightly awkward, self-preening conversation about his current line of work. I've been halfway listening, halfway reading a historical romance novel (to avoid thinking about the tragedy of my own romantic state), but the more they talk the louder they get, and I eventually give up on the French Revolution.

"I miss the rush," says my Subway Nemesis. "The excitement of the floor."

"You mean the terror," says the other. "But I get it. Trading's so addictive, sometimes it feels illegal."

I roll my eyes. Okay, Jordan Belfort.

"What do you do now?" the trader asks.

"Financial consulting," says my Subway Nemesis, and I roll my eyes again.

"What sort of consulting?" the trader asks.

"We work with clients looking to break into new markets."

I look at his computer bag.

I look at my Subway Nemesis.

I look back at his computer bag.

And then, I remember.

That symbol was *on the Strauss website.*

In a perfectly Elle Woods moment, a lightbulb glows bright in my mind, and I gasp out loud, causing both men to glance down where I'm sitting. My hands clutch my book as the train hauls to a stop, and shakily, I rise to standing.

"That's the Strauss logo, right? Is Strauss one of your clients?" I ask. "A client you're trying to help break into a new market?"

Subway Nemesis glares at me. He looks down at his bag, then back up. "It's not against our company policy to accept gifts worth less than fifty dollars. And stop eavesdropping, you teenaged SEC narc."

"That's not what I . . . I'm not going to report your gift to the . . . Whatever."

I walk out the doors. Up the stairs.

My brain is swimming.

That's the Strauss logo, and it was in Robert Harrison's house, and Strauss is employing a consulting firm to help it break into new markets, and oh my God oh my God oh my God.

The tall windows of FiDi refract sunlight all around me, but it does nothing to stave off the sharp cold. Pink salt crunches beneath my boots as I start to walk, chewing on my lip while my mind rolls over the puzzle pieces that are suddenly fitting together. In a daze, I'm in the building, then the elevator. Then Tracy Garcia's office. Gloves still on. Brain still swimming.

Tracy is standing behind her desk in a dusty-blue long-sleeve dress. When she sees me, she smiles. And when she *really* sees me—focused eyes, racing mind, here without an appointment or an offer of explanation—her smile slips into a smirk. "Yes?"

My voice comes out soft but confident. "You said Strauss Holdings' offer was high. Higher than Little Cooper is worth."

She doesn't miss a beat. "I did. And they went even higher last week. They probably thought we'd have accepted by now and upped their offer to speed things along."

I start pacing. "What if Strauss knew our growth strategy for *Bite the Hand*? What if they factored it into their offer? Strauss is mostly a print magazine company, but I think it's wanting to . . . break into a new market."

"How would they know about *Bite the Hand*'s growth plan?" Tracy asks. *Taunts.* "That whole project is privileged information."

"Someone told them."

"Who?" If leading the witness was a thing in the finance world, she'd be doing it.

My laugh comes out slightly deranged. "This is why you asked me to get information from Alex. *This is why* you told *me,* a lowly analyst, about the acquisition. Why you *pretended* to let the Strauss name slip from your mouth in front of me when it was probably no accident at all."

Tracy shrugs. "Calculated risks."

"You suspected it was Robert who leaked information to Strauss. It was never about being in the weeds of our numbers to spot a solution. *It was about being with Alex to spot a clue.*"

"So you spotted a clue, then?" she asks.

"Tracy!"

She sighs and sits down, and gestures for me to do the same. Hollowly, I thunk down in the chair across from her. "The day you and Alex filmed with Saanvi outside of our building? I was there, across the street, coming back from a meeting nearby. I saw you two together, the way you looked at each other, and . . ." She winces. "I used you. Just like you used him."

She phrased it like that precisely so I wouldn't have room to get angry.

"What exactly do you suspect Robert Harrison of?" I whisper.

She gives me a flat look. "I suspect him of preferring to see LC torn apart than in the hands of his college enemy. I suspect him of cutting a deal with Strauss—maybe a seat on their board in exchange for proof that LC is a good investment. Something like *Bite the Hand,* for example. I suspect him of violating his noncompete and breaking confidentiality. And I suspect that's just the tip of the iceberg."

I scoff. "That all?"

"Casey," she says. "What. Do. You. Know?"

I shake my head, ignoring the question. "You were hoping I'd come to you like this one day. I was your Hail Mary. All those bread crumbs you left me—"

"Casey," Tracy says again, growing impatient. "I'm not going to apologize for doing every last thing I can to save this company. I don't think you would, either, in my shoes. Now, tell me what you know. You're here for a reason, and it isn't because you read my diary."

All of a sudden, I'm blinking back tears. "The Strauss logo was in Robert's house," I whisper.

"And?" Tracy probes.

And Alex gave the entire launch plan to his father on a silver platter. I bite my lip. "That's all I know."

She narrows her eyes. "You're lying. You're very easy to read."

"That's all I'm *saying*," I amend. "That's all you're getting."

Tracy rubs her forehead. "If Alex is involved, you should tell me. What's happening to Little Cooper is manipulative and wrong—"

"Alex knows nothing about this," I spit. "If anyone's doing the manipulating here, it's you and Robert Harrison."

She looks at me for a long moment and sighs, defeated. "Well. I guess I had a hand in why you're protecting that kid. I pushed you toward him myself. But all you gave me today is a rumor." She opens her laptop, signaling the end of our chat. "To stop this acquisition, I'm going to need proof."

"This," Alex says, low and careful. "Is ridiculous. *Ridiculous,* Casey."

"Robert said the words 'Don't be so sure about that,'" I argue. "When you called him an early retiree. I was there that day. I heard it."

Alex exhales a hollow laugh, throwing up his hands. "You think when he said that, he was giving me some vague, familial clue he's planning a hostile corporate takeover—"

"Not a takeover—"

"Of a company he *chose* to step down from—"

"And willingly left to his *nemesis?*"

"After spending twenty-five years at LC—"

"I saw the Strauss Holdings logo in his town house. What are the odds, Alex? What are the odds the acquiring company's logo—"

"Don't even get me *started* on that," Alex interrupts, pointing at me. "I can't believe you spoke to Tracy about this before you spoke to me."

Because you would have talked me out of it, I think. *And I would have let you.*

He groans loudly. Outside the conference room we're in, an intern stops to stare at us. I glance at her out of the corner of my eye before stepping back from Alex. Like a magnet, I drew too close. He's looking at me with molten eyes, his defenses on full guard. But he's not just angry. He's hurt. And like a wounded animal, he's lashing out.

"Alex," I whisper. "Robert didn't want you working here, and then all of a sudden he did."

He shudders, stepping farther back from me, and I know I'm hurting him worse, but I have to get this out.

"Because he realized your job description fit into his agenda. He's probably been planning this from the moment Dougie weaseled his way into the CEO seat. If he couldn't have LC unspoiled, Robert was going to dismantle it. All he needed was the right opportunity and a motivated buyer."

Alex's voice is rocky. "What does any of that have to do with me?"

"In your apartment, he challenged you to see this launch through. He offered to help you with the presentation not because he thought you would succeed, but because *he was deliberately setting you up to fail.* Think about it. I'd put money on him leaking that presentation, and then Strauss upping their offer of purchase after they saw it. Tracy confirmed as much."

I say my piece, then snap my lips together. There's no sense of victory here. No thrill at possibly cracking this case. But I can't keep secrets anymore, and that includes what's going through my mind.

He sighs, like the fight's gone out of him. "I want you to consider," he says, "the possibility that this is a story you concocted in your head, a loose end you want wrapped up before you go to London, so you won't think of Tracy Garcia as a mentor you never proved your worth to."

My nose wrinkles, his blow landing. We're slicing each other open right now, trading wounds. I picture Tracy and me in the break room—how eager I was to please her, how she *knew* it, how it's coming back to ruin me now. But as frustrated as I am at being used, I can't even deny that she's anything other a fighter, and a leader.

"It wasn't about proving myself," I say. "I'm trying to keep this company alive so I'm not in a constant panic over everybody's job security, including mine. I just accepted a new job! In a foreign country! And Molly *told* me it was a risk, but I did it anyway! Fari and Brijesh—they have good situations here, which I know because *they've told me*—"

"Companies get bought," he says. "It's *normal*. You're desperate to find a villain, but there *isn't one*. It's just business."

"If I'm desperate to find a villain, you're desperate *not* to find one," I counter. "But maybe it's closer to somewhere in the middle. Your father might not be all bad. But from what you've told me, he isn't all good, either."

Alex's mouth pulls into a flat line. He stares at a spot over my shoulder, unseeing. "Can you blame me for searching for the good in him, Casey? Please don't act like you don't understand. I've seen the way you try to measure up to your own parents."

And I do. Understand. I've always wanted to be the type of person they would be proud of. When it comes to his dad, Alex wants exactly the same. But him saying it—him *naming* the feeling—is what finally cracks open the lie.

I'm not *supposed* to follow in their footsteps. I'm not responsible for continuing their legacy. It's mine to choose, and unlike theirs, it doesn't even have to be tangible. It could start with this exact moment: refusing to stay quiet, to be complicit. Fighting to protect the people I care about.

It could be that small. That huge. But I don't think there's anything that would make my parents prouder of me.

"I love you, Alex." Tears well in my eyes, and his expression softens. "I love you on purpose. Not situationally. Not when it's convenient. No strings attached, no conditions. I know I hurt you with all of this, and I promise I won't ever keep secrets from you again. I swear it, up and down, back and forth, with every part of me. But please, just think about everyone you care about here, in this building. Believe me just for a little while. Follow through with it for *their* sake, and if I'm wrong, I'm wrong, and if I'm right . . . at least we'll know."

Alex comes to me, cups my face in his hands. We're both quiet for the span of a few breaths, holding each other and saying nothing and *thinking everything*.

"I'm so sorry," I whisper again. "You deserved better. From everyone."

His thumbs brush my wet cheeks, and he pushes his forehead against mine. "Did you tell Tracy . . ." He gulps. "Did you tell Tracy I sent Robert the presentation?"

I look up, his words transmuting into something different as they register. "You believe it," I whisper. "You believe me."

"Did you tell Tracy?" he asks me again.

"No." I shake my head. "Of course not. I love you, and that means I'll protect you at all costs, so of course I didn't tell her. Is there something else I don't know?"

For a while he says nothing. Then, "I'm not sure. Maybe. I'm not sure."

Hope blooms in my chest. "Can it help Tracy get her proof?" I ask him, carefully as I'm able. "Can it invalidate the acquisition?"

"I'm not sure," he says again, shaking his head.

But it's not because he really isn't sure. It's because what I'm suggesting he do, ultimately, is betray his father. I know it, and he knows it.

I've been planning this for a while.

The timing's right.

Spare no expense.

If I gave you anything, it's the Harrison hustle.

"I wanted your job." The words jump out of me from nowhere, but I'm glad I said them. This was the last secret between us. The very last one.

His voice is quiet, almost nonexistent. "What?"

"I applied for your job, because . . . I don't know. Because I was under a false impression about what I was supposed to want, and so I pushed myself toward a path that wasn't a natural fit for me." I look up at his blurry face, a kaleidoscope of caramel color through my wet eyes.

Alex gulps. "I didn't know."

I laugh darkly. "I *know* you didn't know."

"That's why you . . ."

"Yeah." I nod. "That's why I hated you. But I came around, because I realized you were meant for that job, and I was meant for something else. And then I fell in love with you, because . . . because how could I *not*? You're wonderful. You're funny and charming and you carry so much life, and you never forget anything I tell you, no matter how offhand. You *listen,* and you make people feel seen, heard, understood. Not just me, everyone. You're just . . ." I sniff, and Alex presses his lips to my temple. "You're really worth loving. Like, so worth it. I hope you know that. But it's *because* I love you that I can't look the other way. Alex, your own team could get splintered in an acquisition. Maybe they replace Gus with someone *they* want as *Bite the Hand*'s editor in chief. Maybe Andre gets laid off, maybe Fari does. I can't live with that. Not knowing I could have done something to stop it."

There are ten full seconds of silence. I hold my breath.

He steps away, leaving me, and rubs two hands over his face, looking positively miserable. I want to be a wallflower inside his brain.

His voice comes out broken. "I don't know what it is you want from me right now. You say you'd protect me at all costs, then expect me to turn around and not to do the same for him?"

"I'm not expecting anything from you," I whisper. Which is the truth. Alex doesn't owe us anything, and if he chooses to sit with this information and do nothing about it, I wouldn't blame him. After so much of being used, he's earned the right to stop participating altogether. "I just wanted you to know. I didn't want you to be in the dark anymore, or ever again."

Alex turns away. He pushes his palms against the table, the muscles in his back flexing. "When I was eleven, Robert Harrison said he'd never turn his back on me. And he never has. I can't turn mine on him."

It's the best he can come up with, and to Alex, that's enough. Even though it comes in a package of unanswered phone calls and traditions you never formed, money that patches bandages it shouldn't have to. Alex is worth something so much fiercer than what his father is willing to offer—and he *just can't see it.* If I could fill that void myself, I would. I'm sure his aunt and his cousins and Freddy have tried. But the love Alex wants the most was never mine to give. I was just the first person he threw his broken heart at who was naive enough to pick it up.

"My flight to London is on the last Monday of January," I say, wiping my eyes. "Ten o'clock at night. I'm not asking you to choose between me and your father. I don't want it to have to be that way. But you loved me hard enough to make me feel more than enough just like this, who I am, without changing a thing. And I love you hard enough to ask you to finally choose yourself over any of us."

Alex parts his lips as he exhales. His jaw tenses like it does whenever he's working through what he wants to say. He comes up with "I love you."

"Yeah," I say, laughing a little. "I love you, too."

We stand there, not looking at each other on the ninety-eighth floor, both of us crying, swirled up in a love that is more than enough and still isn't even close.

CHAPTER THIRTY-FOUR

My last weekend in the city is dedicated to the Fuck It List. It's like a bucket list, but for things that cost a lot of money, and you're just kind of feeling like *Fuck it*.

Tickets and a champagne voucher at the Edge. The Roosevelt Island Tramway—which we hop on, off, and then immediately back on again, because I'm not trying to spend my last days in New York on Roosevelt Island. Dinner at a David Chang restaurant (to this request, Brijesh offers a disgruntled but acquiescent "Fine").

By Sunday night, we lie flat on our backs on Sasha's rooftop for six whole freezing minutes. The sky is backlit with golden orbs, a million city lights bleeding together to lighten it a bluish purple. We ooh and aah like lunatics, pretending we can see even one single star. After, we go inside in a heap of giggles and drink hot toddies until we're plastered.

"Casey," Sasha says. Her eyes go cross-eyed as she looks at me. "Sorry I was gone so often during college."

I smile. "Wasn't that often. And anyway, I never minded while

I walked around naked and listened to niche podcasts on the Bluetooth speaker."

"And did the dishes. You were a great roommate. Always put the dirty dishes in the dishwasher." She shoots Miguel a dirty look.

"I'm not your roommate," he retorts. He's lying flat on his back on her living room carpet. "I'm desperate to live with you, and you won't let me."

"We can reevaluate once you learn to put the dirty dishes in the dishwasher."

"Thanks for letting me be your friend, Casey," Brijesh says. "I'll never forget working up the courage to talk to you in that laptop-training class."

I giggle. "Thanks for not giving up on me based on how awkward I was during our first three encounters."

When everyone else is passed out, sprawled in various states of disarray around the living room, Miriam leans over and whispers, "Want to get a tattoo?"

"Bitch, *yes.*"

Forty-five minutes later, we stumble out of a random tattoo parlor with matching flowers on our left wrists—delicate, thin-lined forget-me-nots, freshly inked, impulsive, perfect. We wander down the sidewalk with no real hurry in our steps, reminiscing about funny memories from all the years of our lives we've shared.

"I gotta say," Miriam says, "I never thought you'd be doing something like this. I'm here for it, but the summer after high school, your big graduation trip? Remember how terrified you were to go out west for a month with Marty and Jerry because you thought you'd be homesick—"

"Okay, but we were sharing one mobile bedroom. My concerns were extensive, and as it turns out, mostly valid—"

"Still, I just really never thought."

I laugh. "Well, you did this to me."

"Did I?" Miriam asks.

"Yeah! You brought me to New York. That was all you."

We settle onto a bench near the edge of Central Park, and Miriam scrutinizes me between kind, serious eyes. "It was good while it lasted, right?"

I nod and lean my head against hers. "Better than good. It's been the best two and a half years of my life."

"Yeah. Mine too."

Which invites the question: *If it's been so good, why would you change a thing?* But I think that would be the biggest shame in the world. Not chasing the very feeling that made you so happy to start with.

"You're going to be okay. Right, Mir?"

"If I say no, will you stay?"

"Probably."

She laughs. "I'm going to be okay. I've got all my nursing friends, and Sasha in the very few moments she's sick of men."

"Very few moments," I emphasize. "Love her, though."

"Love her, though." After a minute, Miriam adds, "I don't think I ever told you this, but thank you for introducing me and Brijesh. I'm just . . . really glad we met."

My mouth pulls into a wry grin. "I, too, am glad you fell hard—harder than you care to admit—for a South Indian food connoisseur who won't ever let you go hungry when I stop putting leftovers in the fridge."

"And who makes two reservations he lets me choose between."

"That too. Speaking of, are you guys dating?"

"Getting there." Miriam looks down at her tattoo, just visible between the cuff of her coat and the edge of her purple wool gloves. "You realize this'll be the first time in our whole lives we won't be living in the same city?"

I throw her an impish grin. "Probably for the best. We're too codependent."

"Cheers to that."

Miriam is visiting me for St. Patrick's Day. Already booked her ticket to Dublin. We'll meet there, and then she'll come stay with me in London for a few days.

One of her nursing friends—Ellie 2, I'm pretty sure—is moving into our apartment. She even bought all my furniture. Miriam and I spent last week consolidating, selling, and donating my things until all that remained would fit in two massive suitcases and one large bin. I had this urge to call Alex, ask if he was proud of me for Marie Kondo–ing my lifestyle, but we haven't spoken since the conference room when everything unraveled.

Maybe we won't again.

I've enjoyed this time with my friends. The past two days have been good. But I haven't heard from Alex in weeks, and it's just been so hard to breathe.

January wind whips through the trees, a cacophony of nature at total odds with this city I've grown to love—which smells like sewage and cinnamon, feels engulfing, metamorphic, and also kind of flimsy. I shiver, hugging my knees to my chest and tucking my chin into the Madewell scarf looped around my neck.

"Do you think you can have more than one love of your life?" I ask.

"Um." She cocks her head at me. "That's a stumper. We're both twenty-five."

I laugh and look down at my tattoo. "You're one of mine."

"Same, babe. What about Alex?"

I frown. "Is he a love of my life?"

Miriam nods.

I told her the truth about our breakup, and about the acquisition. Actually, I told *everyone* about the acquisition. Brijesh, Benny, Fari, the YouTube crew. Once the secret was out with Alex, my morals dictated it was out with everyone, and I really don't give a fuck anymore if it gets back to Tracy and she comes after me for it. Apparently, I'm a very big risk-taker now.

"I don't think Alex counts," I tell Mir. "We didn't last."

But in my head, I picture Freddy's bar. Drinking the Jack and Jills. The shape of Alex's lips when he smiles, the color of his eyes in the moments before he would kiss me. The two of us bent over the chocolate cosmos, Koreatown, the Parthenon, the elevator, Eataly. All of it, some kind of epic montage that makes up the beginning stages of love-of-your-life-level happiness with a cataclysmic, unforgettable love interest.

"He counts," Miriam says.

I sigh. "If you say so."

"He *counts*." She stretches her arms upward and stands. "You wouldn't have asked me if you could have more than one love of your life if he didn't."

CHAPTER THIRTY-FIVE

Alex doesn't make an appearance on my last day of work. Benny cobbles together a goodbye gathering—he even made cupcakes with iced Union Jack decorations, which he passes out while everyone sneakily signs my going-away card—but Alex doesn't show.

"What flavor?" I ask, sticking my pinkie into the frosting.

"Boring old vanilla," says Benny. "I wanted to bake something more interesting, but I wasn't sure what all your weak-ass immune system could handle besides *vanilla*. Never thought I'd be an anti-Darwinist, but here we are."

I smirk. "I take it you're happy you can start gorging on Reese's again?"

"Honestly. I can't get rid of you fast enough."

Don pops a bottle of champagne. Not the sparkling grape juice we reserve for software upgrades—real champagne!

"Casey," he says while my coworkers all hold their plastic flutes aloft in the ninety-eighth-floor break room, "I have learned so much from you. Including spreadsheet styling." He grins, and Fari laughs. "I can't wait to see what you achieve next."

If all men could be more like Don, less like Robert and Dougie, I think our world would be a marginally better place.

A while later, Gus comes up to me and says, "By the way." He's got a number two pencil tucked behind one ear and ink on the collar of his shirt. "Alex told me about your idea. Holiday-triggered fast fashion? That was good stuff. If you have other ideas, about anything at all, don't hesitate to email me. Seriously." He stares at me, waiting for my affirmation. I think he's trying to make it clear that even though he didn't choose me for Alex's job, it doesn't mean he thinks I'm not valuable.

"Um." I blink three times, thrown out of the moment as I recall that conversation on the subway with Alex last month. *You're doing it again. Acting like you're not an inspiration for people.* "Yeah, um, okay."

"Cool," Gus says, tossing his empty flute in the trash. "Sorry he's not here, by the way. Think he had a family thing. His dad just got back from Australia."

"Oh. That's fine," I say. But the floor slides out from under me, and I feel more unsteady than I have since I was young. My insides twist into a mangled, broken thing.

Alex knew what day I was leaving. He's clearly made up his mind on what he wants to do.

Gus's forehead scrunches. I can see the thought forming behind his eyes. He's wondering why I look so upset all of a sudden. Drawing conclusions.

"You should look into featuring Revenant," I blurt.

Gus cocks his head. "Revenant?"

"Yeah, it's a clothing brand. The CEO is named Josephine Davis, and she's, um, doing some pretty cool stuff with capsule wardrobes, and negative carbon footprints, and exposing greenwashing, and stuff." My vomit-spiel ends in a wince.

"Okay," Gus says. "Revenant? I will."

He turns for the door, but his easy expression melts off his face at the glare Saanvi is shooting him. He shrinks under her stare. "I am going back to my desk right now to work on that thing I promised you—"

"Thursday, Gus. You promised it would be ready *last Thursday.*"

Gus winces and steps sideways toward the door. "To my office, right now, working on that write-up and that write-up alone. Swear!"

He scurries off. Saanvi crosses her arms, staring after him with a soft smirk on her face. "Creatives," she says.

I shrug like, *What can ya do?*

Saanvi steps closer. "I got wind through Amanda, who got wind through Instagram, that you and your cohost spent the holidays together. Our account got tagged in a photo of you and Alex taking shots at some Nashville honky-tonk."

The color drains from my cheeks, which makes Saanvi laugh. She observes me, tilting her head. "Tell me, Casey. Did I orchestrate that?"

"Partially."

"Hmm. That's cute. Inadvisable but cute."

"It's not . . ." I shake my head. "We're not . . . together, anymore."

Saanvi looks unconvinced, but with a quick glance around, she seems to realize Alex isn't here. "Regardless. Your YouTube contract is terminated due to the fact that I say so."

"Right," I say. "Makes sense."

After the party, I stop by Tracy's office to clear the air. She's pacing in Vince Camuto kitten heels, one hand pressing her phone to her ear and the other gesturing wildly. I watch her for a minute—the nonstop hustle—until she sees me outside her glass walls and mutters something, then hangs up the phone.

Now that my initial emotions have quelled, I've admitted to myself that Tracy wouldn't have gotten where she is if she didn't have a cutthroat side to her. She used me—but in the end, she owned it, and even though I can't put her on a pedestal anymore, she's more human to me than ever before. And I'm still rooting for her.

She opens the door and gives me a weary smile.

"What will you do next?" I ask softly.

Tracy pulls the door open wider, beckoning me inside. "I was just on the phone with Harold Cooper's wife, begging her to call for a vote of no confidence in Mr. Dawson. Besides that? There's not much I *can* do. I have no proof of anything, no evidence of wrongdoing or ill intent I'd be able to pin to Robert or Dougie's sleeve."

"I'm sorry," I say, meaning it. Guilt slithers through my veins like a cold shot of espresso. "I just . . . can't help you more than I already have."

Her eyes turn pitying. "What did I tell you all those years ago about that unnecessary apologizing, Casey?" She steps forward and puts a hand on my shoulder. "I don't know what Alex did, what exactly you're protecting him from. But I *do* know you tried your best to break a pattern of complicity. That's something to be proud of."

"I'm still keeping secrets," I whisper.

"Because you love him." She smiles softly.

"He's with Robert now, today," I tell her. "I think it's too late."

Tracy sighs. "Then it's too late."

To stop myself from crying, I redirect. "You didn't seem at all surprised when Don said it should have been me that got Alex's job. Did you know I applied for that?"

Tracy nods. "Of course I knew one of my own was looking around."

I nod. "Did you put me up for the travel cost manager position?" I ask.

After a beat, she admits, "Of course I did."

I nod again and breathe out, "Thank you," accompanied by half a sob. "For pulling me up the ladder."

"You know the CEO of CycleBar just got divorced?" Benny says. He picks up my pencil holder, upturns it, and shakes out a unicorn-shaped eraser he proceeds to glare at. "I'll be sure to keep you updated on her whereabouts in proximity to our COO."

"You better," I say, dumping an entire drawer full of paperwork into the recycling bin.

"Casey," Fari says, her tone stressed. "I really don't know if I have room for *all* these plants—"

"Ohmigod*fine*." Benny grabs the heartleaf philodendron and the monstera and storms back to his desk.

"Don't say I never gave you anything!" I call after him.

"Don't say I never gave *you* anything!" he shouts back.

My tote bag of meager office belongings comes with me to my HR exit interview. It's boring and stupid, but Molly is nice and not boring *or* stupid, so I answer all her questions even though they are basically the same question rephrased every time.

On my way out, I run into Dougie Dawson.

He's walking in the opposite direction and nods once before his eyes catch mine in recognition. His face is still purple, and his belly is still round. We both slow, watching each other from half a foot away.

"You," he says. "The finance girl."

"Hello, Mr. Dawson. Casey Maitland, yes."

"You're friendly with Alex Harrison." His eyes cloud with bitter resentment he's so clearly incapable of keeping at bay. "Be careful with that family, girl. Robert Harrison is the sneakiest son of a bitch New York City ever saw. His son is no different."

"They're not a family," I say quietly. "And Alex is nothing like his father."

Dougie makes a disbelieving face. "He is just as ambitious. That much was made obvious during the BTH presentation."

In a split-second decision that I quite literally make on my way out the door, I decide to poke the bear. "Yes, well, I suppose that kind of professional drive isn't for everyone. I hear you're planning to retire soon?"

Dougie narrows his eyes. "That's not for you to know."

"Well. Anyway."

My hand sticks out for him to shake. He raises an eyebrow but places his palm in mine. I think about leaving it alone—and part of me still wants to—but Tracy's words ring out clear and powerful, urging me on: *You tried your best to break a pattern of complicity. That's something to be proud of.*

"This is the way you should have greeted me at that Yankees happy hour," I say. "And I am the last person who should have to teach you this."

His purple face goes violet—all fear, no room left for retaliatory, finger-wagging anger—and the only word I manage to think as I walk away is *Good*.

I kept it together the whole day until now. I thought for *sure* he'd want to see me—even if it was only to say goodbye—but Alex didn't even give me that. On the subway back to Brooklyn Heights, I full-on melt down in tears. Beside me, Brijesh doesn't say a word. He just rubs my back and waits out the five minutes it takes me to be able to breathe normally again.

"If it makes you feel any better," Brijesh says softly, "he's been a walking ghost."

I sigh. "Am I a horrible person if that does make me feel a little better?"

Brijesh laughs. "It makes you an honest one."

When Miriam gets home from the hospital, all three of us go eat together one last time at the same place we went the night I introduced them.

"You got my shared note of East London restaurants?" Brijesh asks.

"Yes," I say. "I'll go somewhere new every week, sit at the bar until someone with impeccable taste in food forces me into his friendship."

Brijesh grins, spinning a lock of Miriam's hair around his finger. "Fate."

"Coercion," I counter.

"Fate," Miriam agrees.

My flight is at 10:00 P.M. Miriam and Brijesh want to stay with me until then, but I have to call my parents and I want to be alone doing it, so I hug and kiss them goodbye after dinner and tell Miriam to sleep at Brijesh's place.

In our apartment, I say goodbye to silly inanimate things, like my air-conditioning unit and the stove we've never turned on. Just for fun, I try to turn it on now and realize it doesn't even work, which makes a gurgle of deranged laughter peal out of me.

I sit on the floor, legs crossed, and call Dad. Jerry's holding the phone, but it's pointed at Dad, who is holding a guitar and waving.

"Hi, guys."

"I wrote a song for you, honey," says Dad. "Want to hear it?"

"Is it going to make me cry?"

"You're already crying," Jerry notes dryly.

"I'm having a moment."

Jerry snorts. "Is this like your teenage years when you would look out the window whenever it was raining and listen to sad music on purpose?"

My lips quirk. "A little."

"Oh, then this'll be *perfect*," Jerry extrapolates. "Play the song, Marty!"

It's in the realm of "Cinderella" by Steven Curtis Chapman or "My Wish" by Rascal Flatts. Slow and melodic, deep and achy, and halfway through, I realize I've heard scraps of this song before. A string of chords after my high school graduation, a lyric in the car ride home from Baskin-Robbins. I can hear *this song, that day,* on the front patio when Jerry explained to me that I like sure things. Or that I used to, anyway.

I think maybe Dad's been working on this song my whole life.

I hold it together through the lyrics about the little girl he took backstage with him at concerts, eyes sparkling at the pretty lights but quiet all the same. But I break down in tears that push hard against my eyes when he gets to the part about how I learned to trust the sound of my own voice: singing to myself in a room all alone, him and Jerry one wall away, out of sight but there to catch me if I faltered.

And I just really hope he knows. I hope he knows he's the best dad in the world, and I'm not running away. I'm just trusting the sound of my own voice, like he taught me. I hope he knows I loved sharing music with him as a kid, even though I flaked on the talent show, even though I can't *make* it like he does.

But just because you don't make art doesn't mean you don't inspire it.

CHAPTER THIRTY-SIX

The thing I never took into consideration when I envisioned myself moving abroad was doing it with a broken heart. It colors everything in a different shade.

My hotel room has a canopy bed and green velvet cushions on the window seat. It is quaint and luxurious without being opulent, only a couple of blocks away from Covent Garden. The bedding is itchy, and I almost ask the maid not to change it anymore after the first night when I come back from exploring to freshly stiff sheets, but I'm not exaggerating when I say she's my best friend right now, and saying hello to her in the mornings is the most human interaction I have all day. I can live with itchy sheets for another two weeks.

My fourth day in London—after a coffee from a fancy espresso place that's honestly terrible, a FaceTime with Miriam, a tour of an apartment I can't afford in Shoreditch followed by a tour of an apartment I can *probably* afford in Clapham—I break down in tears and ask myself what the *hell* I was thinking.

It's not that I don't love London, because I can already feel the city marking me the same way I felt when I first moved to New York. Every neighborhood is busting at the seams with individualist personality, and the history is almost tangible. But this is a place where *he* lived first. No matter where I go, I feel like an intruder. Like something unwanted.

I read four books in four days. Some meals I eat at restaurant bars—which hasn't bothered me since my college days—and some I take to go so I can eat in bed with the TV for company. I email Gran to let her know I'm in town (I omit telling her I've moved here; that will probably go over better in person).

Did you download Bumble BFF yet??? Join a gym? Employee resource group?? Meet a kind stranger in a bookstore? Miriam texts me.

Give me some time to miss human interaction and then we'll see, I text back.

On Friday, I have lunch with my new boss, Sinclair Austin (who I am *not* going to idolize beyond human fallibility the way I idolized Tracy). But despite my best efforts, I like her instantly. She has blue streaks in her black hair and is curvy, short, and engaged to be married to a woman named Austin (ha). She doesn't even make fun of me when I mispronounce items on the café menu.

After we eat, she takes me on a tour of our office building, shows me the desk I'll be claiming after orientation next Monday.

"What's your first impression of the city?" she asks.

I smile at her, internally cataloging that Brits call London "the city" the same way New Yorkers call Manhattan "the city." I'm gathering details one at a time to flesh this place out until I know it enough to call it home.

But I really, genuinely mean it when I tell her, "I think I've fallen in love. Again."

London is cleaner than Manhattan, and much more sprawling. The beer isn't pretentious, and the food is comforting—which will probably get tiresome but right now is exactly the vibe I need.

Every block is steeped in centuries, giving the atmosphere a kind of transcendence. In fact, the only flaw I can hold to the city isn't the city's fault at all: if I had to assign London a feeling, it couldn't be anything other than lovesick.

Sinclair is walking me to the front elevators when I spot a directory.

Archives: Floor 12.

"The *Take Me There* archives are kept here?" I ask. I had assumed they were all at the flagship office.

"Yes," she confirms. "We've got every issue ever printed, all digitized."

Like a broken record, my heart starts to skip. "Can I go?"

"Sure." Sinclair shrugs. "You've got your badge now. Be my guest."

"Thank you," I murmur, calling the elevator.

This is some seriously masochistic behavior. Because whether I find Charlotte Yoon down there or not, it's going to wreck me either way. But the pain has started to fade to numbness, and I'm not ready to feel numb when I think of Alex yet.

The archivist is a gray-haired cottage fairy, helpful as ever as she takes down the name I request and my best guess for when Charlotte may have started writing for the magazine. My hopes aren't high. The woman disappears and leaves me at the front desk. The longer she's gone, the farther my hopes fall. I sit down and bounce my knee, biting my lip until it bleeds.

"Well then," the archivist says. "I've got some photocopies for you."

I stand shakily, hands outstretched.

Nine. There are *nine* of them. All written by Alex's mom.

"Can I stay and read for a minute?" I ask.

The archivist smiles. "Of course, dear."

I sit back down, leafing through the articles. THE BEST HOTEL IN EACH DISTRICT OF SEOUL, AND HOW TO CHOOSE ONE. TIPPING

ETIQUETTE IN THE 10 MOST POPULOUS COUNTRIES. PLANNING YOUR
VACATION BASED ON FOREIGN EXCHANGE RATES.

EVERY THOUGHT YOU'LL HAVE WHEN YOU MOVE ABROAD ALONE.
I cannot believe this is real. And I also can't believe my tear ducts
haven't declared a state of emergency based on drought. But when
I start to read, the tears just flow. Because it's not only Alex's mom
I feel with me right now. Mine is here, too.

> It's going to start with being overwhelmed and under-
> whelmed at the exact same time. Maybe you get lost on pub-
> lic transportation. Maybe you spot a spider in the corner the
> first night you move in. Or possibly, you overhear a couple
> having a fight about something totally ordinary. It's going to
> humanize the place, demystify it from the version you built
> up in your head. And somehow, you're going to think, *This
> city is kind of a letdown, but also more enchanting than it
> was before.* I can't explain what I mean, but when you feel it,
> you'll feel it.
>
> At some point, you're going to cry. Just trust me on this
> one. Maybe it's because you're trying to raise a toddler, or
> brokenhearted (or both, in my case). Maybe it's because
> you're leaving something important behind where you came
> from. Maybe it's because you cannot find the right diapers to
> save your life. Whatever the reason, just cry, and don't hold
> back if you're in public. Nobody knows you yet, and I promise
> it's cathartic.
>
> Things are looking up now, right? You've mostly figured
> out how to get around, and you've nailed down all your
> "spots": coffee, takeout, groceries, where to get pesticide.
> That one tourist attraction—the one you were worried might
> be oversold in all the travel guides—*is* actually stunning after
> all, and you've learned the main turns of phrase the locals
> use.

Hear me out. You'll regress a little when you get lonely. And without a doubt, you are going to get lonely. It will feel like everyone around you has a fleshed-out life, and you're only pretending to be a full human for a handful of hours per day.

To my knowledge, there is exactly one remedy for this sense of outsideness: time. None of us were born feeling at home—on the contrary, we were born being ripped out of the only home we'd ever known—but we've all got one. Maybe, in this place, you haven't felt that way yet. It'll probably take a while because home isn't something you find. It's something you build. But eventually, it happened for me, and I'm hopeful it'll happen for you: the completely ordinary, totally mundane, absolutely sparkling day that comes when you first think to yourself, *This place feels like home.*

I'm in the lobby on my way out of the building, the photocopies of Charlotte's articles clutched tight to my chest, when I hear the most unexpected thing in the world.

My name.

"Casey?" The voice is feminine, vaguely familiar, and definitely aimed right at me. I do a one-eighty, quickly wiping a thumb under each eye.

It takes me a minute to place her. The image comes slow: girlfriend of one of Alex's college friends. Grew up in Alabama, graduated from Dartmouth. She looks the same—puffed hair, flawless black skin, tall and delicate boned—but she's subbed out her Christmas getup for a dark mauve jumpsuit.

"Hey," I say, somewhat shocked.

She smiles. "Hey." I realize right then that I don't know her name. "Jada." She points at herself.

"Right," I lie. "I knew that."

She smirks. "It's fine. There were a lot of us that night."

"What are you doing in London?"

She steps closer, her heels clapping against marble tile. "I work in home technology sales. We've got a satellite branch here."

I gesture around. "Same, kind of. I got transferred here for a new job."

Jada arches her eyebrows. "Full-time? That's brave."

"Yeah." I shuffle Charlotte's articles. "I guess."

Jada crosses her arms, dissecting me. "Makes sense you're with Alex. I don't know him well, but Josh describes him as the type whose feet don't always touch the ground."

I'm not sure what to say to that except for "We broke up."

Her face draws up in confusion. Or maybe pity. "Oh. He's not in London for you?"

"He's." It takes me several, painful seconds to grasp what she said. "What?"

"He's here." Jada points at the ground, like Alex is going to emerge from beneath the floor. Two women carrying briefcases walk between us, and a gust of sterile lobby air hits my nose. "In London. I don't know how, but he managed to get a seat on our company's corporate jet, and we just landed, like, two and a half hours ago."

My ears hear her words, and my eyes see her lips move, but I'm still not comprehending.

I've spent the last thirty minutes letting Alex's mother console me from beyond the grave. The cottage fairy archivist literally asked me if she needed to call an ambulance because I was crying so hard. And now Jada is telling me I might have to *face* him?

I can think of only one worse possibility. What if he's here for some other purpose and has no intention to see me at all?

Jada's mouth presses into a thin line. If she spent a whole plane ride with Alex and still isn't sure of the intent behind his visit, she's not going to give me false hope.

She fishes her cell phone out of her bag, offers it to me. "Put your number in. Josh and I are here for work once every couple of months. Even when we're not, there are tons of people I can set you up with. Not romantically!" she clarifies, voice jumping. "I mean, maybe, I guess. But I imagine you could use a friend or two. I can help with that, at least."

I grab her phone and put my number in. "Thank you."

She nods, taking it back. "We're going for drinks and small plates tonight at this meze place in Shoreditch. You interested?"

This—right here—is the point with most of my awkward acquaintances where I'd normally say no. A polite but firm "Thanks *so* much for offering, but I'm exhausted and should probably rest up. I wouldn't want to bring the group down!" Part of me wants to play out the old song and dance out of fear, and anxiety, and my introverted belief that I don't need anyone new. But this time, I have to say yes. I *have* to give myself a fighting chance at friendship here, push myself into scary waters. I came this far. It's what Charlotte would want me to do.

Home is something you build.

"I'd like that," I say. "Text me the details."

Outside, I push past the text reading jada <3 go auburn!! to pull up Find My Friends. Hands shaking, I wait for the app to load.

Alex's contact says *Location Unavailable.*

Which means he either (*a*) doesn't want me to know he's here or, (*b*) doesn't have an international phone plan. Optimistically I'm hoping for the latter, but realistically it's the former. Alex Harrison was *raised* on international phone plans.

Still, there is a nettlesome thump in my heart all the way back to my hotel. I have no reason to believe Alex will be there. I also have no reason to believe that my heart has been yanked out and stuffed with magnets instead. But in the lobby, I admit to myself I'm looking for his unruly mop of black hair about a fraction of a second before I see it.

He's dressed in a gray Patagonia coat that's too lightweight for this weather, and the same jeans and tennis shoes we went hiking in a few days after Christmas. Ganier Ridge, the hike was called. That day, the wind blew his hair back from his forehead in one smooth sweep, but today it's been tugged in every direction. He's wringing his hands in knots, seated on the edge of an ottoman, staring at the floor so intently I'm convinced he's counting the stains on the Persian rug. There is a mostly empty weekender bag beside his feet.

"Alex?"

His head snaps up. That's when I see the bruisy half-moons under his eyes. The shadow of his stubble is more pronounced than I've ever seen it. He stands in one smooth movement, then pushes a hand to his forehead like the motion made him dizzy.

"Hi," he says as he takes a step toward me. "God, you're so fucking beautiful. How—"

I back away. Alex frowns and goes still, not coming any closer.

He should have warned me. This isn't fair. I'm too vulnerable right now, doing my best to adjust, and Alex knows it.

"Two days ago, my phone fell in the toilet," he tries again. "At the office."

"Your . . ." My head tilts. "The toilet."

"Yeah," he articulates, but all I really acknowledge is how much I missed the sound of his voice. "I tracked you because you weren't at the all-hands meeting Wednesday. And I saw you were already here, which kind of took me by surprise enough to drop my phone in the fucking toilet."

I frown. "What took you by surprise?"

He blinks at me. Blinks again. "That you moved up your flight."

"No, I didn't," I mutter.

Alex takes another step forward. This time, I hold my ground, keep my eyes on his.

"The last Monday in January, Case. That's the day you said you were leaving. Ten at night on Monday during the last week of

January. That's three days from now. I was going to go all the way to the airport with you. I wanted to be the first person you called when you landed. When I realized you'd left without me, I got on the literal first flight I could."

I open my mouth, close it again. I'm too fixated on the second part of what he said to wrap my head around the first. "I guess . . ." I rub my forehead. "I guess I meant the last Monday of January according to Little Cooper's fiscal calendar. Which was four days ago."

We stare at each other for a few seconds, dumbfounded at the misunderstanding.

Alex's mouth pulls into the outline of a smile, some of the strain eclipsed by it. "You would have meant that." A laugh slips through his teeth. "I honestly should have known."

I muster an equally thin smile for about two point five seconds before it falls back off my face. "Did you come all the way here to say goodbye?"

"I don't want to say goodbye," Alex murmurs, closing the distance between us. "Never did. I needed space, but not a whole ocean of it." His voice digs in, deep, *straining*. "I fucking *love* you, Casey."

I press a hand to his chest, trying to put aside the feeling of the pounding heart beneath it. "Okay. But we can't just ignore—"

"I know." Alex shudders against me, his eyes sweeping over my neck and lips. "I know it wouldn't have been right for me to come here if I hadn't done some reflection first." He pauses. "I met with Robert."

I refocus. "You did?"

Alex nods, the muscles in his jaw flexing. "The day of your party, which—yep, makes sense now that it was a week early." He sighs and shakes his head. "You asked if I knew something you didn't. Remember?"

I nod.

"Well, I did. On my birthday, I got this email from my father. He told me I inspired him to come out of retirement and explore digital media."

"Oh." My hands come to rest against my lips.

He winces, dropping my eyes. "You were right about everything," he whispers. "The day you left New York . . . that's the day I finally worked up the courage to go to his town house. I saw the same piece of paper from Strauss you saw, right there on the entryway table. Guess what it was? A proposed outline of his future share. He got home later that night, and I confronted him about it. He didn't want to fess up at first, but when he could tell I was onto him, he just sort of . . . broke open. Started talking about how Dougie deserved it, how it was a matter of honor." Alex laughs darkly. "He manipulated not one, but two whole businesses so he could get a leg up on a man who is, objectively, his own mirror image."

"Alex—"

"And *then*," Alex says, hand on his neck, "he started promising me things. He said he always planned to bring me into a position of power in the new company. Money, a better job title. He even dangled his own mentorship in my face like a carrot. Said now that I was grown, we could be partners. But it was all just too little, too late."

I didn't want to be right about this. I can tell just looking at Alex that he's exhausted, defeated. He hasn't had it as bad as me over the last few weeks. He's had it worse.

Alex scratches at his jaw, still not meeting my eyes. "I stood there in that town house, inwardly fuming, staring at the spot where I made love to you on the floor, with his wife in the next room hating me loudly, and realized. I could put up with that type of behavior when it was only me Robert was undoing. Not when it was everyone else." He shakes his head, eyes on the floor. "I told him I wanted no part in any of it."

My thoughts are stumbling over themselves, rapid-fire, begging for attention at the front of my brain, but I am present enough to recognize that Robert wouldn't have liked that response. "How did he take it?" I ask.

Alex frowns. "He was frustrated. But funny enough, I think part of him understood. Maybe he even respected me for it." He scrubs a hand over his face. "Robert's never lied to me about who he is, or what his priorities are. But I made it clear it him—and to myself, finally, after all this time—that mine aren't the same." His eyes flash to me. "He knows I'm going to come clean. He's preparing for it."

"No." I shake my head, spiraling at the prospect of Alex in trouble. "That's not . . . *No*."

"I can handle the legal consequences," he rasps. "I did what I did."

For a few long seconds he says nothing, and I know in my bones we could stay like this for hours. Remembering each other. He doesn't make any move to touch me. But his gaze lingers. "You really are so beautiful," he murmurs. "Whip-smart. Funny. Inspiring. And the way you quietly care about people is just . . . completely unbound." His eyes dip down to the papers in my hand, his mother's name in bold under the titles at the top. "Don't think I haven't noticed what you're holding."

"I—I just found them—"

"You don't have to explain right now," he says. "I think I already know." Alex slips a hand into his coat pocket and withdraws two pieces of paper. They're folded up tight, wrinkled at the corners, creased with fraying edges. "I'll trade you." He presses them into my hands, taking the articles in his. "Read the letter first. I wrote it on the plane. And then this. Gus wrote it with my help, and with Tracy Garcia's help, too. I told him he couldn't publish it anywhere until you read it first."

Alex steps back. His caramel eyes are warm. They devour me like he is starving for the sight. "I know it doesn't make up for missing seeing you off. But maybe it'll help you understand why I needed time."

CHAPTER THIRTY-SEVEN

Casey,

I'm on my way to you right now. I'm locked out of iCloud because memorizing passwords is impossible, and for the same reason I haven't memorized your number, so I decided to write you this letter instead. Even though you might not read it, which would be within your right since I let you board a plane without saying goodbye.

The first time I ever saw you in that elevator, I knew something was wrong. Your face was split up with nerves and I could tell your heart was in knots. I cracked a joke because I wanted to make you laugh, but I didn't manage that until that late September day on the balcony. That was the first laugh you let me keep.

Here's the thing. When you told me you loved me too, I wasn't sure I deserved it. I couldn't escape the feeling that I had no right to even be with you until I could somehow win him over too. Because why would someone as perfect as you love me